GREEK EPIC POETRY

GREEK
EPIC POETRY

from Eumelos
to Panyassis

G. L. HUXLEY

HARVARD UNIVERSITY PRESS
Cambridge, Massachusetts
1969

SBN 674-36238-1

TO
DAVINA

Acknowledgements

I am grateful to Dr L. H. Jeffery who read the entire manuscript of the book. From her deep literary and historical scholarship I have profited greatly. Mr James Grainger, who also read the draft, made many helpful suggestions in matters of detail; and Miss Pauline Lisney accurately carried out the typewriting of the English text. To my publisher, Mr Charles Monteith, I owe more than I can say for his gentle encouragement over many years.

I have had to explore many rarely-trodden bye-ways of Greek literature; so my book, I know, has defects; that there are not more is due to the painstaking kindness of the persons named above. Lastly, I have to thank Professor Myles Dillon, most learned of Hibernians, for reading the appendix, the draft of which was improved by his authoritative criticism.

Contents

Abbreviations

References to F. Jacoby's *Die Fragmente der griechischen Historiker* (*F.Gr.Hist.*) are made in the form 'Epimenides 457 F 1'. References to Diels and Kranz, *Die Fragmente der Vorsokratiker* (9th ed. Berlin 1960) are given according to their system: e.g. Epimenides 3 B 1 or D.K. 3 B 1. The following abbreviations will also be found in the notes:

Abh.	Abhandlungen
A.B.S.A.	*Annual of the British School at Athens*
A.B.V.	J. D. Beazley, *Attic Black-Figure Vase-Painters* (Oxford 1956)
A.C.	*L'Antiquité classique*
A.J.A.	*American Journal of Archaeology*
A.R.	*Archaeological Reports* (Annual Supplement to *J.H.S.*)
A.R.V.	J. D. Beazley, *Attic Red-Figure Vase-Painters* (Oxford 1963)
B.C.H.	*Bulletin de Correspondance hellénique*
C.Q.	*The Classical Quarterly*
C.R.	*The Classical Review*
F.H.G.	*Fragmenta Historicorum Graecorum* ed. C. and T. Müller and V. Langlois. Vol. I–V (1848–1870)
G.R.B.S.	*Greek, Roman and Byzantine Studies*
H.S.C.P.	*Harvard Studies in Classical Philology*
J.d.I.	*Jahrbuch des deutschen archäologischen Instituts*
J.H.S.	*The Journal of Hellenic Studies*
M.W.	See Merkelbach and West *infra*.
P. Oxy.	*The Oxyrhynchus Papyri*
P.P.	*La Parola del Passato*
P.U.	*Philologische Untersuchungen*
R.E.	*Pauly's Real-Encyclopädie der classichen Altertums-wissenschaft*, ed. G. Wissowa
R.E.A.	*Revue des Études anciennes*

Abbreviations

R.F.   *Rivista di filologia classica*

R.M.   *Rheinisches Museum*

T.A.P.A. *Transactions and Proceedings of the American Philological Association*

Works Cited by Author's Name Only

T. W. Allen, *Homeri Opera, Tomus V Hymnos Cyclum Fragmenta Margiten Batrachomyomachiam Vitas Continens* (Oxon. 1946).

E. Bethe, *Homer 2: Odyssee, Kyklos, Zeitbestimmung* (Berlin 1922).

D. von Bothmer, *Amazons in Greek Art* (Oxford 1957).

C. M. Bowra, *Greek Lyric Poetry* (²Oxford 1961).

E. T. H. Brann, *The Athenian Agora VIII. Late Geometric and Protoattic Pottery* (Princeton 1962).

F. Brommer, *Herakles* (Münster 1953).

J. Dörig and O. Gigon, *Der Kampf der Götter und Titanen* (Olten and Lausanne 1961).

T. J. Dunbabin, *The Greeks and their Eastern Neighbours* (London 1957).

E. Heitsch, *Die griechischen Dichterfragmente der römischen Kaiserzeit* (2 Vol. Göttingen 1963 and 1964).

F. Jacoby, *Abhandlungen zur griechischen Geschichtschreibung* (Leiden 1956).

L. H. Jeffery, *The Local Scripts of Archaic Greece* (Oxford 1961).

K. F. Johansen, *The Iliad in Early Greek Art* (Copenhagen 1967).

G. Kinkel, *Epicorum Graecorum Fragmenta I* (Leipzig 1877).

G. S. Kirk (ed.), *The Language and Background of Homer* (Cambridge 1964).

I. Löffler, *Die Melampodie* (Meisenheim-an-Glan 1963).

J. G. G. Marcksheffel, *Hesiodi, Eumeli, Cinaethonis, Asii et Carminis Naupactii Fragmenta* (Leipzig 1840).

R. Merkelbach, 'Die Hesiodfragmente auf Papyrus', *Archiv für Papyrusforschung* 16 (1957).

R. Merkelbach and M. L. West, *Fragmenta Hesiodea* (Oxon. 1967).

D. L. Page, *Poetae Melici Graeci* (Oxford 1962).

J. U. Powell, *Collectanea Alexandrina* (Oxon. 1925).

Greek Epic Poetry

A. Rzach, *Hesiodus. Carmina* (³Stutgard. 1958).

K. Schefold, *Myth and Legend in Early Greek Art* (London 1966).

J. Schwartz, *Pseudo-Hesiodeia* (Leiden 1960).

E. Schwyzer, *Dialectorum Graecarum exempla epigraphica potiora* (Hildesheim 1960).

A. Severyns, *Le Cycle épique dans l'École d'Aristarque* (Paris/Liège 1928).

M. N. Tod, *A Selection of Greek Historical Inscriptions* I (²Oxford 1946).

H. T. Wade-Gery, *The Poet of the Iliad* (Cambridge 1952).

T. B. L. Webster, *From Mycenae to Homer* (London 1958).

F. G. Welcker, *Der epische Cyclus* (2 Vol. Bonn 1835 and 1849).

C. Wendel, *Scholia in Apollonium Rhodium Vetera* (Berlin 1935).

M. L. West, *Hesiod. Theogony* (Oxford 1966).

U. von Wilamowitz-Moellendorff, *Homerische Untersuchungen* (*P.U.* 7. Berlin 1884).

B. Wyss, *Antimachi Colophonii reliquiae* (Berol. 1936).

Preface

Of the making of books on Homer there is no end, because each
generation interprets anew the *Iliad* and the *Odyssey*, as evidence grows;
the poems and fragments of Hesiod, too, have been illuminated by
devoted commentators, ancient and modern; and the Homeric Hymns
have not lacked competent editors. But the fragmentary lost epics of
early Hellas have been given less attention, because their remains are so
sparse, their authors so obscure, and the circumstances of their composition, in song, speech or script, so uncertain. Yet, as the fragments
show, these lost poems lack neither historical interest nor literary merit.

In the belief that an introduction to the lost hexametric epic poetry of
the three centuries from the first age of colonisation to the rise of the
Athenian empire would be helpful to my pupils and to other students of
Greek literature and history, I have written this book. I do not presume
to instruct learned Hellenists, but even they may find here recondite
facts to amuse, or new ideas to stimulate, their capacious intellects. My
aims have been to decide what the chief fragments mean, so that they
may be placed in their likely contexts, and to determine the scope of
each lost poem. Where archaeological evidence has proved illuminating,
it has been noted; but not often can vase-paintings, sculpture or bronze-
reliefs be proved to represent specific literary versions of the stories. To
examine here all the tales likely to have featured in the earliest written
epics would have entailed the writing of a comprehensive genealogical
treatise on Hellenic myth and legend. As it is, this study, with its
emphasis on attributable non-Hesiodic fragments, is quite long enough;
if there are any readers who in turning the last page think that the book
is too long, I beg their forgiveness.

Belfast   G. L. H.
March 1969

I

Theogonies and Theomachies

We begin at the beginning, with the births and the battles of the gods. The early Greeks, like other peoples possessing mature imaginations, attempted to explain the origins of the world in terms of the matings and offspring of primaeval divinities. The earliest complete theogony, Hesiod's, dates from about 700 B.C.,[1] but there is evidence for theogonical poems contemporary with his which differed markedly from the Hesiodic scheme. A cosmogonical system is also implicit in the *Iliad*; and this too differs from Hesiod's.

Two passages, both from the fourteenth book of the *Iliad*, are evidence of the Homeric cosmogony. In one (14.201) Hera speaks of 'Okeanos, the begetter of the gods, and mother Tethys' –

$$\text{'}\Omega\kappa\epsilon\alpha\nu\acute{o}\nu \ \tau\epsilon \ \theta\epsilon\hat{\omega}\nu \ \gamma\acute{\epsilon}\nu\epsilon\sigma\iota\nu \ \kappa\alpha\grave{\iota} \ \mu\eta\tau\acute{\epsilon}\rho\alpha \ \textbf{\textit{T}}\eta\theta\acute{\nu}\nu.$$

In the other (14.245–246) Hypnos declares that he would easily send to sleep 'even the streams of river Okeanos who is the creator of all things' –

$$\pi\text{ο}\tau\alpha\mu\text{ο}\hat{\iota}\text{ο} \ \dot{\rho}\acute{\epsilon}\epsilon\theta\rho\alpha$$
$$\text{'}\Omega\kappa\epsilon\alpha\nu\text{ο}\hat{\upsilon}, \ \ddot{\text{ο}}\varsigma \ \pi\epsilon\rho \ \gamma\acute{\epsilon}\nu\epsilon\sigma\iota\varsigma \ \pi\acute{\alpha}\nu\tau\epsilon\sigma\sigma\iota \ \tau\acute{\epsilon}\tau\upsilon\kappa\tau\alpha\iota.$$

The two expressions strongly suggest that in Homer's view the male Okeanos and the female Tethys were primaeval progenitors of the world. The opinion was held also by the author of some verses ascribed to Orpheus and quoted by Plato (*Cratylus* 402B): 'Okeanos of the fair stream first began wedlock, who married Tethys his sister by the same mother.'

$$\text{'}\Omega\kappa\epsilon\alpha\nu\grave{o}\varsigma \ \pi\rho\hat{\omega}\tau\text{ο}\varsigma \ \kappa\alpha\lambda\lambda\acute{\iota}\rho\text{ο}\text{ο}\varsigma \ \hat{\eta}\rho\xi\epsilon \ \gamma\acute{\alpha}\mu\text{ο}\iota\text{ο}$$
$$\ddot{\text{ο}}\varsigma \ \dot{\rho}\alpha \ \kappa\alpha\sigma\iota\gamma\nu\acute{\eta}\tau\eta\nu \ \dot{o}\mu\text{ο}\mu\acute{\eta}\tau\text{ο}\rho\alpha \ \textbf{\textit{T}}\eta\theta\grave{\nu}\nu \ \ddot{\text{ο}}\pi\upsilon\iota\epsilon\nu.$$

These words may have been written down as long as two centuries after Homer, but they are consistent with the Homeric scheme. Homer

---

[1] The epoch of Hesiod and Homer is discussed in Chapter X.

Greek Epic Poetry

does not speak of Okeanos and Tethys having one mother; but the mother's place was perhaps reserved by him for Night, who, the poet suggests, was mightier even than Zeus. Hypnos says (*Iliad* 14.259-261) that Zeus would have thrown him out of sight into the sea 'if Night, subduer of gods and men, had not saved me; to her I came fleeing, and Zeus, though he was angry, did cease; for he shrank from doing what would be displeasing to swift Night'. This view of the primacy of Night in the Homeric cosmogony was maintained, against the Peripatetics, by Damaskios (*De Principiis* 124 [D.K. 1 B 12]); it is not demonstrably incorrect.

The Hesiodic cosmogony is, in any case, widely divergent from the Homeric. Hesiod states at the beginning of his genealogies: 'Verily at the first did Chasm come into being, and then broad-bosomed Earth, a sure seat of all things for ever, ... and the murky realms of Tartaros in a hollow of the broad-pathed earth, and Eros who is most beauteous amongst the undying gods ...' (*Theogony* 116 and 118–120).

> ἦ τοι μὲν πρώτιστα Χάος γένετ', αὐτὰρ ἔπειτα
> Γαῖ' εὐρύστερνος, πάντων ἕδος ἀσφαλὲς αἰεί,
> Τάρταρά τ' ἠερόεντα μυχῷ χθονὸς εὐρυοδείης,
> ἠδ' Ἔρος, ὃς κάλλιστος ἐν ἀθανάτοισι θεοῖσι.

Χάος, Chasm[1] or Chaos, is cognate with the root χα- meaning 'gape'. Hesiod is perhaps guilty of a slight illogicality here since there cannot have been a gaping Chasm before the separation of Earth (Gaia) and Tartaros; so Χάος cannot have 'come to be' 'first and foremost' – πρώτιστα ... γένετο. Eros is perhaps Hesiod's own invention, a divinity to preside over the generation of the other gods; but Tartaros and Earth are ancient, traditional elements, whose separation is also an essential feature of the Homeric picture of the world. In Homer dark Tartaros is at least as far below the earth as the sky is above it (*Iliad* 8.13–16).

We can now examine the separation of Sky (Ouranos) and Earth. Neither in Hesiod nor in Homer is their division the primary cosmogonical event. In Homer primal Okeanos is distinguished from Tethys; in Hesiod Chasm brought into being Erebos and black Night, and from Night and Erebos, again, came Aither and Day; not until these four

[1] For this translation see West, p. 192.

Theogonies and Theomachies

divinities have been created does Hesiod mention the bringing-forth of Ouranos out of Earth (*Theogony* 126–128).

126   Γαῖα δέ τοι πρῶτον μὲν ἐγείνατο ἶσον ἑαυτῇ
     Οὐρανὸν ἀστερόενθ', ἵνα μιν περὶ πάντα καλύπτοι
     ὄφρ' εἴη μακάρεσσι θεοῖς ἕδος ἀσφαλὲς αἰεί.

'And Earth first brought forth starry Ouranos, equal to herself, to cover her all over, that there might be a firm seat for the blessed gods for ever.' Thus Ouranos, like the Mountains and Pontos the sea, whom Earth next brings forth–again 'without delightful love' (lines 129–132) – is in Hesiod a being of secondary cosmogonical importance.[1]

Hesiod's view of Ouranos was however not universally held; and there is evidence that in some early Greek cosmologies the separation of Gaia and Ouranos was the first event. In *Melanippe the Wise* Euripides (F 484 Nauck[2]) recalled a creation story through a character (Melanippe herself) who claims to have heard it from her mother; thus the poet presents a traditional story: 'And the tale is not mine but from my mother, how Sky and Earth were one shape; but since they have been separated apart from each other they bring forth all things and give them up into the light – trees, birds, beasts and those whom the briny sea doth nourish, and the breed of mortals.' Here the absence of gods is noteworthy; perhaps they were reserved for special mention later, since they can hardly have been omitted entirely from the cosmogony followed by the poet, who shows that Sky and Earth were at first undifferentiated, till they separated to create offspring bisexually. The primaeval mating of Sky and Earth was described in a cycle of epics mentioned by Proklos, and from their mating, Proklos added, 'they beget three hundred-handed sons and three Kyklopes':

διαλαμβάνει δὲ καὶ περὶ τοῦ λεγομένου ἐπικοῦ κύκλου, ὃς ἄρχεται μὲν ἐκ τῆς Οὐρανοῦ καὶ Γῆς μυθολογουμένης μίξεως, ἐξ ἧς αὐτοὶ καὶ τρεῖς παῖδας ἑκατοντάχειρας καὶ τρεῖς γεννῶσι Κύκλωπας.

(Photios p. 319a Bekker). Here we may perhaps, with Welcker (2.556), discern a paraphrase of a hexameter:

[1] Ouranos is also secondary in a cosmogony accepted by Alkman (F 61 Page), Antimachos of Kolophon (F 44 Wyss) and 'Hesiod' (Frag. fals. 6 Rzach[3]), who declare him to be a son of Akmon; ἄκμων originally meant a meteoric stone (cf. Sanskrit *áśman* 'sling-stone') and the affiliation of Heaven to Thunderbolt may well be very ancient.

τρεῖς Ἑκατόγχειρας καὶ τρεῖς γεννῶσι Κύκλωπας.

Proklos held that the epic cycle began from the mating of Sky and Earth; he does not say that it began from their separation. That he perhaps represents here a genuine tradition, in which the two had been for ever distinct, may be seen from the parallel narrative at the beginning of the *Library* of Apollodoros who states that Sky was the first to rule over the whole world; 'and having wedded Earth, he begat first the Hundred-handers, as they are called; Briareos, Gy⟨g⟩es, Kottos, who were unsurpassed in size and might, each of them having a hundred hands and fifty heads. After them Earth bore to him the Kyklopes, Arges, Steropes, Brontes, each of whom had one eye on his forehead' (1.1.1–2). The dreadful Kyklopes personify thunder, their names representing two aspects of the same event, the bright flash of lightning (ἀργός, στεροπή) and the clap (βροντή). They must have proved to be a threat to Sky, who cast them down to Tartaros before he begat the Titans by Earth. Of the Titans listed by Apollodoros (*Lib.* 1.1.3) Okeanos, Hyperion and Kronos amongst the males and Tethys, Rhea and Dione amongst the females are most relevant to an examination of the lost *Titanomachia*, to which we may now pass.

The authorship of the lost poem or poems called 'The Battle of the Titans' was a matter of doubt to Athenaios, who knew of ascriptions to Eumelos of Corinth and to Arktinos of Miletos or to 'anyone else who rejoices in being called author' (277D cf. 22C). Such bare ascriptions are unverifiable and the very title *Titanomachia* may be no earlier than the Hellenistic age; but the remarks of Athenaios do show that the poem was thought to be early, because Arktinos was reputed to be a pupil of Homer (Artemon 443 F 2) and Eumelos is said to have overlapped in time Archias who founded Syracuse from Corinth in 734 B.C. (see Clement Alex. *Strom.* 1.131 Dindorf and T. J. Dunbabin, *J.H.S.* 68 (1948) 67 n. 73). Nor is the mention of Eumelos as author quite implausible; he is said to have described the Sun (that is, a son of the Titan Hyperion) and the horses of his chariot, two males and two mares;[1]

[1] Hyginus, *Fab.* 183 (p. 128 Rose). *Equorum solis et horarum nomina. Eous; per hunc caelum verti solet. Aethiops quasi flammeus est, concoquit fruges. hi funales sunt mares. 2. feminae iugariae, Bronte quae nos tonitrua appellamus, Sterope quae fulgitrua.* (These seem to be adaptations of the names of the Kyklopes.) *Huic rei auctor est Eumelus Corinthius. Aethiops: Aethops* Severyns 174.

and the two pairs are elsewhere supposed to have been named in the *Titanomachia*.[1] The Sun, who was a divinity much favoured at Corinth, recurs prominently in a verse fragment ascribed to Eumelos (Schol. Pindar *Ol.* 13.74).[2]

Another fragment, ascribed to 'Eumelos in the *Titanomachia*', is more illuminating. We are told (by a scholiast on Apollonios Rhodios, *Argonautika* 1.1165c p. 106, Wendel) that Eumelos declared Aigaion to be a son of Earth and Pontos; the poet said that he dwelt in the sea and fought as an ally of the Titans.[3] Εὔμηλος δὲ ἐν τῇ Τιτανομαχίᾳ τὸν Αἰγαίωνα Γῆς καὶ Πόντου φησὶ παῖδα, κατοικοῦντα δὲ ἐν τῇ θαλάσσῃ τοῖς Τιτᾶσι συμμαχεῖν. Here is a different theogony from that surviving in the *Library* of Apollodoros. For Aigaion is the same creature as Briareos and is so identified by Homer (*Iliad* 1.403–404): '... the hundred-handed one ... whom gods call Briareos, but all men Aigaion', ἑκατόγχειρον ... | ὃν Βριάρεων καλέουσι θεοί, ἄνδρες δέ τε πάντες | Αἰγαίων'.... In Hesiod (*Theogony* 147 ff) the monster is, as in Apollodoros, son of Sky and Earth, but in Eumelos he is son of Pontos and Earth. It is worth asking whether in the opinion of Eumelos Pontos was a third primal element beside Earth and Sky; one piece of evidence, indeed, suggests that he may have been: in his *Argonautika* Apollonios Rhodios told how Orpheus sang a theogony, presumably the earliest or most primitive-looking known to the learned Hellenistic poet.[4] Apollonios wrote: 'He sang how Earth and Sky and Sea, being formerly fitted together in one guise, were divided from each other through baneful strife' (1.496–498).

ἤειδεν δ' ὡς γαῖα καὶ οὐρανὸς ἠδὲ θάλασσα,
τὸ πρὶν ἔτ' ἀλλήλοισι μιῇ συναρηρότα μορφῇ,
νείκεος ἐξ ὀλοοῖο διέκριθεν ἀμφὶς ἕκαστα.

(p. 21 Fränkel)

In writing the *Argonautika* Apollonios is said to have made use of poetry ascribed to Eumelos, and it is possible that he does so here; Sea in the song of Orpheus corresponds to Pontos in the fragment of Eumelos about Aigaion, but in the version of Apollonios Earth, Sky and Sea

---

[1] Schol. Ven. B. *Iliad* 23.295.   [2] See Chapter V *infra*.
[3] See also Antimachos of Kolophon F 14 Wyss.
[4] G. S. Kirk and J. Raven, *The Presocratic Philosophers* (Cambridge 1957) 33.

23

were, it seems, originally undifferentiated. As for Eumelos's views on their separation, we have no evidence whatsoever.

The mention of Aigaion by Eumelos recalls an anonymous hexameter verse which may also be the work of the Corinthian poet. Phavorinos in his Corinthian oration (Dion. Chr. 37, II Para. 11 p. 170 ff Arnim) states that Poseidon and the Sun quarrelled over the city. They appointed as arbitrator a god older than themselves, a being who had 'very many heads and very many hands'

$$\dots \pi\lambda\epsilon\hat{\iota}\sigma\tau\alpha\iota \ \mu\grave{\epsilon}\nu \ \kappa\epsilon\phi\alpha\lambda\alpha\acute{\iota}, \ \pi\lambda\epsilon\hat{\iota}\sigma\tau\alpha\iota \ \delta\acute{\epsilon} \ \tau\epsilon \ \chi\epsilon\hat{\iota}\rho\epsilon\varsigma.^{1}$$

This being was Briareos-Aigaion, son of Earth and Sea according to Eumelos, who may have mentioned the arbitration, not in the *Titanomachia*, but in his patriotic poem the *Korinthiaka*.

Eumelos is reported to have called Aigaion an ally of the Titans (Schol. Ap. Rhod. *Arg.* 1.1165c). How Eumelos treated this alliance we do not know, but a fragment ascribed to him or to Arktinos by Athenaios (22C) may well record the victory celebrations of Zeus after the Titans had been shut up in Tartaros: 'in the midst of them' that is, of the other gods 'did the father of men and gods dance';

$$\mu\acute{\epsilon}\sigma\sigma\sigma\iota\sigma\iota\nu \ \delta' \ \acute{\omega}\rho\chi\epsilon\hat{\iota}\tau\sigma \ \pi\alpha\tau\grave{\eta}\rho \ \acute{\alpha}\nu\delta\rho\hat{\omega}\nu \ \tau\epsilon \ \theta\epsilon\hat{\omega}\nu \ \tau\epsilon.$$

Secure at last after the victory, the children of Kronos and Rhea cast lots for the sovereignty. To Zeus went the lordship of the sky and clouds, to Poseidon the rule over the waves, and to Hades the dominion under the earth. Earth and high Olympos were common to them all (Homer, *Iliad* 15.187–193). The sharing of Earth seems to have been presupposed by Eumelos if the story of the arbitration of Aigaion is his; Aigaion again intervened in the affairs of the gods above the earth when he was summoned from the sea by Thetis to put down a revolt of Hera, Poseidon and Athena against Zeus (*Iliad* 1.399–405).

The remaining fragments ascribed without author's name to a *Titanomachia* do not fit a coherent pattern, but they are individually of interest. It is alleged that Sky (Ouranos) was called in the poem a son of Aither, which is perhaps best translated as 'the ether of heaven': $A\grave{\iota}\theta\acute{\epsilon}\rho\sigma\varsigma \ \delta' \ \upsilon\acute{\iota}\grave{\sigma}\varsigma \ O\grave{\upsilon}\rho\alpha\nu\acute{\sigma}\varsigma, \ \acute{\omega}\varsigma \ \acute{\sigma} \ \tau\grave{\eta}\nu \ T\iota\tau\alpha\nu\sigma\mu\alpha\chi\acute{\iota}\alpha\nu \ \gamma\rho\acute{\alpha}\psi\alpha\varsigma$ (Cramer, *Anecdota Oxon.* 1.75.12); it is also asserted that Aither is the source of

---

[1] See A. Barigazzi, *R.F.* 94 (1966) 131.

Theogonies and Theomachies

all things (Philodemos, περὶ εὐσεβείας p. 61 Gomperz).[1] Aither is here the undifferentiated original stuff also implicit in the theogony ascribed to Orpheus by Apollonios Rhodios; but how the *Titanomachia* described the separation of Aither into Ouranos (and other entities including, presumably, Earth and perhaps Pontos) we have no evidence. A beautiful fragment, said by Athenaios (277D) to come from the second book of the *Titanomachia*, describes fish playing in the sea:

ἐν δ᾽ αὐτῇ πλωτοὶ χρυσώπιδες ἰχθύες ἐλλοὶ
νήχοντες παίζουσι δι᾽ ὕδατος ἀμβροσίοιο.[2]

'In her the swimming, scaly fishes with their golden faces do sport as they slip through the water divine.' To guess at the context is pointless, but the choice of epithets delights by its elegance.

Two fragments of a *Titanomachia* are concerned with the centaur Cheiron. In one (Schol. Ap. Rhod. 1.554 p. 47, 20–48, 2 Wendel) it is stated: 'The poet of the Gigantomachia' (the variant title need have no special significance)[3] 'says that Kronos, having been changed into a horse, mated with Philyra, daughter of Okeanos; this is why Cheiron was born a hippocentaur': ὁ δὲ τὴν Γιγαντομαχίαν ποιήσας (*Titanomachiae fg.* 7 Kinkel) φησίν, ὅτι Κρόνος μεταμορφωθεὶς εἰς ἵππον ἐμίγη Φιλύρᾳ τῇ Ὠκεανοῦ, διόπερ ἱπποκένταυρος ἐγεννήθη Χείρων. The second fragment introduces Cheiron as an educator and culture-hero: 'the author of the *Titanomachia* says that he was the first who "brought the race of mortals to justice, having explained to them oaths and holy sacrifices and the patterns of Olympos"' (Clem. Alex. *Strom.* 1.73 = *Titanomachia* F 6 Kinkel): . . . καὶ ὁ τὴν Τιτανομαχίαν γράψας φησὶν ὡς πρῶτος οὗτος

εἴς τε δικαιοσύνην θνητῶν γένος ἤγαγε δείξας
ὅρκους καὶ θυσίας ἱλαρὰς καὶ σχήματ᾽ Ὀλύμπου.

The patterns of Olympos are the constellations, the identification and

---

[1] See also Ziegler in Roscher's *Lexikon der Mythologie* 5 (Leipzig 1916–1924) 1524.

[2] παίζοντες νήχοντο Bergk.

[3] J. Dietze, *R.M.* 69 (1914) 535. Note however that according to Eudokia (ap. p. 7 Kinkel) Briareos and Kottos sided with the gods in a war against the *Giants*. Cf. Dörig/Gigon 10–11 and Wilamowitz, *Kronos und die Titanen* (repr. Darmstadt 1964) 15. F. Vian in *La Guerre des Géants* (Paris 1952) Ch. viii offers a reconstruction of the contents of an archaic epic *Titanomachia*.

mythology of which formed a substantial part of early Greek hexametric poetry, as can be seen from Hesiod's *Works and Days* and from the fragments of the *Astronomy* ascribed to him (M.W. F 288–293).[1] Cheiron's precepts were also the subject of a poem specially devoted to them (Hesiod F 170–173 Rzach). One fragment (170) enjoins the pupil to sacrifice to the gods whenever he returns home, and is thus consistent with the remark in the *Titanomachia* about holy sacrifices. Since centaurs appear in Greek bronzework as early as 750 B.C.,[2] the creatures may well have appeared in epic Titanomachies even earlier still. According to Athenaios (470C) the poet of the *Titanomachia* was the first to state that the Sun sailed across the world (from west to east at the end of the day) in a cauldron (Kinkel p. 312): Θεόλυτος δ' ἐν δευτέρῳ "Ωρων (*F.Gr.Hist.* 478 F 1) ἐπὶ λέβητός φησιν αὐτὸν (scil. "Ηλιον) διαπλεῦσαι, τοῦτο πρώτου εἰπόντος τοῦ τὴν Τιτανομαχίαν ποιήσαντος. This remark, if true, would help to date the composition of the fragments, other than those ascribed to Eumelos: for the bowl or cup of the Sun was mentioned by the Ionian poet Mimnermos (F 10 Diehl = Athenaios 470A) who, speaking in a riddle, called the hollow of the cup a golden bed (αἰνισσόμενος τὸ κοῖλον τοῦ ποτηρίου, says Athenaios); and Stesichoros in a magnificent fragment also describes the vessel (F 8 Page = Athenaios 469E).

---

[1] There may well have been an astronomical excursus in the *Titanomachia*, because Atlas was a Titan, and his daughters, the seven Pleiades, became a prominent constellation. Severyns (171–173) therefore suggested that some anonymous hexameters about them come from the *Titanomachia*, but the lines would also be at home in a Hesiodic *Astronomy* ('Hesiod' F 275 and 276 Rzach); all four verses are quoted by a Scholiast to Pindar's second *Nemean* (2.16) and may well come from the same poem; they tell the names of the Pleiades and how one of them Maia became the mother of Hermes.

Τηϋγέτη τ' ἐρόεσσα καὶ Ἠλέκτρη κυανῶπις,
Ἀλκυόνη τε καὶ Ἀστερόπη, δίη τε Κελαινώ,
Μαῖά τε καὶ Μερόπη, τὰς γείνατο φαίδιμος "Ατλας.   (F 275)
Κυλλήνης ἐν ὄρεσσι θεῶν κήρυκα τέχ' Ἑρμῆν.   (F 276)

Later one of the seven Pleiades, Elektra, abandoned her place in the sky because she did not wish to see the Sack of Ilios. This tale may also originate in early epic poetry; Schol. AD on *Iliad* 18.486 ascribe it to the κυκλικοί (cf. Severyns 171).

[2] Boardman, *Pre-Classical* (Pelican, 1967) Plate 36 provides a good illustration of a bronze centaur *ca.* 750 B.C. with a hero. There is an even earlier, Protogeometric, centaur from Kos: R. A. Higgins, *Greek Terracottas* (London 1967) 20.

Theogonies and Theomachies

Mimnermos flourished about 600 B.C. and Stesichoros about 550; so if a version of the *Titanomachia* first described the cup of the Sun (not just, as perhaps in Eumelos, his horses) then the poem must be dated in the second half of the seventh century B.C. at the latest. It is indeed possible that Stesichoros, whose melic poetry had exceptionally close ties with traditional epic, was indebted to a *Titanomachia*. The Himeran's lines noted above (F 8) set the scene at the western edge of the world where the Sun ends his day's work.[1] Here Herakles departs to look for the cattle of Geryon (or possibly for the apples of the Hesperides), not far from the streams of Tartessos, which are mentioned in another fragment of Stesichoros (F 7 Page); nearby was the land of the Hesperides, where Mimnermos has the Sun begin his journey in the cup, χώρου ἀφ' 'Εσπερίδων (F 10, 8 Diehl). In view of this western episode in Stesichoros it is significant that the apples of the Hesperides are said to have been mentioned in the *Titanomachia* (Philodemos, περὶ εὐσεβ. 92.24 p. 43 Gomperz): καὶ τὰς 'Αρπυίας τὰ μῆ[λα φ]υλάττειν 'Ακο[υσίλ]αος (2 F 10). 'Επιμενίδης (D.K. 68 B 9) δὲ καὶ τοῦτο, καὶ τὰς αὐτὰς εἶναι ταῖς 'Εσπερίσιν. ὁ δὲ τὴν Τι[τα]νομαχίαν ⟨τὰ⟩ μὲν μῆλα φυλάτ[τειν. ... 'Akousilaos' – the fifth century B.C. historian, of Argos – 'says that the Harpies guard the apples. But Epimenides says this and also that the Harpies are the same as the Hesperides. But the poet of the *Titanomachia* says that the apples are guarded by. ...' Who or what guarded the apples in the *Titanomachia*? The train of the wording in Philodemos suggests that the guardians of the apples were neither Harpies nor Hesperides. This makes a likely candidate the snake who guards them in Hesiod's *Theogony* (334–335), 'the dread serpent who in the lairs of the dark earth at the mighty bounds of the world watches the all-golden apples'. ...

δεινὸν ὄφιν, ὃς ἐρεμνῆς κεύθεσι γαίης
πείρασιν ἐν μεγάλοις παγχρύσεα μῆλα φυλάσσει.

We are not told in what context the guardian or guardians of the apples were mentioned in the *Titanomachia*; the adventures of Herakles in the far west provide one occasion; the journeys of the sun, westwards in his chariot, eastwards in his bowl, another; but the poet may have been concerned only with the watcher's place in the genealogical scheme.

[1] C. M. Bowra, *Greek Lyric Poetry* (²Oxford 1961) 92.

27

Summing up the conclusions to be drawn from the pitiful remnants of the lost hexameter poems on the battles of the Titans and related themes we may claim: (1) Eumelos almost certainly composed theogonical poetry including a *Titanomachia* (though this may not be the name he gave to his poem); (2) even if Arktinos treated the subject, nothing is known about his poem;[1] (3) the divine genealogies in these lost poems differed from those in Homer and Hesiod, especially in the account of the creation of the world; (4) Herodotos' statement[2] that Homer and Hesiod made 'a theogony' for the Greeks is only partly true; primaeval genealogies are explicit in Hesiod, and to be inferred from certain passages in Homer; but there was much traditional lore not only inconsistent with the Homeric and Hesiodic schemes but also quite as ancient as those two outstanding poets. Much of this lore came down to the Greeks of the eighth century in oral tradition, beginning perhaps in the Mycenaean age. Herodotos's remark is true only in the sense that Hesiod (and, less deliberately, Homer too) was an intelligent systematiser of a great mass of inherited tales. His role as an inventor of gods is much less significant.

The antiquity of parts of the *Theogony* of Hesiod, and the striking divergence of that poem from other traditional epics, can most clearly be seen in the legend of the birth of Aphrodite. In Hesiod (*Theogony* 188–192) the goddess is born of the foam created when the genitals of Ouranos, having been severed by Kronos with an adamantine sickle, are cast into the sea. This important stage in the succession myth is closely akin to the Hittite, and originally Hurrian, myth of the kings of heaven recorded in a cuneiform text at Hattušaš, the Hittite capital in Asia Minor, in the thirteenth or fourteenth century B.C.[3] The text relates that the Babylonian sky-god Anu reigned for nine years, but then fought with the god Kumarbi, who chased him to heaven and after seizing his feet bit off his genitals. Kumarbi spat out as much of

---

[1] A mere name, too, is Telesis of Methymna in Lesbos who may have composed a *Gigantomachia* or *Titanomachia*: Tabula Borgiana ap. Kink. p. 4]μαχίας οὐχ ἦν Τέλεσις ὁ Μηθυμναῖος υ[. See Wilamowitz, 334⁴.

[2] 2.53.2. οὗτοι δέ (sc. Homerus et Hesiodus) εἰσι οἱ ποιήσαντες θεογονίην "Ελλησι καὶ τοῖσι θεοῖσι τὰς ἐπωνυμίας δόντες καὶ τιμάς τε καὶ τέχνας διελόντες καὶ εἴδεα αὐτῶν σημήναντες.

[3] The relevant documents are cited by West, pp. 20–21.

them as he could, but the Storm-god, the chief deity of the Hittite pantheon, grew within his body and eventually emerged. The similarities to the Hesiodic succession are remarkable. Anu, like Ouranos, is castrated by his successor, and gods are born from the severed genitals. Kronos swallows his offspring, except the infant Zeus for whom a stone wrapped in swaddling clothes is substituted; similarly Kumarbi has within him the son who emerges to overthrow him. It is an open question how this near eastern myth came to Hesiod. Greeks may have heard it in the Levantine emporia, at Al Mina in Syria or elsewhere, from 800 B.C. onwards;[1] or Aeolians and Ionians may have picked it up from the successors to the Hittites in Asia Minor (though the Ionian Homer ignores it); or it may have entered the tradition in Mycenaean times and have been passed down orally with little change for half a millennium or more to Hesiod – a tale undigested because indigestible.[2]

The contrast with the Homeric version of Aphrodite's birth is remarkable. In the *Iliad* (5.370 ff and 428) Homer shows that Aphrodite was the child of Zeus and Dione. In Hesiod's *Theogony* (353) Dione is one of the numerous progeny of Okeanos and Tethys, no hint being given that she is also a consort of Zeus. She was specially at home at Dodona where she was worshipped with Zeus, but otherwise plays a small part in Greek myth.[3] Her name $Δι-ώνη$ is but the feminine form of Zeus, to whom she is a foil, and her principal function is to be the mother of Aphrodite. She may well have been selected for this role by poets who refused to accept the tale of Aphrodite's birth as reported by Hesiod; but even so, Dione's consortship with Zeus may still be very ancient; it may not be an invention of Hesiod's and Homer's day, but one designed to compete with an unacceptable, and originally non-Hellenic, myth. The *Library* of Apollodoros, behind the early chapters of which, we have suggested, lay a non-Hesiodic tradition, also chooses the Homeric version of the parentage of Aphrodite (1.3.1).[4] Since the

---

[1] T. J. Dunbabin, *The Greeks and their Eastern Neighbours* (London 1957) 56–57.

[2] Cf. P. Walcot, *Hesiod and Near Eastern Epic* (Cardiff 1966) 129.

[3] W. Potscher, *Mnemosyne* 19[4] (1966) 135–145.

[4] Apollodoros (1.1.4), however, agrees with Hesiod (*Theogony* 183–185) in stating that the Furies were born from the drops of Sky's blood which fell on Earth and impregnated her.

two traditions were irreconcilable, poets had to choose between them, just as they had to choose between the primaeval parentage of Ouranos and Earth in one system or Okeanos and Tethys in another. The Greeks, indeed, were well aware of the sound principle that in religion there is much merit in system, but none in uniformity.

II

Phoronis and *Danais*

The first writer known to have set down systematically in prose the local traditions of Argos and the Argolid was Akousilaos the Argive, who worked in the middle of the fifth century B.C. or a little earlier (*F.Gr.Hist.* 2 T 2 and 3). The existence of a lively oral tradition in the Argolid is attested by the abundance of stories about Argos, Tiryns and Mycenae with their heroic dynasties, and by the words of Thucydides describing the establishment of the Pelopid dynasty at Mycenae: 'those of the Peloponnesians who accept in oral tradition from their forerunners the clearest evidence declare'. . . .[1] Here the historian may even be alluding to Akousilaos who is known to have devoted part of his work, the *Genealogies*, to the royal lines of the land.

A principal source of evidence used by Akousilaos was the lost epic called the *Phoronis*, of which a few significant details survive. It was pleasing to Argive patriotism that Phoroneus was said to be first man and ancestor of the human race – πατέρα θνητῶν ἀνθρώπων (F 1 Kinkel); as though he were another Cheiron, Phoroneus is said to have been the instructor of mankind in civilised life (Pausanias 2.15.5). This son of the Argive river god Inachos and grandson of Okeanos and Tethys[2] was, it seems, even thought to be an Argive Prometheus, who enabled mankind to work with fire. A fragment of the *Phoronis* describes the Idaians, the smiths of Phrygia (Schol. Ap. Rhod. 1.1126–31b, p. 102 Wendel) – or of Crete, as some believed. In the verses the smiths are called 'men', so they presumably were said in the poem to have been born later than Phoroneus himself. One of them is fitly named Anvil (Akmon). The scene is perhaps the smithy on Mount Ida, 'where the

---

[1] 1.9.2 λέγουσι δὲ καὶ οἱ τὰ σαφέστατα Πελοποννησίων μνήμῃ παρὰ τῶν πρότερον δεδεγμένοι. See also J. B. Bury, *The Ancient Greek Historians* (Reprint. New York 1958) 103.

[2] Apollodoros, *Library* 2.1.1.

Idaian sorcerers, the Phrygian men of the mountains, did dwell, Kelmis and mighty Damnameneus and Akmon exceeding in strength, the skilful attendants of Adresteia of the highlands, they who first discovered the craft of Hephaistos of the many counsels, dark iron, in the mountain dells, and brought it to the fire and wrought a conspicuous task.'

ἔνθα γόητες

Ἰδαῖοι Φρύγες ἄνδρες ὀρέστεροι οἰκί' ἔναιον,
Κέλμις Δαμναμενεύς τε μέγας καὶ ὑπέρβιος Ἄκμων,
εὐπάλαμοι θεράποντες ὀρείης Ἀδρηστείης,
οἳ πρῶτοι τέχνην πολυμήτιος Ἡφαίστοιο
εὗρον ἐν οὐρείῃσι νάπαις ἰόεντα σίδηρον,
ἤνεγκάν τ' εἰς πῦρ καὶ ἀριπρεπὲς ἔργον ἔτευξαν.

Adresteia was a nurse of the infant Zeus (Ap. Rhod. *Arg.* 3.133). Pausanias (2.19.5) remarks that Phoroneus was reputed to be the discoverer of fire; the point of this fragment may therefore be that the hero taught the Idaians about fire, which they then adopted for metal working, their own discovery. The parochial emphasis on 'first discovery' or 'first achievement' was, evidently, strong in the poem; it is the Argive equivalent of Soviet cultural propaganda of the Stalinist era. The first man's daughter, Niobe, was also the first mortal woman to mate with Zeus, according to Akousilaos (2 F 25a), who may well have taken the claim from the *Phoronis*. In a papyrus fragment (*P. Oxy.* 1241 Col. iv 3 ff) Phoroneus is even said to have been the first to set up a court of law, a notion which was no doubt gratifying to the vigorous Argive democrats of the mid-fifth century. [ἐδίκασε] δὲ τοὺς ἐμφυλίους [πρῶτος δικασ]τήριον ποιήσας [Φορωνεύ]ς ὁ Ἰνάχου. But that detail may not have originated as early as the *Phoronis*.

The context of a fragment in Strabo (471 = F 3 Kinkel) is quite lost: 'The writer of the *Phoronis* says that the Kouretes were flute players and Phrygians.' The recurrence of Phrygians is noteworthy, and it may be relevant that Strabo here quotes a Hesiodic fragment (F 198 Rzach) in which the Kouretes are called offspring of a daughter of Phoroneus – . . . 'The Kouretes, gods who delight in play and are dancers.' The verses may be part of the Argive genealogy, but, if so, it is surprising that the first man, Phoroneus, had descendants, the dancing Kouretes, who are here said to be gods.

Phoronis and Danais

The most significant fragment concerns Argive cult (F 4 Kinkel =
Clem. Alex. *Strom.* 1.164) and the first priestess of Argive Hera.
Clement remarks that the ancients set up pillars and worshipped them
as abodes (ἀμφιδρύματα) of the god: 'at any rate the poet of the
Phoronis writes: "Kallithoe, the custodian for the Olympian queen,
Argive Hera, who first with chaplets and tassels did adorn the lofty
pillar of the lady." '

Καλλιθόη κλειδοῦχος Ὀλυμπιάδος βασιλείης
"Ηρης Ἀργείης, ἣ στέμμασι καὶ θυσάνοισι
πρώτη κόσμησεν περὶ κίονα μακρὸν ἀνάσσης.

Kallithoe (or Kallithye) became identified with Io who was also a
priestess of Argive Hera.[1] At the Argive Heraion Pausanias (2.17.5) saw
a small pearwood seated statue of Hera which had been taken thither
from Tiryns when the Argives had captured Tiryns. Beside the statue
he saw what he calls an old ἄγαλμα ἐπὶ κίονος of Hera. This could well
be the pillar-type statue described in the *Phoronis*, which Pausanias
perhaps mistakenly saw as a statue on a pillar.[2]

To determine when the Argives took Tiryns and expelled part at
least of the inhabitants to Halieis is not easy, since the ancient authorities
are not explicit; but the recent American excavations at Halieis suggest
that the settlement of Tirynthians there may well have occurred as
early as 470 B.C.[3] Unless therefore the *Phoronis* was composed later than
about 470 B.C. (and there is no reason to think that it was),[4] the verses
about the pillar are alluding to Tirynthian cult, not to the worship of the
wooden column at the Argive Heraion. All the more remarkable
therefore is the epithet of Hera, ᾽Αργείη, in line 2.[5] The reason may well

[1] Hesychius: Ἰὼ Καλλιθύεσσα· καλλιθύεσσα ἐκαλεῖτο ἡ πρώτη ἱέρεια τῆς Ἀθηνᾶς
[τῆς ἐν ῎Αργει ῞Ηρας Knaack]. Cf. Wilamowitz, *Aischylos, Interpretationen* (Berlin
1914) 25 and Jacoby, *Abh.* 335.

[2] I am grateful to Dr L. H. Jeffery for this illuminating suggestion.

[3] Herodotos 7.137.2. Ephoros 70 F 56. Strabo 373. On the problem see
M. Wörrle, *Untersuchungen zur Verfassungsgeschichte von Argos im 5 Jahrhundert vor
Christus* (1964) 114, note 41.

[4] Akousilaos, who made use of the *Phoronis*, may already have been active before
470 B.C. (cf. Jacoby on *F.Gr.Hist.* 2 T 1).

[5] F. Stoessl, *R.E.* 20.1 (1941) 649, notes the difficulty. Cf. G. Kaibel, *Göttingen
Nachrichten* 1901, 504 and F. Wehrli, 'Io, Dichtung und Kultlegend' in *Festschrift
Schefold* (Bern 1967) 196.

be that Hera is not of Argos, the city, but of the grove of the hero Argos, near Tiryns, which Kleomenes I of Sparta caused to be burned down (Herodotos 6.76–80). This, surely, is the grove from which the wooden column, adorned in honour of Hera, came, first to Tiryns, and later to the Heraion, between Tiryns and Mycenae. A pendant to this story may be seen in a fragment of Akousilaos (2 F 28), who reported that when the all-seeing herdsman Argos was set by Hera to watch over Io, who had by then been transformed into a heifer, Argos bound the creature to an olive tree in the grove of the Mycenaeans. The original version of the story, it may be suggested, had told how Io was tied to a tree in the grove near Tiryns.

One last fragment of the *Phoronis* cannot be placed in context. It tells how Hermes was named by Zeus. 'His father called Hermeias Eriounios because he surpassed all the blessed gods and mortal men in wiles and cunning thievings' (F 5 Kinkel = Etym. Mag. 374.18, which feebly tries to link Eriounios with ἐρεύνησις, 'searching').[1] The poet would have provided a folk-etymology of his own to explain the epithet Eriounios, whose true meaning is uncertain. The occasion of the verses is perhaps the birth of Hermes to Maia in a cave on Mount Kyllene in Arkadia, not so far from Argos. If the *Phoronis* included the story of Io, then Hermes had a prominent part in the epic, because at the command of Zeus he stole Io away and killed Argos who had been set to watch over her (Apollodoros, *Library* 2.1.3).

The conclusions to be drawn from the *Phoronis* are tenuous; but even less may be asserted with confidence about the *Danais*. Since this epic may be supposed to have been a principal source of the Danaid tetralogy of Aeschylus, the Argolid was almost certainly the main scene of the tale, and the flight of Danaos and his daughters from Egypt to Argos, whither they were pursued by the sons of Aigyptos, a feature of the plot.[2]

[1] Ἑρμείαν δὲ πατὴρ Ἐριούνιον ὠνόμασ' αὐτόν·/πάντας γὰρ μάκαράς τε θεοὺς θνητούς τ' ἀνθρώπους/κέρδεσι κλεπτοσύνῃσί τ' ἐκαίνυτο τεχνηέσσαις.

[2] Euripides [F 846 Nauck²] seems to have known of a version of the tale according to which Aigyptos did not come with his sons to Argos; this can be inferred from his statement that *most* people declare Aigyptos to have accompanied them:

Αἴγυπτος, ὡς ὁ πλεῖστος ἔσπαρται λόγος,
ξὺν παισὶ πεντήκοντα ναυτίλῳ πλάτῃ
Ἄργος κατασχών.

34

Phoronis and Danais

The Tabula Borgiana, a Roman inscription written in Greek, names in a list of epics a *Danaides* allegedly of 6,500 verses, καὶ Δαναΐδας ͵ϛφ′ ἐπῶν (Kinkel p. 4). The plural *Danaides* perhaps is due to a confusion with the lost play of that name, 'Daughters of Danaos', by Aeschylus (F 122–127 Mette). Both Clement of Alexandria (*Strom.* 4.120= *Danais* F 1 Kinkel) and Harpokration (s.v. αὐτόχθονες) refer to ὁ τὴν Δαναΐδα πεποιηκώς; the title *Danais* may be compared with *Alkmaionis*, the epic about Alkmaion, or *Phoronis*, the epic about Phoroneus. Danaos is likely therefore to have been the chief character. Clement quotes two verses about the hero's daughters: 'Then swiftly did the daughters of Danaos equip themselves before the flowing river, the Lord Nile.'

καὶ τότ' ἄρ' ὡπλίζοντο θοῶς Δαναοῖο θύγατρες
πρόσθεν ἐϋρρεῖος ποταμοῦ Νείλοιο ἄνακτος.

(*Strom.* 4.120 = *Danais* F 1 Kinkel)

The context may well be the preparation of the fugitives for their voyage to Greece from Egypt, and their arming against the sons of Aigyptos. 'Lord Nile' here may well be Aigyptos, since the two names were often equated.[1]

One fragment (F 2 Kinkel = Harpokration s.v. αὐτόχθονες) states that Pindar (F 180 Turyn) and the poet of the *Danais* declared Erichthonios son of Hephaistos to have appeared from the earth: ὁ δὲ Πίνδαρος καὶ ὁ τὴν Δαναΐδα πεποιηκώς φασιν Ἐριχθόνιον †καὶ Ἥφαιστον† (τὸν Ἡφαίστου Schroeder) ἐκ γῆς φανῆναι. The allusion is to the story of Hephaistos and his attempt upon the virginity of Athena.

Schol. MTAB on Euripides, *Or.* 872 seem to regard Danaos and Aigyptos as natives of Argos, and so do Schol. MB on *Hec.* 886 (1.185 and 1.69 Schwartz). But this variant of the story is almost certainly secondary since in the *Danais*, the earliest known account of Danaos, his daughters were clearly immigrants from Egypt. In tragedy as early as Phrynichos (p. 720 Nauck²) Aigyptos comes from Egypt to Argos: Φρύνιχος δὲ ὁ τραγικὸς φησὶ σὺν (fort. ἐν) Αἰγυπτίοις τὸν Αἴγυπτον ἥκειν εἰς Ἄργος. But in Aeschylus (*Suppl.* 928) the sons of Aigyptos arrive in Argos without their father; here Aeschylus agrees with Hekataios (1 F 19) against Phrynichos. Hekataios doubted that Aigyptos had fifty, or even twenty, sons, but not that the Danaids and the sons of Aigyptos were foreign immigrants to Argos (see also 1 F 21). For discussion of these rival versions see Wilamowitz, *Aischylos, Interpretationen* (Berlin 1914) 20 with note 3. Cf. J. T. Hooker, *A.J.A.* 71 (1967) 277.

[1] Schol. EV, *Od.* 4.477.

35

Greek Epic Poetry

The maiden goddess escaped from the lame craftsman's embrace, but his seed fell on the ground. From it sprang Erichthonios who became king of Athens. The story is mentioned in the Tabula Borgiana and evidently was not deemed unsuitable for epic. What place this Athenian tale can have had in the *Danais* is beyond conjecture. As Athena avoids marriage, so the daughters of Danaos shun the sons of Aigyptos; and Aeschylus in his *Danaides* wrote, in a renowned passage, of rain falling from Sky to Earth to create the growth of herds and crops. 'Holy Sky' says Aphrodite 'yearns to penetrate the ground and a passion seizes Earth to achieve wedlock' (Aeschylus F 125, 20–21 Mette). The conflict between the sublime power of Aphrodite and the horror of enforced marriage is central in the epic theme Aeschylus inherited; but, re-grettably, these analogies do not show what was the context of the Erichthonios episode in the *Danais*.

When Danaos became king of Argos (either by the replacement, or after the death, of his indigenous predecessor Gelanor or, as he was also called, Pelasgos) the future of the immigrants was secure. In his succession lies the true unfolding of the tale. No fragment identifiable as part of the *Danais* describes the event, but a Hesiodic verse recalls one of his principal achievements – the irrigation of waterless Argos: "Ἄργος ἄνυδρον ἐὸν Δαναὸς ποίησεν ἔνυδρον (Hesiod F 24 Rzach). A variant twice quoted without author's name by Strabo (370 and 371) makes the hero's daughters responsible: "Ἄργος ἄνυδρον ἐὸν Δανααὶ θέσαν "Ἄργος ἔνυδρον. Strabo believed that Argos town with its wells was indicated here, because the plain of the Argolis was amply watered by nature; but in one early version of the story a Danaid Amymone was led by Poseidon to discover the springs of Lerna out in the countryside (Aeschylus F 130 Mette), which thus was saved from drought. If the *Danais* in fact extended to 6,500 verses, there was plenty of scope for taking the traditional tale so far down in time as the new dynasty's waterworks or discovery of springs.[1]

The prime link between the *Phoronis* and the *Danais* is Io; for she was a blood relation of Phoroneus, being according to some a daughter of Inachos (Aeschylus *P.V.* 705), to others, of Peiren son of Phoroneus

---

[1] Kerchneia (Aeschylus *P.V.* 676) may have been another fountain discovered by the family.

(Akousilaos 2 F 26); and genealogists tied the offspring, Epaphos, born to her in Egypt to the royal line of Danaos (Aeschylus, *Supplices* 300–321). Since both Akousilaos and Aeschylus were aware, and made use, of this link, some epic poet may have dwelt on it before them; but not necessarily in the *Danais* or the *Phoronis*.

Such was the power and renown of the house of Danaos that Danaoi was used in epic to mean 'all the Greeks'. It is so used from Homer onwards, but the meaning may well have originated in Mycenaean times. A Levantine people called Danuna is mentioned in documents at Tell-el-Amarna in Egypt *ca.* 1365 B.C.; if these are a branch of the Danaoi, the legend is at least consistent in implying that Danaos was an immigrant to Argos and a foreigner. One of the most famous princesses of the dynasty was Danae, daughter of Akrisios, king of Argos. Homer makes Zeus speak of his passion for her to Hera in a long list of his lady-loves, divine and human (*Iliad* 14.319–320). Since the princess is called by Zeus daughter of Akrisios and mother of Perseus, elements of the story were well known to Homer; they may well have been very ancient indeed. The tale recurred in the Hesiodic *Catalogues of Women*, of which a fragment survives with an allusion to her being cast in a chest into the sea by Akrisios, and to Zeus's having visited her in the form of golden rain;[1] but this brings us far from the extant fragments of the *Danais*. One more fragment of the *Danais* overlaps the *Phoronis*. Philodemos (περὶ εὐσεβ. p. 42 Gomperz) remarks that according to the author of the *Danais* the Kouretes were attendants of the Mother of the Gods, and in the *Phoronis* (F 3 Kinkel) the Kouretes are called flute-players; their instruments they may well have played in honour of the Great Mother of Phrygia, the country whence the Phrygian mode of music came to the Greeks. Amongst the innovations ascribed to Phoroneus in the *Phoronis* and the *Danais* were perhaps the art of flute playing and the worship of the Phrygian Great Mother. Phrygian musical and other influences were strong amongst the Greeks *ca.* 700 B.C. [see *G.R.B.S.* 2 (1959) 94–99], but this fact provides no pointer to the time when the *Phoronis* and *Danais* were composed. All we can say is that these, to us, obscure poems on illustrious dynasties were earlier than the prose writer Akousilaos, who made use of them as well as of

[1] (F 135, 2–4 Merkelbach/West.)

the great mass of genealogical poetry ascribed to Hesiod (see *F.Gr.Hist.* 2 T 5).

Finally, an affinity and a conflict between the *Phoronis* and the Prometheus legend must be noted. Amongst the innovations ascribed to Phoroneus was, as we have seen, the introduction of fire or of means of conveying (μετάγειν) it (Pausanias 2.19.5 ἐς Φορωνέα τοῦ πυρὸς μετάγειν ἐθέλουσι τὴν εὕρεσιν). Argive chauvinism may well have led to the inclusion of this achievement, amongst the hero's many discoveries, in the *Phoronis*. But if so, the poet deliberately rejected the Hesiodic story according to which Prometheus was punished by Zeus for having brought fire to men in a hollow fennel stalk (*Theogony* 565–570; *Works and Days* 50–52). This does not entail however that the *Phoronis* ignored Prometheus entirely, since Aeschylus in the *Prometheus Vinctus* may not have been the first to bring Io to Egypt by way of the rock in Skythia to which Prometheus was fastened. If another reason for the punishment of Prometheus was needed, then the attempt to deceive Zeus into choosing the worst helping of ox in the sacrificial meal at Mekone (Hesiod, *Theogony* 535 ff) was an equally punishable offence of *lèse-majesté*. As an opponent of Zeus and a son of the Titan Iapetos, Prometheus may well have been prominent in the *Titanomachia* also; but it is remarkable that no epic *Prometheia*, devoted entirely to his crime, punishment and release is reliably attested.

III

The Theban Epics

The story of Thebes in legend begins with Kadmos the founder, an immigrant from Phoenicia, and continues with Amphion and Zethos who on becoming kings fortified the city, the stones following Amphion's lyre (Apollodoros, *Library* 3.5.5). Homer knows the fortifiers but says nothing of the miracle of the lyre (*Od.* 11.260–265): Odysseus reporting his visit to the oracle of the dead relates, 'And next I saw Antiope, daughter of Asopos, who was proud to have enjoyed the embrace of Zeus and brought forth two sons, Amphion and Zethos, who first did stablish the seat of seven-gated Thebes and towered it about, since, mighty pair though they were, they could not dwell in Thebe of the wide dancing floor unless it had bastions.' To the two brothers we return when we come to Asios of Samos.

Homer alludes also to the birth of the god Dionysos, son of Zeus, to Semele, daughter of Kadmos (*Iliad* 14.323 and 325), a theme of local interest to the Boiotian Hesiod (*Theogony* 940–942); and both poets mention that Herakles was born to Zeus out of Alkmene, wife of Amphitryon of Thebes (*Theogony* 943–944. *Iliad* 19.94–124). Homer relates how Hera hastened the birth of Eurystheus in the seventh month to a grand-daughter of Perseus, but delayed the birth of Herakles to Alkmene, being aided in this by the Eileithyiai, goddesses of childbirth. Hera thus ensured that Eurystheus, not Herakles, would, as Zeus had promised for the prince born that very day, be overlord of his neighbours. Eurystheus duly became king of Mycenae and charged Herakles with the labours.

Thus there was already in Homer's day much detailed legend concerned with Kadmos, his descendants and his successors at Thebes. Some of this genealogical evidence was presented systematically in the Hesiodic *Catalogues of Women*,[1] but there were also three great epic

[1] Cf. the Hesiodic *Shield* 27–56.

poems devoted to Thebes and her bloody history – the *Oidipodeia*, the *Thebais* and the *Epigonoi*. Each epic is closely connected with the others, and since the earliest evidence for the tales is of special interest, the poems must be taken together.

An *Oidipodeia* was ascribed to Kinaithon, a Lakedaimonian poet, by the author of the Tabula Borgiana (Kinkel p. 4). Kinaithon is dated before the middle of the eighth century B.C. by Eusebius (Olympiad 4, 2), but the epoch is almost certainly too high and in any case does not depend upon local records but upon calculation of generations. Two fragments of the *Oidipodeia* show the outlines of the story. One alludes to the devouring of Thebans by the Sphinx whose riddle they could not solve: 'yet again the most beauteous and delightful of them, the dear son of blameless Kreion, noble Haimon' did the Sphinx devour.

> ἀλλ' ἔτι κάλλιστόν τε καὶ ἱμεροέστατον ἄλλων
> παῖδα φίλον Κρείοντος ἀμύμονος, Αἵμονα δῖον
> . . . .   [*Oidipodeia* F 2 Allen]

Hesiod knows the Sphinx by her Boiotian name Phix (*Theogony* 326) and the Phikian hill on which she sat to tease, and to devour, the unfortunate Kadmeian victims is mentioned in the Hesiodic *Shield* (33). The two lines show that others had been eaten before Haimon, king Kreion's son, but the loss of his heir was the cruellest blow of all. When Oidipous solved the riddle – that which has one voice and yet becomes four-footed and two-footed and three-footed is Man – he became king and unwittingly married his mother Epikaste. Homer in his report of the heroes and heroines seen by Odysseus in Hades shows knowledge of this incest, but as Pausanias was at pains to point out (9.5.11) Homer does not state that Oidipous had children by Epikaste, or, as she was usually called, Iokaste. Pausanias, who had seen at Plataia a painting of Euryganeia bewailing the mutual slaughter of her sons Eteokles and Polyneikes, maintained that she was the mother of the children of Oidipous. Harmonisers, such as the Athenian historian Pherekydes, who wrote *ca.* 500 B.C., maintained that Oidipous had had progeny by both ladies (*F.Gr.Hist.* 3 F 95). The gods, according to Homer (*Odyssey* 11.271–274), made the incest of Oidipous with his mother 'notorious at once', so that Pausanias's remark that Oidipous cannot have had time before the exposure to beget four children by

Epikaste has substance. Moreover, dynasts such as Theron of Akragas, who claimed descent from Oidipous (Pindar, *Ol.* 2.35), must have preferred not to think of themselves as descended from an incestuous marriage.

Homer knows of the killing by Oidipous of his father and of Epikaste's suicide when the incest was revealed, but there is no sign in the *Odyssey* of the Aeschylean and Sophoclean theme of the blinding of Oidipous. After Epikaste had hanged herself, Homer states, Oidipous remained king 'suffering anguish by the baneful counsels of the gods ... and to him she bequeathed many a sorrow, even all that a mother's Furies bring to pass' (*Odyssey* 11.275–280). The tale of Oidipous is touched on once in the *Iliad* (23.679–680), where we are told that Mekisteus attended at Thebes the funeral games celebrated after the death of Oidipous:

ὅς ποτε Θήβασδ' ἦλθε δεδουπότος Οἰδιπόδαο
ἐς τάφον,–

'who came long ago to Thebes, when Oidipous had fallen, to the wake'. The strong word δεδουπότος, 'thudded to the ground', suggests that Oidipous was thought to have been assassinated.[1] Early epic gives no sign of the wandering of the blind Oidipous to Athens, a strictly Athenian and secondary development of the legend. As for the name *Oidipodeia*, Pausanias, who gives the name of no author of the poem called it Οἰδιπόδεια (sc. ἔπη), neuter plural; but the Tabula Borgiana knows it as τὴν Οἰδιπόδειαν. The variants may reflect differing versions of the poem, one Boiotian, the other Lakedaimonian.

As if the mother's curse of Epikaste upon Oidipous had not been enough, Oidipous himself twice cursed his sons Polyneikes and Eteokles, whose dispute over their patrimony was the theme of the *Thebais*. This poem was, as early as the time of Kallinos of Ephesos, in the seventh century B.C., ascribed to Homer, if we may trust Pausanias (9.9.5) who had evidently read a substantial part of it, because he declares the epic to be inferior only to the *Iliad* and the *Odyssey*. Athenaios and other writers call the poem the 'cyclic' *Thebais* to distinguish it from the long poem, also a *Thebais*, by Antimachos of Kolophon who flourished about 400 B.C.

[1] See R. C. Jebb, *Sophocles. The Oedipus Tyrannus* (Cambridge 1887) xii.

41

The first curse of Oidipous was uttered because his sons had disobeyed his command not to place on his table the wine-cups of Laios his father. This fragment, extending to ten lines (Athenaios 465 F: F 2 Kinkel), relates both the disobedience and the curse: 'Then did the nobly born hero, fair haired Polyneikes, first place by Oidipous a fine table of silver, that had belonged to Kadmos of the divine thought. Next he filled with sweet wine a beautiful golden bowl. But when Oidipous recognised the costly property of his father lying beside him, mighty trouble fell upon his spirit and forthwith did he curse both his sons with wasting imprecations as they stood by – and the divine Fury did not fail to hear them – that they should divide their patrimony in no friendly spirit, but that war and strife should ever be between them.'

αὐτὰρ ὁ διογενὴς ἥρως ξανθὸς Πολυνείκης
πρῶτα μὲν Οἰδιπόδῃ καλὴν παρέθηκε τράπεζαν
ἀργυρέην Κάδμοιο θεόφρονος· αὐτὰρ ἔπειτα
χρύσεον ἔμπλησεν καλὸν δέπας ἡδέος οἴνου.
5   αὐτὰρ ὅ γ' ὡς φράσθη παρακείμενα πατρὸς ἑοῖο
τιμήεντα γέρα, μέγα οἱ κακὸν ἔμπεσε θυμῷ,
αἶψα δὲ παισὶν ἑοῖσι μετ' ἀμφοτέροισιν ἐπαρὰς
ἀργαλέας ἠρᾶτο· θεῶν δ' οὐ λάνθαν' ἐρινύν.
ὡς οὔ οἱ πατρώϊ' ἐν ἠθείῃ φιλότητι
10   δάσσαιντ', ἀμφοτέροισι δ' ἀεὶ πολεμοί τε μάχαί τε
. . . .

9 πατρωιαν εἴη φιλότητι cod. A. Athen.
ἐνηέι ⟨ἐν⟩ φιλότητι W. Ribbeck.

The second curse upon the sons was uttered when they sent to their father a haunch instead of a shoulder of a sacrificed animal. 'The author of the cyclic *Thebais* tells the story as follows' remarks a scholiast on Sophocles, *Oedipus Coloneus* 1375; 'when he perceived the haunch, he threw it to the ground and declared. Alas for me! my sons have sent it to shame me. He prayed to Zeus the king and to the other immortals that at each other's hands they should go down within Hades.' The mutual slaughter of the brothers gave the internecine strife of the war against Thebes a special poignancy, which Pindar had in mind when he wrote of the swift Fury who slew his warlike progeny, each murdered by the other: ἰδοῖσα δ' ὀξεῖ' Ἐρινὺς | ἔπεφνέ οἱ σὺν ἀλλαλοφονίᾳ γένος ἀρήϊον (Olympian 2.45–46).

It may perhaps be inferred from Hesiod that the dispute centered upon the division of the flocks of Oidipous. War, says the poet, destroyed the demigod race of heroes. 'Some it ruined beneath seven-gated Thebes, the Kadmeian land, as they fought for the sheep of Oidipous, others too it destroyed even in their ships as it brought them above the mighty surge of the sea to Troy, because of Helen of the fair locks' (Works and Days 161–165).

Polyneikes departed to Argos to recruit an army which would take Thebes by storm. It is an open question whether in the legend Thebes first had seven-gates, or Polyneikes recruited an army of seven leaders including himself, and there had to be seven gates to match them.[1] Excavation of Late Helladic Thebes would perhaps decide whether the city in fact had seven gates at the time of the historical core of the legend.[2] In Aeschylus (Septem 375 ff) Polyneikes and six comrades face Eteokles and his six at each of the seven gates, but that there were two bands of seven already in the Cyclic Thebais we do not know. The significance of Argos in the poem as base for the attack on Thebes is emphasised by its mention in the first line:

Ἄργος ἄειδε θεὰ πολυδίψιον ἔνθεν ἄνακτες

(Certamen Homeri et Hesiodi p. 235 Allen)

The ascription of a Thebais to the Ionian Homer should not be ignored, because there were immigrants from Boiotia in Ionia (Herodotos 1.146.1) who would have found the exploits of their Kadmeian ancestors of deep interest. Homer reveals in the Iliad and the Odyssey detailed knowledge of Theban legend to which he many times digresses. Thus Agamemnon relates how, when Polyneikes came with Tydeus to Mycenae to muster troops for the war against Thebes, help was refused because Zeus sent unfavourable omens (Iliad 4.376–38). The poet makes Diomedes recall how his father Tydeus had come from Aitolia to Argos, where he had married a daughter of King Adrastos; later Tydeus had died before Thebes and was buried there (Iliad

[1] Cf. P. Friedländer, R.M. 69 (1914) 323–324.
[2] A. Schachter, 'The Theban Wars', Phoenix 21 (1967) 1–10 examines the historical origins of the legends.

14.113–121). Homer glances at the escape of Adrastos, after the defeat at Thebes, with his steed Arion and alludes to the animal's divine progenitors Poseidon and Demeter (who consorted with him in the likeness of a Fury. *Iliad* 23.346–347, cf. Apollodoros, *Library* 3.6.8.). He knows the story of how Eriphyle was bribed by Polyneikes to persuade her husband Amphiaraos the seer to go to war against Thebes (*Odyssey* 11.326–327 and 15.247); and it is even asserted in the quaint pseudo-Herodotean *Life of Homer* that there was a poem devoted to the *Expedition of Amphiaraos to Thebes* (᾿Αμφιαράου ἐξέλασις: see also Suda s.v. ῝Ομηρος), but that this was a poem distinct from the *Thebais* is doubtful. Two anonymous verses have been ascribed tentatively to the *Expedition* (Powell, *Collectanea Alexandrina* 246):

πουλύποδός μοι, τέκνον, ἔχων νόον, ᾿Αμφίλοχ᾿ ἥρως
τοῖσιν ἐφαρμόζου τῶν κεν <κατὰ> δῆμον ἵκηαι.

(Athen. 317A)

'Amphilochos my son, be minded like the cuttle-fish and fit yourself to those to whose land you may ever come.' The words are perhaps spoken to his son by Amphiaraos just as he is about to depart for Thebes.[1] Tydeus's challenge to the Kadmeians dining in the house of Eteokles, and the failure of the Thebans to kill him in an ambush before battle commenced, while the Argive army was halted at the river Asopos (*Iliad* 4.387–400), are well known to Homer. The links between the *Iliad* and the *Thebais* are therefore close; they can be used to elucidate the fragments of the lost poem.

Pausanias, discussing Arion the horse, quotes a line about him from the *Thebais* (8.25.8).

εἵματα λυγρὰ φέρων σὺν ᾿Αρείονι κυανοχαίτῃ.

Adrastos fled 'wearing his baneful garments with dark-maned Arion'. The significance of the clothing here is lost – the verse may mean

---

[1] Some versions add the line

ἄλλοτε δ᾿ ἀλλοῖος τελέθειν καὶ χώρῃ ἕπεσθαι.

See Löffler 57, who considers the alternative explanation that the words were addressed to his son Amphilochos (II) by Alkmaion. This Amphilochos seems to be a late addition to the Melampodid genealogy and may reflect Corinthian settlement on the Ambrakiot gulf; he is the eponymous hero of Argos Amphilochikon (Apollod. *Lib.* 3.7.7.). Thucydides (2.68.3), however, thought that the eponymous hero of Amphilochian Argos was Amphilochos (I), brother of Alkmaion, for whose ties with the district see Chapter IV.

The Theban Epics

simply that the hero's clothes were dirty after the battle – but, as Pausanias saw, the epithet κυανοχαίτης 'dark haired' is regularly given to Poseidon. The poet may thus be noting Arion's parentage in passing.

As Amphiaraos fled from defeat at Thebes, Zeus split the earth by throwing a thunderbolt and the hero vanished with his chariot before Periklymenos could strike him in the back, as Pindar, who made use of the *Thebais*, relates (*Nemean* 9.23–24). In one passage Pindar followed the wording of the epic closely, as Asklepiades informs us (*F.H.G.* 3.299): in *Olympian* 6 (16–17) Adrastos speaking of the lost Amphiaraos says 'I yearn for the eye of my army, doubly skilled as seer and champion with the spear'.

πoθέω στρατιᾶς ὀφθαλμὸν ἐμᾶς
ἀμφότερον μάντιν τ' ἀγαθὸν καὶ δουρὶ μάρνασθαι.

Echoes of epic versification survive here, e.g. ὄμμα τ' ἐμῆς ποθέω στρατιῆς and, as Leutsch noted, the second line presupposes such a hexameter as ἀμφότερον μάντιν τ' ἀγαθὸν καὶ δουρὶ μάχεσθαι.[1] The thought is echoed in a fragment of the Hesiodic *Catalogues of Women* where Amphiaraos is called 'excellent in valour and in war, noble in spirit and beloved of the immortals' (Merkelbach p. 19, 37–38). The gods who specially loved him were Zeus (who saved him by opening the ground) and Apollo (because he was a seer), so Homer reports (*Odyssey* 15.244–245).

In the manner of all early Greek epic the *Thebais* was concerned with the ancestry of the heroes who fought in the war. One fragment (Apollod. *Library* 1.8.4) shows that the family of Tydeus received special treatment: his mother, it is there stated, was taken as a prize by Oineus in the war against Olenos (in Achaia). The poet would next have related how Tydeus, having grown to manhood in Kalydon, committed murder, for which reason he had to flee to Argos, where he married a daughter of Adrastos and begat Diomedes. Another fragment shows that the epic did not always agree with local Theban legend. Pausanias (9.18.6) mentions the tomb of Asphodikos, a hero who killed Parthenopaios son of Talaos, according to the Thebans; but, says Pausanias, the verses in the *Thebais* on the death of Partheno-

---

[1] See also C. M. Bowra, *Pindar* (Oxford 1964) 254 and Wilamowitz, *Pindaros* 310, n. 3.

paios say that Periklymenos slew him. We may have here a hint that the *Thebais* was not composed in Boiotia, but elsewhere, in Ionia, for example.

A story about the Teumesian vixen is assigned vaguely to 'the writers of the *Thebaika* . . . who took the tale from the epic cycle' (Photios and Suda s.v. *Τευμησία* = Aristodemos 383 F 2). It may belong either to the *Oidipodeia* or to the *Thebais*. In the tale Kephalos came from Athens with his dog and pursued the pest; but dog and vixen were fated never to be caught; so Zeus turned them both into stone. It may be questioned whether this was the earliest form of the tale; for the Boiotian poetess Korinna (F 22 Page) remarks that *Oidipous* destroyed not only the Sphinx but the Teumesian vixen as well. This was the local version; but why the story was transferred to Kephalos is not clear. Oidipous needed but one success – the defeat of the Sphinx – to become king; so the vixen could be dissociated from him and introduced as a pest sent by the gods so as to force the Thebans to exclude the descendants of Kadmos from the kingship (see Aristodemos of Thebes *loc. cit.*). To set this story securely in the context of either epic, or of the *Epigonoi* with which it is sometimes associated, is impossible.

To the fragments of the *Epigonoi* we may now address ourselves. The theme is set out in the first line: 'And now, Muses, let us begin to sing of younger men. . . .'

νῦν αὖθ' ὁπλοτέρων ἀνδρῶν ἀρχώμεθα, Μοῦσαι.

The word ὁπλοτέρων originally meant 'more capable of bearing arms', and that may be the implication here: the men of Tydeus's generation in the *Thebais* had failed to take Thebes, but the heroes of the *Epigonoi* in the next were yet more martial and so succeeded. Both poems were alleged to have been 7,000 verses long;[1] each dealt with a popular theme as can be seen from the *Iliad*.

The theme of the greater valour of the *Epigonoi* is taken up by Sthenelos in the *Iliad* (4.403 ff): 'We claim that we are better than our fathers; we took even the seat of seven-gated Thebes, leading a weaker force beneath a stronger wall, putting our trust in the portents of the gods. . . .' Diomedes rebukes his Argive colleague for this unseemly

---

[1] *Contest of Homer and Hesiod* p. 235 Allen. See also J. U. Powell, *Collectanea Alexandrina* 248.

boasting in the presence of Agamemnon whose army has failed as yet to take Troy; but Homer makes a shrewd comparison here: Thebes was an even greater opponent than Troy, though Troy still stands. (The meaning of the boast is not, surely, that the walls of Thebes had been strengthened after the defeat of Polyneikes, Adrastos and their army. Nor is Homer necessarily saying that the victorious army of the *Epigonoi* was smaller than the force defeated in the previous generation.)

Herodotos (4.32), who doubted that Homer was author of the *Epigonoi*, states that the Hyperboreans of the North 'beyond the North Wind' were mentioned in the poem and by Hesiod. A Hesiodic fragment (p. 37 Merkelbach) does in fact mention the Hyperboreans in connexion with other remote peoples such as Aithiopes and Pygmies; but the context of their appearance in the *Epigonoi* is quite unknown. One may note, however, that Kadmeians in the time of King Laodamas son of Eteokles were thought to have fled far to the north – to Illyria (Herodotos 5.61.2). One other fugitive had a prominent place in the poem – Manto daughter of Teiresias who was dedicated by the Epigonoi at Delphi as a spoil of war (Schol. Ap. Rhod. 1.308 p. 35 Wendel). There she married Rhakios a Mycenaean, before migrating to Kolophon in Asia Minor. This story is another Theban episode of obvious interest to Ionians. The fragment concerning Manto is introduced as coming from 'those who wrote the *Thebais*', but this is a loose way of referring to the Theban cycle as a whole. We do not have to suppose that one of the poems called *Thebais* took the story all the way down to the fate of the defeated Thebans. Their lot was one of the subjects treated in the *Epigonoi*.

It would be easy, but unprofitable, to fill out the bare frame provided by the epic fragments with details from Attic tragedy. For we would thereby obtain a continuous narrative of Theban legend at the cost of introducing themes alien to the early hexameter poems upon which the tragic poets drew so copiously in reworking the stories to suit their purposes. Homer and Hesiod however show clearly that even in their early written forms the stories were long and complex. With the help of those two poets, as we have seen, most of the remaining fragments of the *Oidipodeia*, *Thebais* and *Epigonoi* can be placed in their likely contexts.

The Theban epics provided powerful ammunition for the mytho-logical warfare continuously waged by Greek city states, and the Argives were specially prominent in the exploitation of the *Thebais* and *Epigonoi* as propaganda. Thus sometime between about 480 and 465 B.C. they set up at Delphi a group of statues of the Seven against Thebes by the Theban sculptors Hypatodoros and Aristogeiton; at the same time, so Pausanias believed (10.10.3–4), they also set up a group of the *Epigonoi*. The letter forms of the associated inscriptions are too early for the battle of Oinoe with which Pausanias connected these dedications;[1] but the monuments may well recall the Argives' destruc-tion of their neighbours in Mycenae – aptly, for had not Mycenae failed to help the Seven against Thebes and so, perhaps, rendered their defeat more likely? The victorious Epigonoi also had gone to war without Mycenaean aid.

The *Epigonoi* also lies behind the celebrated mythological campaign-ing against Argos by Kleisthenes tyrant of Sikyon about a century earlier than the sack of Mycenae. 'Kleisthenes', Herodotos reports (5.67.1), '. . . after fighting the Argives stopped rhapsodes competing in Sikyon because of the Homeric poems, since the Argives and Argos are everywhere praised in them.' Now it is true that Argos is frequently named in the *Iliad* and the *Odyssey*, but most often in the old generic sense of 'mainland Greece', not with the meaning 'the city of Argos'. Likewise Argeioi is most frequently in Homer a synonym for Danaoi and Achaioi; but Argos itself is not singled out for exceptional praise in the poems. Kleisthenes' objection therefore would have been poorly directed if it were aimed at the *Iliad* and the *Odyssey*, though the refer-ence to the kingship of an Adrastos (almost certainly the Argive) in Sikyon (*Iliad* 2.572) would, it is true, have been galling. Grote suggested that the tyrant's ban was upon Homeric reciters of the *Thebais* and the *Epigonoi*,[2] a notion which would help to explain why the two epics were ascribed to Homer – they formed part of the repertoire of Homeric rhapsodes who also sang the *Iliad* and the *Odyssey*.

[1] Jeffery 163.
[2] *History of Greece* 2.242 n. 1 of the Everyman Edition. This view is however rejected by Johansen 233, who notes that Herodotos doubted the Homeric author-ship of the *Epigonoi*.

The Theban Epics

Herodotos adds that Kleisthenes stripped the Argive Adrastos of the heroic honours formerly paid to him in Sikyon. In his stead the tyrant set up with Theban help a precinct of Melanippos, who in the war of the Seven had killed Mekisteus and Tydeus, respectively brother and son-in-law of Adrastos (5.67.2–5). Here too Kleisthenes patently invoked epic tradition to further his anti-Argive policies. Delphi bluntly objected to the changes; the Pythia told Kleisthenes, who had gone to ask her whether he should throw out Adrastos, 'Adrastos is king of the Sikyonians, but you are a mere slinger-of-stones.' Pindar in *Pythian* 8 (50–53) implies that Adrastos took part in both the expedition of the Seven and that of the *Epigonoi*; if this version was generally accepted in Thebes, Adrastos must have been specially hateful to the Theban friends of Kleisthenes. But we do not know that Adrastos had a part in the epic *Epigonoi*.

The Argive mythologists could not ignore the arrogance of Kleisthenes. To them is surely due the assertion that Adrastos was a founder of the heroic Nemean games. The games themselves, first held in 573 B.C. under the presidency of Kleonai but with the approval of Argos, were plainly intended as a challenge to Kleisthenes and his reformed Sikyonian festivals (M. F. McGregor, *T.A.P.A.* 72 (1941) 277–283). It is significant, therefore, that Pindar in *Nemean* 2 before 480 B.C. gives special prominence to the Homeridai and speaks of their composing *prooimia* in honour of Zeus, who in the context may well be Zeus of Nemea. The link of the Homeridai with the festival of Nemea can reasonably be supposed to have begun at the time of their expulsion from Sikyon. At Nemea the poets would fitly have sung the *Thebais* and the *Epigonoi*; but the additional verses in praise of Argos in the Homeric Catalogue of Ships may well have been introduced to the *Iliad* by the Homeridai about the time of Kleisthenes' war with Argos:

ἐν δ' ἄνδρες πολέμοιο δαήμονες ἐστιχόωντο
Ἀργεῖοι λινοθώρηκες κέντρα πτολέμοιο

(*Iliad* 2.568a.b.)

'And in the ships were ranked men well-versed in warfare, the Argives with their linen corselets, goads of war.' Pindar's words in *Nemean* 2 ὅθεν περ καὶ Ὁμηρίδαι | ῥαπτῶν ἐπέων τὰ πόλλ' ἀοιδοί | ἄρχονται, Διὸς ἐκ προοιμίου suggests that the Homeridai at Nemea began by invoking Zeus.[1] No Homeric hymn to Zeus (of Nemea or elsewhere) survives, however; and it is possible that Pindar has in mind here the Διὸς βουλή, the plan of Zeus which led to the Trojan war; Zeus's plan was mentioned at the start of the *Kypria* and again at the beginning of the *Iliad*. The Theban wars too could be regarded as part of the divine plan to lessen the population of the earth. Pindar here speaks of the Homeridai as singers of 'stitched epics'; the manner in which the *Epigonoi* was tied to the *Thebais* by an allusion backwards in its first line – ὁπλοτέρων ἀνδρῶν – is an instance of such stitching. Not only the Theban epics, but the *Iliad* too, would have been welcome at Nemea, for scenes from that poem had been popular with northeast Peloponnesian artists from about 625 B.C. onwards.[2] Thus the Homeridai would have been assured of an instructed and appreciative audience for rhapsodic performances at the festival of Zeus.

[1] Wade-Gery however (p. 78) thinks of a Zeus-prelude in an Athenian festival of Zeus, because *Nemean* 2 is written for an Athenian.

[2] See especially Johansen 84.

IV

Two Mantic Poems

As a pendant to the *Thebais* the tale of Alkmaion, son of the seer
Amphiaraos, was treated in a distinct poem, the *Alkmaionis*, which,
like the *Melampod(e)ia*, was much concerned with prophecy; indeed it
may well have been composed by a *mantis*. The elements of the story
are given by Thucydides in an excursus from his account of the silting
of the mouth of the river Acheloos in Akarnania (2.102.5–6). Amphiaraos, who had been compelled to go to his death in war against
Thebes by his wife Eriphyle, had bidden his son to kill her. This
Alkmaion did, but being now under a taint (and according to some
versions having been driven mad by a Fury) he was ordered by Apollo
to settle in a part of the world not seen by the Sun at the time of the
matricide. After many wanderings the hero came to the mouth of the
Acheloos and settled on land formed by the river silt in the period since
the murder. There he ruled, in the neighbourhood of Oiniadai, and
left the name Akarnania to the land from his son Akarnan.[1] 'This is the
tradition we have inherited concerning Alkmaion' writes Thucydides.

The historian's authority for these remarks may well have been the
epic *Alkmaionis*, in which Akarnania was mentioned, as we learn from
Strabo (452 = F 5 Kinkel). The geographer remarks that Penelope's
father Ikarios had two sons Alyzeus and Leukadios, who ruled after
their father in Akarnania. These were, like Akarnan son of Alkmaion,
eponymous heroes, and gave their names to the town of Leukas (which
at that time was still not an island but part of the mainland) and to
Alyzeia (Ephoros 70 F 124).[2] Ikarios is at home in Lakedaimon, but

---

[1] Akarnan was son of Kallirhoe, daughter of the river Acheloos. His brother was
Amphoteros, whose name comes from the disputed territories on either side of the
wandering course of the river, at the bounds of Aitolia and Akarnania. Apollodoros 3.7.6–7. Löffler 56.

[2] Ephoros also explained how Alkmaion went with Diomedes to Aitolia to

according to some authors he migrated thence to northwest Greece; the context of the fragment of the *Alkmaionis* may well be Alkmaion's conquest of Akarnania shortly before the Trojan war (Ephoros 70 F 123).

The remaining fragments of the epic do not deal with events in Akarnania, but suggest, rather, that the poem was wide in scope and diffuse in content. One fragment (F 4 Kinkel: Apollodoros, *Lib.* 1.8.5.) shows that the presence of Tydeus in Argos was explained by his having left Kalydon after a homicide. Another (F 6 Kinkel: Schol. Eur. *Or.* 997) touched on the story of the shepherd who brought the golden lamb to Atreus, which, having become a token of the kingship at Mycenae, was stolen from him by Thyestes.

At least a plausible guess may be made about the invocation to 'Lady Earth, and Zagreus highest of all the gods'

πότνια Γῆ Ζαγρεῦ τε θεῶν πανυπέρτατε πάντων

(F 3 Kinkel).

Zagreus is Dionysos in an older guise, as son of Persephone, not of Semele. He was torn to pieces by the Titans and buried near the oracular tripod at Delphi (Kallimachos F 43, 117 Pfeiffer and F 643). The speaker is surely Alkmaion at Delphi, where the oracle has just told him that he must go to the land upon which the Sun has not cast his gaze. In the circumstances the tainted hero's prayer to Earth and the buried Zagreus for help in his seemingly impossible search for land hidden from the Sun was intelligently apt. In the end the two divinities did not fail him.

Three verses quoted from the *Alkmaionis* (Schol. Eur. *Andr.* 687) cannot easily be placed in context. They tell how Peleus and Telamon killed their brother Phokos who excelled them in athletics. 'There did

---

punish the enemies of Oineus, after the destruction of Thebes by the Epigonoi. In their absence Agamemnon easily won Argos, because most of the army was absent in Aitolia. Later Diomedes returned home, and followed Agamemnon to Troy, but Alkmaion stayed in the Northwest (*F.Gr.Hist.* 70 F 123 *a, b*). This looks to be an attempt to explain the absence of the Akarnanians from the expeditionary force to Troy. All these details in Ephoros may well come from the *Alkmaionis*, which may also have inspired a Hellenistic hexameter poem on the theme of Agamemnon's capture of Argos (see the fragment in *Collectanea Alexandrina* pp. 72–76 Powell).

god-like Telamon strike his head with the wheel-shaped disc and Peleus quickly stretching his arm on high with the brazen axe did strike the small of his back.'

> ἔνθα μὲν ἀντίθεος Τελαμὼν τροχοειδέϊ δίσκῳ
> πλῆξε κάρη, Πηλεὺς δὲ θοῶς ἀνὰ χεῖρα τανύσσας
> ἀξίνῃ εὐχάλκῳ ἐπεπλήγει μέσα νώτων.

Like Alkmaion, though with less excuse, the sons of Aiakos of Aigina, Telamon and Peleus, had incurred blood guilt from the murder of kin. Phokos was their half-brother by a different mother (Pausanias 2.29.9). Pausanias (2.29.10) relates that after the murder Telamon and Peleus fled from Aigina. Telamon later attempted to return to the island, but his father refused to let him land; Aiakos said that if he cared to stand in the ship and pour earth into the sea he could plead his case from the mole so formed. The story is an *aition* designed to explain the presence of the mole in the 'hidden' harbour, Kryptos Limen, at Aigina. The comparison with the newly formed land at the mouth of the Acheloos is obvious and may well have been made in the *Alkmaionis*.

Another quotation preserves three verses about a feast for the dead. Here the context is again unspecified (Athenaios 460 B). 'After laying out the corpses on the wide straw bed spread upon the ground he laid beside them a plentiful feast and put out cups and chaplets on their heads':

> νέκυς δὲ χαμαιστρώτου ἔπι τείνας
> εὐρείης στιβάδος, παρέθηκ' αὐτοῖσι θάλειαν
> δαῖτα ποτήριά τε στεφάνους τ' ἐπὶ κρασὶν ἔθηκεν.

The feast was for the benefit of the dead; but who attended them, who they were, and where the feast was held we are not informed. A possible context is the honouring of the dead after the victory of the Epigonoi; in one account Laodamas King of Thebes killed Aigialeus but did not flee to Illyria, as Herodotos may imply (5.61); instead he was killed by Alkmaion (Apollod. *Lib.* 3.7.3). If the context is correctly identified, then Alkmaion is here the subject of ἔθηκε and αὐτοῖσι are Laodamas, Aigialeus and perhaps other corpses of warriors too.

According to the developed legend Alkmaion was murdered in Arkadia by the sons of Phegeus, from whom the hero had recovered the fatal necklace of Harmonia and Eriphyle. The death of Alkmaion was avenged by his sons Amphoteros and Akarnan (Apollod. *Lib.* 3.7.6.) who were mentioned in the poem, perhaps in connexion with the vengeance. Finally, it is possible that the author of the *Alkmaionis*, like Hesiod, declared that life in the time of Kronos was utterly blessed: κα[ὶ τῆς ἐπ]ὶ Κρόνου ζω[ῆς εὐ]δαιμονεστά[της οὔσ]ης, ὡς ἔγραψ[αν 'Ησί]οδος καὶ ὁ τὴν ['Ἀλκμ]εωνίδα ποή[σας].[1] To speculate on the context of this assertion (Philodemos περὶ εὐσεβ. p. 42 Gomperz) is pointless.

The tale in the *Alkmaionis* that Akarnan was a grandson of the seer Amphiaraos has an obvious bearing on the long tradition of prophecy amongst the Akarnanians. Herodotos reports that an Akarnanian diviner, Amphilytos, predicted the victory of Peisistratos the Athenian shortly before the battle near the sanctuary of Athena Pallenis, and quotes a hexameter couplet (1.62.4):

ἔρριπται δ' ὁ βόλος, τὸ δὲ δίκτυον ἐκπεπέτασται,

θύννοι δ' οἰμήσουσι σεληναίης διὰ νυκτός.

'The throw is made, the net is spread, and the tunnies shall dart along through the moonlit night.' This story suggests that Akarnanian seers were, like the priesthood of Delphi,[2] capable of oral improvisation in verse. A second Akarnanian seer in the *Histories* of Herodotos is Megistias who chose to stay with the Leonidas at Thermopylai, though the king had sent him back, to meet the death he had foreseen (7.221). Megistias claimed descent from the hero Melampous, himself a distinguished prophet, who gives his name to an epic about prophecy, the *Melampodeia*. It is an attractive and likely suggestion that this poem was composed by a *mantis*,[3] who, like Amphilytos, could compose hexameters.

Certain fragments of oracular stamp are ascribed simply to Hesiod; a second group is said to come from 'Hesiod in the *Melampodeia*'; and a third from 'the author of the *Melampodeia*'. It is relevant here that Hesiod was thought to have been given tuition in soothsaying by

[1] The forms of the hero's name 'Ἀλκμάων, 'Ἀλκμαίων and 'Ἀλκμέων are attested; the last was preferred in Athens, perhaps because of the Alkmeonid family name there.

[2] On whose use of clichés of epic character see W. McLeod in *T.A.P.A.* 92 (1961) 317–325.

[3] Löffler, Vorwort.

Two Mantic Poems

Akarnanians; and it is reported that mantic verses and expositions of portents were ascribed to him locally in Boiotia (Pausanias 9.31.5).

A prophecy by Melampous himself is not named amongst the extant fragments, but the hero was certainly not omitted from a poem named after him. His most splendid achievement was the curing of the madness of the Argive women, for which he was paid with a third of the kingship for himself and a third for his brother Bias (Herodotos 9.34, but in some versions Melampous was not responsible for the cure, as for instance in the eleventh *Epinician* of Bacchylides).[1]

Homer does not mention the cure, but the versatile hero's other great success, the driving of the cattle of Phylakos to Pylos for Neleus, is recalled in the *Odyssey* (15.235–236). In this passage the seer Theoklymenos recounts his descent from Melampous (15.223–255). He gives this stemma, which itself provides a convenient framework in which to examine the fragments of the *Melampodeia*:[2]

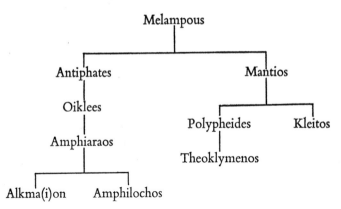

Second-sight ran through many generations of this family. When Amphiaraos died, Apollo made Polypheides the best of prophets amongst mortals (*Odyssey* 15.252–253) and in the other line Amphilochos was renowned for his oracular powers. From which line the brave Megistias who stayed behind at Thermopylai descended we do not know; but since he was an Akarnanian he may well have claimed kinship with Melampous through Akarnan son of Alkmaion.

[1] See Jebb, *Bacchylides* p. 211.
[2] For a different Melampodid stemma see Hesiod F 136 M.W.

The curing of the Argive women or, specifically, of the daughters of King Proitos is mentioned in a Hesiodic fragment (Merkelbach D. 10–15) where their folly is ascribed to the anger of a god or goddess – either Hera, whose image they had despised (Akousilaos 2 F 28), or Dionysos whose rites they had rejected (Hesiod F 27 Rzach).[1] The family of Melampous stayed in Argos after his death, but of their lives in the kingdom we learn nothing from the fragments of the *Melampodeia*. Homer adds a small detail – that Polypheides quarrelled with his father Mantios and migrated to Hyperesia in northern Peloponnese (*Odyssey* 15.254). Melampous himself appears in a fragment of the *Melampodeia*.

καὶ τότε μάντις μὲν δεσμὸν βοὸς αἴνυτο χερσίν,
Ἴφικλος δ' ἐπὶ νῶτ' ἐπεμαίετο. τῷ δ' ἐπ' ὄπισθεν
σκύπφον ἔχων ἑτέρῃ, ἑτέρῃ δὲ σκῆπτρον ἀείρας
ἔστειχεν Φύλακος καὶ ἐνὶ δμώεσσιν ἔειπεν.

(Athenaios 498 B)

Μάντης Meineke μάντης cod. μάντις M.W. F 272.

'Then did the seer take the halter of the ox in his hands. Iphiklos touched its back, and behind it with a cup in one hand and with his sceptre held high in the other Phylakos marched and spoke to his slaves about him.'[2] The scene, we may suggest, is Phylake, the home of Phylakos, inland from the gulf of Pagasai. Iphiklos is his son, whose impotence Melampous cured (Apollodoros, *Lib.* 1.9.12). Iphiklos walks beside the ox. The seer is by its head, and King Phylakos follows behind with his servants. The animal is being led to sacrifice.

Immediately before, Athenaios has quoted (498 AB) two more verses as being from the second book of Hesiod's *Melampodeia*.

τῷ δὲ Μάρης θοὸς ἄγγελος ἦλθε δι' οἴκου,
πλήσας δ' ἀργύρεον σκύπφον φέρε, δῶκε δ' ἄνακτι.

Μάρις Löffler, cf. Π319.   (M.W. F 271)

'To him did the rapid messenger, Mares, come through the house; he had filled the silvery cup, brought it, and given it to his lord.' If this is

[1] The Proitides in their madness wandered to Sikyon and were cured there: Apollod. *Lib.* 2.2.2, and see F. Vian, *R.E.A.* 67 (1965) 27. No doubt Melampous cured them of the itch and baldness, their second affliction, before Bias married Lysippe the Proitid and he himself took Iphianassa her sister to wife (M.W. F 133).

[2] ἐπεμαίετο perhaps means 'touched with the whip' as, for example, in *Iliad* 5.748.

the cup carried by Phylakos behind the ox, then τῷ will be Phylakos and ἄνακτι the same person. The cup will have been brought out of the house to the field by the messenger. This fragment at least shows that there were not fewer than two books of the poem in the edition known to Athenaios. There was also a Hesiodic *Melampodeia* in at least three books (Athen. 609E) in which Chalkis in Euboia was called a place of fair women – καλλιγύναικα,[1] an epithet normally given in epic to Sparta, Hellas or Achaia; but the context of this remark is lost.

One fragment shows that Teiresias the Theban seer was mentioned in the *Melampodeia*, which therefore was not only concerned with the family of Melampous. Tzetzes quotes from the poem five lines spoken by Teiresias himself; they show that the prophet was believed to have lived at least seven generations, from the time of Kadmos to the sack of Thebes (according to some writers he expired during the flight from the stricken city). 'Father Zeus, would that you had granted me a shorter span of life and to have knowledge equal to mortal men's. But you have paid me not the slightest honour, who have caused me to have a long span of life and to live for seven generations amongst mankind.'

> Ζεῦ πάτερ, εἴθε μοι ἧσσον᾿ ⟨ἔχειν⟩ αἰῶνα βίοιο
> ὤφελλες δοῦναι καὶ ἴσα φρεσὶ μήδεα ἴδμεν
> θνητοῖς ἀνθρώποις· νῦν δ᾿ οὐδέ με τυτθὸν ἔτισας
> ὃς μακρόν γέ μ᾿ ἔθηκας ἔχειν αἰῶνα βίοιο
> ἑπτά τ᾿ ἐπὶ ζώειν γενεὰς μερόπων ἀνθρώπων.

(Hesiod F 161 Rzach)

Another remark ascribed to Teiresias by the Scholia to Lykophron (v. 683. Vol. 2 p. 226 Scheer) is alleged to come from the *Melampodeia*: in sexual intercourse, said the Theban, nine parts of pleasure were enjoyed by the woman, but the male has the tenth:

> ἐννέα μὲν μοίρας, δεκάτην δέ τε τέρπεται ἀνήρ.

(F 162 Rzach, after Schenkl)

This was said in response to an enquiry from Zeus and Hera who had discussed the matter. Teiresias was asked because once he had killed a female snake which he had seen mating on Mount Kithairon, whereupon he became a woman; when he killed the male, he became a man once more (Schol. Ambros. Hom. *Od*. 10.494). The strangeness of this

[1] M.W. F 277. Cf. F 64, 2.

story should not draw attention away from its inconsistency: Teiresias was not fully competent to answer the god's question unless he had mated both as man and as woman. There may therefore have been a version of the tale in which the hero spent a long time as a female before reverting to his former state.

Hera found the seer's reply offensive and blinded him; but Zeus, delighted with it, made him a gift of prophecy and bestowed a life of great length. The remark on copulation thus belongs to a time early in his life; the complaint about his age came much later. Apollodoros (*Library* 3.6.7) declares that Teiresias saw the snakes mating on Mount Kyllene; having wounded them he became a woman, but when he observed the same snakes again mating he turned into a man. This version perhaps allows him enough time to gain the experience needed to answer the god's question. Ovid consistently allowed the hero to remain a woman for seven years (*Metamorphoses* 3.316 ff).

Two small quotations (F 163 and 164 Rzach), one on the sweetness of knowing what lot the gods have assigned to mortals, the other on the delights of story-telling after a good meal, do not help in the reconstruction of the poem. Nor can we be sure that because Teiresias was prominent in the *Melampodeia*, his grandson, Mopsos son of Manto, another diviner, was also mentioned in it. Strabo (654) tells how Mopsos defeated Kalchas in a guessing contest at Klaros[1] shortly after the fall of Troy; he also relates that, according to Hesiod, Amphilochos, a brother of Alkmaion and like him a seer, was put to death by Apollo at Soloi in Kilikia (Strabo 676 = Hesiod F 167 Rzach); but in default of other evidence these legends cannot be proved to belong to the *Melampodeia*. From the few fragments definitely to be ascribed to the poem we can see however that its author's purpose was to recount the surpassing wisdom, and so to extol the descendants, of the heroic

[1] The contest was placed at Apollo's sanctuary in Gryneion by Euphorion (F 97 Powell), but the poet may have deliberately innovated. According to Pherekydes (3 F 142) Kalchas asked Mopsos how many piglets a sow would bring forth: Mopsos replied 'ten, and one of them a female' – δέκα ὧν ἕνα θῆλυν. The answer, which contains an interesting play on genders, is part of a hexameter: Pherekydes evidently drew on an epic poem in his account. In the Hesiodic version of the contest (F 278 M.W.) Mopsos correctly estimates the number of fruits on a wild fig tree.

Two Mantic Poems

diviners, especially Melampous and his line. For as Hesiod asserted, Zeus may have given valour to the descendants of Aiakos, and riches to the Atreidai, but to the sons of Amythaon (Bias and Melampous), he gave intellect (Nikolaos of Damascus, *F.Gr.Hist.* 90 F24).

ἀλκὴν μὲν γὰρ ἔδωκεν Ὀλύμπιος Αἰακίδῃσι
νοῦν δ' Ἀμυθαονίδαις, πλοῦτον δ' ἔπορ' Ἀτρεΐδῃσι.

Intellect in heroic, not less than in classical and archaic Greek, times was as highly prized as any other quality in mankind. Melampous and his family stand out, by reason of their skill and percipience, as the true intellectual ancestors of the philosophical pioneers of early Ionia.

V

Eumelos, the early Argonautika and related Epics

The core of our *Odyssey* is the return or *Nostos* of Odysseus, homewards to Ithaka after the sack of Troy. Into the core have been grafted folktales, such as the story of the Lotus-Eaters and of Polyphemos; but the boldest addition, perhaps the work of Homer himself, consists in the introduction to the account of the hero's wanderings of many details from another epic, the *Argonautika*.[1] Homer reminds us of his source when he describes the wandering rocks, between which, before Odysseus came, only *Argo* had passed, with Hera's help because she loved Jason; '*Argo* who is known to all' (12.70). Kirke too belongs to the Argonautic saga; she is, as Homer (*Od.* 10.137–139) tells us, a daughter of the Sun and a sister of Aietes, from whose kingdom the *Argo* sailed homewards. Again, the fountain Artakie (which flowed in the country close to where Kyzikos, the Propontic city, was later founded) is at home in the story of Jason's wanderings, from which it may well have been transferred to our *Odyssey* (10.108). The *Argonautika* had no influence upon the plot of the *Iliad*; but in that poem too Homer glances at an essential part of the saga – the visit of Jason to Lemnos where he begat a son Euenos. This son of Hypsipyle and the Argonauts' leader has, in the *Iliad*, dealings with the Achaeans before Troy, sending them wine (7.467–469) and ransoming a Trojan captive (23.747–748).

The Argonautic tale of courageous navigation through hazardous, unknown seas would naturally have been popular amongst Greek mariners and the citizens of maritime states during the first stage of colonial expansion in the eighth century B.C. The story seems to have

---

[1] Cf. Denys Page, *The Homeric Odyssey* (Oxford 1955) 2, and especially K. Meuli, *Odyssee und Argonautika* (Berlin 1921) 53 ff.

Eumelos, the early Argonautika and related Epics

found especial favour in Corinth, whose ruling nobility the Bacchiads deplored the insignificant place of their city in heroic legend; and it was a Bacchiad, Eumelos, son of Amphilytos, who set out to supply his city with an epic past. His method was ingenious and deliberately propagandist: as Homer had added Argonautic elements to the earlier tales of Odysseus, so Eumelos linked Corinthian local cult with the story of Jason. The details of this process are all but lost: in particular it is well nigh impossible to determine how and when Medea the sorceress, who is not named in the *Odyssey*, entered the Argonautic story. She may be foreshadowed by *Agamede* the daughter of Augeias who knew all the medicines that grow on the earth (*Iliad* 11.739–740 and Walter Leaf *in loco*),[1] but, if so, we have to explain how a north-west Peloponnesian lady was converted into a formidable Kolchian princess.

Corinth's place in the Homeric poems was, to the Corinthian view, depressingly insignificant. The place is not mentioned at all in the *Odyssey*; in the *Iliad* it is named as part of Agamemnon's kingdom (2.570), a fact which brought no comfort in the eighth century to an independent city with colonial pretentions, but the epithet given to Corinth, ἀφνειός, 'rich', perhaps offered a little encouragement. The only other mention is of the Corinthian Euchenor, who dies ingloriously at the hands of Paris, a rich and good man though he was, the son of Polyidos a wise seer (*Iliad* 13.660–672).

To make good these deficiencies Eumelos adopted a strikingly bold expedient; he appropriated to Corinth a large body of epic poetry loosely associated with a place called Ephyre, which according to a vague Homeric expression was situated somewhere 'in a nook of horse-rearing Argos', that is to say somewhere on the Greek mainland. The position of Ephyre or Ephyra became a topic of intense discussion amongst ancient geographers, partly as a result of the confusion created by the tampering with tradition by Eumelos and the Corinthians. In the *Iliad* we learn that the mother of Tlepolemos came from Ephyre by the river Selleeis, but are given no help in finding where the city lay (2.658–9). Bellerophon, his father Glaukos, and his grandfather Sisyphos son of Aiolos are said to live in Ephyre in the nook of Argos

---

[1] Cf. E. Will, *Korinthiaka* (Paris 1955) 122.

(6.152–155) and Eumelos could no doubt have claimed without fear of contradiction that Corinth was meant here, even if that was not Homer's intention. In *Iliad* 15.529–531 a breastplate is mentioned; it had been brought out of Ephyre by Phyleus father of Meges who had an island kingdom in northwestern Greece (2.625–630). Here the Thesprotian Ephyre of Epeiros could be meant, or possibly the even more obscure place of that name in northwest Peloponnese. In the *Odyssey* Athena in the guise of Mentes says that Odysseus has gone up from Ephyre, where he had stayed with Ilos son of Mermeros (1.259), and Ephyre evidently could be reached without great trouble from Ithaka (as can Sparta and Pylos) (2.326–8). The Thesprotian Ephyre is almost certainly meant here, because Mermeros, according to some, lived in Corcyra and the mainland opposite (Pausanias 2.3.9). The impression left by these passages is that the Odyssean Ephyre is not far from Ithaka; so the Thesprotian place, to which we shall return, may well be meant. These very obscurities, however, gave Eumelos his opportunity. His date is, fortunately, not in doubt; for two verses of his quoted by Pausanias (4.33.2) from a processional hymn, composed for the Messenians who went to the festival at Delos and praising Zeus of Ithome, belong to a time shortly before, or at the very outbreak of, the first great war between Sparta and the Messenians *ca.* 730 B.C.[1]

τῷ γὰρ ᾿Ιθωμάτᾳ καταθύμιος ἔπλετο μοῖσα,

ἁ καθαρὰ καὶ ἐλεύθερα σάμβαλ' ἔχοισα.

In the second line an anapaest may be missing after καθαρά. ἔπλετο may mean, 'was' or, as in *Odyssey* 1.225, 'has come to be' –

τίς δαίς, τίς δαὶ ὅμιλος ὅδ' ἔπλετο;

So we do not know whether or not, when Eumelos composed these verses, the festival of Zeus at Ithome had been abandoned owing to the Messenian war. But they are nevertheless a sound guide to the poet's date, the second half of the eighth century B.C. 'By the god of Ithome' says Eumelos 'is the Muse beloved, she who is untainted; unshackled are her dancing-sandals'.

Poetry ascribed to Eumelos was at some time rendered into prose, and it was in this form that Corinthian epic tradition and mythology were known to Pausanias. A few verse fragments survive, notably in

[1] Cf. C. M. Bowra, *C.Q.*, 13 (1963) 145–153.

Eumelos, the early Argonautika and related Epics

the Scholia to Apollonios Rhodios where they are quoted because of
their relevance to the *Argonautika*. We may now turn to an examination
of those verses and fragments ascribed with certainty or likelihood to
Eumelos (apart from the *Titanomachia* which has already been discussed). The change of name from the land of the Ephyraia to Korinthos
was explained by Eumelos by means of a genealogy (Pausanias 2.1.1
= *F.Gr.Hist.* 451 F 1a). Ephyra daughter of Okeanos first dwelt in the
land. But later Marathon (the eponym of the neighbourhood in Attica),
who was the son of Epopeus, son of Aloeus, son of Helios, fled from the
lawlessness and outrages of his father and settled in the coastal part of
Attica. When Epopeus died, Marathon came to Peloponnese and
divided the dominion between his two sons, before he returned to
Attica. From his son Sikyon the land watered by the river Asopos was
called Sikyon, and the land of Ephyra was called after his son Korinthos.
Ephyra had a high antiquity in the Eumelian picture of the world for
she was a daughter of Okeanos and Tethys, the primal deities of Homer
(Schol. Ap. Rhod. 4.1212/14b); her husband Epimetheus links her to
the Prometheus legend, but there is no sign that Ephyra had for
Eumelos anything to do with the Hesiodic Pandora, who caused
Epimetheus so much trouble. The details about Ephyra come from a
prose work known as the *Korinthiaka* or Κορινθία συγγραφή
(*F.Gr.Hist.* 451 T 1), but the true title of the poem is lost.

Helios the Sun-god, declared Eumelos, had given to Aloeus the land
of Asopos, and to his other son Aietes the Ephyraia. But Aietes went
off to Kolchis leaving the land in trust with Bounos who was a son of
the god Hermes and Alkidameia (Pausanias 2.3.10). Here is an ingenious claim to Corinthian prehistoric interest in far eastern Black Sea
coasts, whose promise of riches was already, it seems, being bruited in
Corinth in the time of Eumelos, long before Greek colonists permanently settled thereabouts. Kolchis, thanks to the Argonautic saga,
beckoned as a land offering fabulous rewards to hardy explorers, but in
spite of Eumelos and his tying of Corinthian legend to the *Argonautika*
there is no archaeological evidence that Corinthians pioneered the
passage to the northeast from the Aegean; they were, as it happened,
far too busy in the west, and when finally after 650 the shores of the
Black Sea were colonised, the leading maritime powers in those parts

Greek Epic Poetry

were Miletos and Megara.[1] It is conceivable that exploratory voyages as early as 750 B.C. encouraged poets to elaborate the Argonautic legend with tales about Kolchis, but the hypothesis cannot be proved.

When Bounos died, the story continued, Epopeus ruled over the Ephyraians as well as the Asopians and after him Korinthos ruled in Ephyra. After the death of Korinthos, who had no son, the Corinthians sent for Medea, daughter of Aietes, from Iolkos (where she had settled with Jason after fleeing with him from Kolchis). Medea then ruled at Corinth (Pausanias 2.3.10), inheriting the kingdom which her father had left in trust to Bounos. In one version (Schol. Pindar, Ol. 13.74 f Vol. I p. 373 Drachmann) the mother of Aietes and Aloeus is called Antiope, as indeed we are informed by some verses ascribed to Eumelos himself; the same commentator asserts that Aloeus was given by his father Helios the land in Arkadia – presumably that part of Arkadia in the hinterland of Sikyon, the Stymphalia, is meant. Some of these bequests and migrations are neatly summed up in the verses just mentioned (F.Gr.Hist. 451 F 2c):

ἀλλ' ὅτε δ' Αἰήτης καὶ Ἀλωεὺς ἐξεγένοντο
Ἡελίου τε καὶ Ἀντιόπης, τότε δ' ἄνδιχα χώρην
δάσσατο παισὶν ἑοῖς Ὑπερίονος ἀγλαὸς υἱός·
ἦν μὲν ἔχ' Ἀσωπός, ταύτην πόρε δίῳ Ἀλωεῖ,
5   ἦν δ' Ἐφύρη κτεάτισσ', Αἰήτῃ δῶκεν ἅπασαν.
Αἰήτης δ' ἄρ' ἑκὼν Βούνῳ παρέδωκε φυλάσσειν,
εἰσόκεν αὐτὸς ἵκοιτ' ἢ ἐξ αὐτοῖό τις ἄλλος
ἢ παῖς ἢ υἱωνός· ὁ δ' ἵκετο Κολχίδα γαῖαν.[2]

The last three lines show that Aietes contemplated a return to Corinth from Kolchis, or, failing that, wished a son or grandson of his to inherit the kingdom. In the event his daughter did so. The Eumelian genealogy may now be set out:

---

[1] On the earliest Greek trading voyages to the Black Sea see J. Boardman, *The Greeks Overseas* (Pelican Books 1964) 247.

[2] 'But when Aietes and Aloeus were born to Helios and Antiope, then did the glorious son of Hyperion portion the land apart for his children; the part that Asopos held, that did he give to lordly Aloeus, but that which Ephyre had won, to Aietes did he give it entire. Then did Aietes readily give his share to Bounos to keep safe' (lines 1–6).

Eumelos, the early Argonautika and related Epics

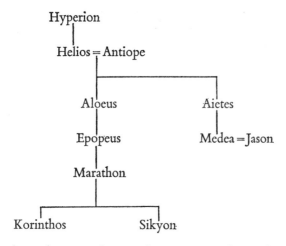

Hyperion
|
Helios = Antiope
|
┌──────────────┴──────────────┐
Aloeus   Aietes
| |
Epopeus   Medea = Jason
|
Marathon
|
┌──────────┴──────────┐
Korinthos   Sikyon

Through Medea Jason became king in Corinth. Medea hid her children by him, successively as they were born, in the temple of Hera, expecting them to become immortal. But she was deceived in this, for they died. When Jason found out, he refused to forgive her and retired to Iolkos. Medea then also went away after handing over the dominion to Sisyphos (who, as we have seen, was in Homer a king of Ephyre). Pausanias (2.3.11) who tells this story ascribes it to Eumelos; there is no reason to doubt that it is genuinely Eumelian, as it provides the link needed to bring into the myth-history of Corinth the family of Sisyphos and Bellerophon. It is remarkable that there is no mention in the Eumelian verses of Kirke, who in Homer is sister of Aietes and, like Aietes, a child of the Sun, Helios. In Homer the mother of Kirke and Aietes is not Antiope but Perse, daughter of Okeanos. There is no sign that Eumelos identified Perse with Antiope. Nor is it certain that in his view Ephyra, who according to Eumelos was a daughter of Okeanos, was wife of Helios, and so Antiope in another guise. The appearance of Marathon, an Attic place name, in the Corinthian genealogy is surprising; Eumelos seems to have staked a mythological claim to a part of Attica remote from, and for long independent of, Athens. With this fiction we may compare the claim to Kolchis implied by the fictitious Corinthian ancestry of Aietes. Similarly, the claim of the poet that the Asopia was ruled by a son of Helios, a divinity specially favoured in

G.E.P.   E

Corinth, at least suggests a mutual interest between Sikyon and Corinth; and there is no need to infer political rivalry between the two cities from the assertion that Epopeus was ill-behaved and lawless.

Having linked Corinth to the *Argonautika* Eumelos would not, with his active imagination, have wished to omit all description of the exciting adventures of Jason in Kolchis. The Scholia to Apollonios Rhodios show that the poet may have dealt with events there in some detail (Schol. 3.1354/6a, displaced to 1372. See pp. 257–258 of Wendel's edition). The Scholiasts say that Apollonios has taken some verses (describing how armed men sprang up when the dragon's teeth were sown) from Eumelos. How many verses were borrowed they do not state, but all five lines of the sentence are worth quoting because their wording is reminiscent of early Greek epic and may well therefore have been borrowed almost verbatim by Apollonios. The motive of the dragon's teeth is itself borrowed into the *Argonautika* from the Kadmos legend (Apollon. Rhod. *Arg.* 3.1354–1358):

> οἱ δ' ἤδη κατὰ πᾶσαν ἀνασταχύεσκον ἄρουραν
> γηγενέες· φρῖξεν δὲ περὶ στιβαροῖς σακέεσσιν
> δούρασί τ' ἀμφιγύοις κορύθεσσί τε λαμπομένῃσιν
> Ἄρηος τέμενος φθισιμβρότου, ἵκετο δ' αἴγλη
> 5 νείοθεν Οὐλυμπόνδε δι' ἠέρος ἀστράπτουσα.

'Now did the earth-born ones grow like corn ears throughout the entire field. The precinct of Ares who wastes mortals away bristled with stout shields and spears for two hands and shining helmets, and their gleam flashing through the air passed from below as far as Olympos.' Epic echoes here, of single words and phrases, suggest, but do not prove, that the Scholiasts are correct in contending that these verses come from Eumelos. For example, ἄρουραν appears in epic frequently in the accusative at the end of Homeric hexameters (e.g. *Od.* 19.593). With φρῖξεν ... σακέεσσιν in line 2 compare σάκεσιν ... πεφρικυῖαι (*Il.* 4.282). στιβαρόν is a regular epithet of σάκος (e.g. *Iliad* 3.335). δούρασί τ' ἀμφιγύοις is analogous with ἔγχεσιν ἀμφιγύοις (*Iliad* 15.386). κορύθεσσί τε λαμπομένῃσι is a variant of κορύθων ἀπὸ λαμπομενάων. Compare λαμπρῇσιν κορύθεσσι at the beginning of a line (*Il.* 17.269). Ἄρηος appears as first word in the famous variant reading in [*Iliad*] 24.805. φθισιμβρότου in line 4 is found at the same position in the line as $\phi\theta\iota\sigma\iota\mu\beta\rho\sigma\tau\sigma\nu$ in *Odyssey* 22.297. The construction in lines 2 to 4 is reminiscent of *Iliad* 13.339:

$$\ddot{\epsilon}\phi\rho\iota\xi\epsilon\nu\ \delta\dot{\epsilon}\ \mu\acute{a}\chi\eta\ \phi\theta\iota\sigma\acute{\iota}\mu\beta\rho\sigma\tau\sigma\varsigma\ \dot{\epsilon}\gamma\chi\epsilon\acute{\iota}\eta\sigma\iota.$$

These observations reveal the traditional character of the verses of Apollonios. But if Eumelos composed the originals, the comment of one Scholiast is mistaken: 'This (i.e. v. 1354) and the following lines are taken from Eumelos, in whose poem Medea speaks to Idmon' ($"I\delta\mu\sigma\nu a$ L $'I\acute{a}\sigma\sigma\nu a$ P). The variant 'Jason' for 'Idmon' cannot be correct, because Medea would not give to Jason a detailed description of events in which he was the protagonist. On the other hand a conversation between Idmon and Medea surprises, because the seer according to Apollonios, who drew on Eumelos, died before the Argo reached Kolchis (see e.g. Apoll. Rhod. *Arg.* 2.815 ff). One possible solution to the seeming paradox is of some interest, namely that Medea is speaking to the dead seer Idmon in these verses in a *nekyomanteia* or consultation of the dead. Eumelos may have had such a consultation in his version of the Argonautic saga. Here would be one more likeness between the early *Argonautika* and the *Odyssey*. In the one poem Medea would consult Idmon and also inform him about events later than his death; in the other poem Odysseus speaks with Teiresias and others and exchanges news. It is relevant to note here that in one story of Medea's death she was said to have been buried in Thesprotia, where, at Ephyra or Kichyros, there was a famous oracle of the dead (Solinus 2.30).[1] To raise the spirit of Idmon was surely not beyond the powers of this omnicompetent sorceress. But it is important to note that in the Naupaktian epic (F 6 and 8 Kinkel) Idmon did travel at least as far as Kolchis.

In his *Argonautika* (2.946–8) Apollonios alludes to the myth of Sinope, daughter of Asopos, who tricked Zeus into promising her lasting maidenhood. The Scholiasts here state (p. 197 Wendel) that Eumelos and Aristotle both called Sinope a daughter of Asopos.[2] So Apollonios may well be following an Argonautic passage of Eumelos here too. It is possible, therefore, that Eumelos already before 700 had mentioned

[1] Cf. Meuli, *Odyssee und Argonautika* 115 on the Argonautic *nekyia*, and West on *Theogony* 992.

[2] The remarks of C. M. Bowra, *Problems in Greek Poetry* (Oxford 1953) 58–59 on this topic may be compared with those of D. L. Page, *Corinna* (London 1953) 25–27.

Sinope, the principal promontory on the south coast of the Black Sea, on the route from the Bosphoros to Kolchis, in his poetry. There is no archaeological evidence for a Greek colony at Sinope earlier than about 600 B.C.,[1] but Eumelos could have mentioned the promontory, a conspicuous sailing-mark, before 700. By making Sinope a daughter of Asopos the poet was attempting to stake yet another Peloponnesian claim to the new lands beyond the northeast passage. One may compare the optimistic manner in which Victorian cartographers coloured red vast, imperfectly explored tracts of Africa or remotest Canada. A similar interest in the Black Sea may be observed in a fragment listing three Muses, daughters of Apollo (F 17 Kinkel): their names are given as Kephisous, Apollonis and Borysthenis. The river Borysthenis is the Dniepr. If the fragment is genuinely Eumelian then the Greeks must have known something about the north shores of the Black Sea before *ca.* 700 B.C. The likelihood of this is increased by the clear reference by Hesiod in the *Theogony* (339) to the river Istros or Danube. Kephisous presumably gets her name from another, less distinguished but also less distant, river, the winding Kephisos, which other poets praised too (Hesiod F 37–39 Rzach). We would expect the second Muse, Apollonis, to have a river name too: G. Hermann's change to Achelois (᾽Αχελωῖδα) here is admirable. The water at Apollo's Kastalian spring at Delphi was said to come from the Acheloos river, in a story supporting the proposed emendation (see Panyassis F 15 Kinkel). Nine other Muses the poet thought to be daughters, not of Apollo, but of Zeus and Memory, if Clement (*Stromateis* 6.2.11) correctly ascribes a verse to him

Μνημοσύνης καὶ Ζηνὸς ᾽Ολυμπίου ἐννέα κοῦραι

(F 16 Kinkel).

That would make twelve Eumelian Muses in all, a large but not unacceptable number. The Muse whom Zeus of Ithome loved was surely one of his own daughters (F 13 Kinkel = Pausanias 4.33.2).

Before we return to examine the rest of the Eumelian fragments, the treatment of the Argonautic story in the *Naupaktian epic* (Ναυπάκτια ἔπη or Ναυπακτικά) demands attention. This was not a story about Naupaktos, which is not named in the extant fragments, but a tale recited at a festival at that place, one of the chief cities of the Western

---

[1] See my *Early Ionians* 66 and the evidence there cited.

Lokrians on the north shore of the Corinthian gulf. Pausanias knew two traditions about the authorship of the epic (10.38.11): according to Charon of Lampsakos (262 F 4), with whom the periegete agreed, the *Naupaktia* was composed by Karkinos a Naupaktian, but most people ascribed the poem to a Milesian. In the age of Pontic exploration and colonisation the Milesians were surely interested in the heroes of the Argo tale, a theme of special concern in the *Naupaktia*; the Milesian authorship doubted by Pausanias may therefore be genuine to this extent – that a wandering Milesian poet came to Naupaktos and performed an Argonautic poem there, perhaps in competition with local poets such as Karkinos. Indeed, a Milesian was believed to have been a fellow guest with Hesiod amongst the Lokrians (Plut. *Mor.* 162 B).

Hesiod himself may well have visited Naupaktos. The best documented version of his death placed it at the sanctuary of Nemeian Zeus in western Lokris (Thucydides 3.96.1). The *Contest of Homer and Hesiod*, it is true, states that Hesiod was murdered in the country of the eastern (or Opountian) Lokrians shortly before a festival of Ariadne (*Hom. Op.* v p. 234 Allen), but this version is secondary and mistaken (see especially Marcksheffel 31). It is an attractive hypothesis that Hesiod died in western Lokris not far from Naupaktos when he was on the way to perform there. The existence of a flourishing epic tradition in the islands and on the coasts of northwest Greece may be inferred, if not from the content of the *Odyssey* itself, then from the late eighth century hexameter inscribed upon an Ithakan sherd (M. Robertson, *ABSA* 43 (1948) 80 ff) and from the epic diction of the epichoric verse epitaphs of the neighbourhood, notably the poem on the warrior Arniadas of Corcyra who died fighting at the mouth of the river Aratthos (Tod 2) and the verses commemorating the Lokrian *proxenos* in Corcyra, Menekrates (Schwyzer 133, 1). The *Naupaktia* was similar in content to the Hesiodic *Catalogues of Women*, if we trust the statement of Pausanias that it was composed about (and perhaps also for) women – ἔπεσιν πεποιημένοις ἐς γυναῖκας. As such it was perhaps well suited to recitation at a festival of Ariadne.[1]

One fragment is plainly akin to Hesiodic catalogue poetry

[1] For this festival see also L. Lérat, *Les Locriens de l'Ouest* 2 (Paris 1952) 167–169.

τὴν δὲ μέθ' ὁπλοτάτην 'Εριώπην ἐξονόμαζεν,
'Αλκιμάχην δὲ πατήρ τε καὶ "Αδμητος καλέεσκεν.

(Schol. *Il.* 15.336 = *Naupaktia* F 1 Kinkel): 'Her youngest sister he named Eriope, but her father and Admetos did call her Alkimache.' 'He' is Oileus, father of the lesser Aias and the most famous hero of the Lokrians, who may be expected to appear in a Naupaktian poem. The father of Eriope or Alkimache, wife of Oileus, was Pheres. Admetos is her brother. Oileus and Admetos were both Argonauts (Ap. Rhod. *Arg.* 1.74 and 1.49), and it is with the Argonautic story that the *Naupaktia* was chiefly concerned: hence the mention of the heroes and Eriope, wife of one and sister of the other, in this fragment. Admetos became king of the country at the head of the gulf of Pagasai, whence *Argo* sailed forth. He therefore had a prime role in the *Naupaktia*.

Two more fragments of the *Naupaktia* refer to the Admetos legend. In one it is said that Asklepios, son of Apollo, restored Hippolytos to life (Apollodoros, *Lib.* 3.10.3); in the other that Zeus struck Asklepios with a thunderbolt (Philodemos, περὶ εὐσ. p. 52 Gomperz). Zeus smote the hero because he feared that men might acquire the art of healing from him and so aid each other. Apollo then killed the sons of the Kyklopes because they had made the bolt for Zeus (Pherekydes 3 F 35a). Now Zeus would have thrown Apollo down to Tartaros, but for the intercession of Leto; instead Apollo had to serve a man for a year. The god therefore went to Admetos whom he served as a herdsman.

The fragments of the *Naupaktia* describing the voyage of the *Argo* can all be placed in their contexts. They come from the scholia to the *Argonautika* of Apollonios Rhodios, who may have made use of the *Naupaktia* as well as of Eumelos. According to Apollonios, the Harpies who had troubled Phineus were chased by Zetes and Kalais to the Strophades islands, where the creatures were made to swear that they would leave Phineus alone and torment him no more. They then disappeared into a lair in Minoan Crete. Now a comment on this passage (Schol. *Arg.* 2.299, p. 150 Wendel) reports that in the *Naupaktia* the Harpies were said to have fled into a cave in Crete beneath the ridge called Arginous. It is possible therefore that in the *Naupaktia*, which Apollonios may well be following here, they also went to the Strophades

Eumelos, the early Argonautika and related Epics

islands on the way from Phineus to Crete. Here would then be a local allusion in the *Naupaktia*, for the Strophades (or Echinades) lie near Naupaktos, not far from the entrance to the Corinthian gulf (cf. Apollodoros, *Lib.* 1.9.21).

In the *Naupaktia* Eurylyte is the name of the wife of Aietes (Schol. *Arg.* 3.240, p. 227 Wendel), but in Apollonios she is Eidyia. There were differences in the plot too: in the poem of Apollonios (3.521) not all the heroes are eager to face the task of yoking the bulls of Aietes, but in the *Naupaktia* all those who sailed in the *Argo* were named as volunteers: ὁ δὲ τὰ Ναυπακτικὰ ⟨ποιήσας⟩ (add. Kinkel) πάντας ἀριθμεῖ τοὺς ὑπ᾿ αὐτοῦ φερομένους ἀριστεῖς, where for αὐτοῦ we should read Ἀργοῦς.[1] Idmon (who in this poem evidently had not died before the heroes arrived in Kolchis) urged Jason to undertake the task (*Naupaktia* F 6 Kinkel = Schol. Ap. Rhod. *Arg.* 3.523–524 p. 234 Wendel). Aietes planned to kill the Argonauts after a feast to which they had been invited, and to burn the ship, but was deflected from his purpose by Aphrodite who filled him with a yearning to lie with his wife. Idmon foreseeing the danger urged the heroes 'to hasten from the hall through the swift black night', from the palace of Aietes to the *Argo*: φευγέμεναι μεγάροιο θοὴν διὰ νύκτα μέλαιναν. (Schol. Ap. Rhod. *Arg.* 4.86 and 66a, pp. 266–267 Wendel). Medea hearing the footsteps of the escaping heroes arose and set off with them.

Four verses are preserved in the scholia (to *Arg.* 4.86) showing how the heroes were enabled by Aphrodite to flee: 'Then did the lady Aphrodite cast a longing upon Aietes to mingle in love with his spouse Eurylyte; for she cared in her heart how that after his task was done Jason might return homewards in the company of his close-fighting companions.'[2] The main task was the taking of the fleece, which according to the *Naupaktia*, was lying in the house of Aietes. When Medea fled, she simply brought the fleece with her to the *Argo*. It is not certain whether in the poem Jason had first to collect the fleece and bring it to Aietes or that the prize was kept permanently in the house.

---

[1] Robert, *Die gr. Heldensage* (Berlin 1920) 795 n. 2.

[2]
δὴ τότ᾿ ἄρ᾿ Αἰήτῃ πόθον ἔμβαλε δῖ᾿ Ἀφροδίτη
Εὐρυλύτης φιλότητι μιγήμεναι ἧς ἀλόχοιο,
κηδομένη φρεσὶν ᾗσιν ὅπως μετ᾿ ἄεθλον Ἰήσων
νοστήσῃ οἰκόνδε σὺν ἀγχεμάχοις ἑτάροισιν.

The mythographer Herodoros (*F.Gr.Hist.* 31 F 52), who agrees with the *Naupaktia* in some points, reported that Jason had to kill the dragon before bringing the fleece to Aietes.

Jason, as Aphrodite had intended, returned home to Iolkos (Pausanias 2.3.9): but by what route the *Naupaktia* brought him back from Kolchis we are not informed. In the earliest *Argonautika* the heroes may well have come home the way they sailed out – through the Propontis, since there is no evidence that elaborate journeys up the Phasis or Istros to outer Okeanos formed part of the Argonautic legend in its earliest form; such deviations first appear in the geography of Hekataios (1 F 18a), but are not likely to have been invented by him. They reflect the growing knowledge of northerly regions amongst epic poets from the mid-seventh century B.C. onwards. Some of this knowledge originated in Aristeas the explorer, who was also the composer of an epic, the *Arimaspea*. He made two journeys to central Asia from the shores of the Black Sea. From the second expedition he did not return.[1]

After the death of Pelias, the *Naupaktia* continued, Jason migrated from Iolkos to Corcyra where he settled. Mermeros the eldest of his children was killed by a lioness when hunting on the mainland opposite to the island (Pausanias 2.3.9). This story may be a variant, suited to a northwestern Greek audience, of the Eumelian or Corinthian tale according to which Medea killed her sons by Jason, Mermeros and Pheres, in Corinth (cf. Apollodoros, *Lib.* 1.9.28). On the other hand, the legend of Mermeros in northwest Greece, on the Epeirot mainland, is early. It already appears in the *Odyssey*, where Homer mentions Ilos son of Mermeros in connexion with Thesprotian Ephyra. Here we may hazard a conjecture that in the *Naupaktia* the witch Medea was associated with the famous oracle of the dead at Thesprotian Ephyra.[2]

Ephyra or Kichyros now lies some distance from the sea in the Acheron valley, whose marsh has silted up since antiquity. In early

[1] Herodotos 4.13–15. See also J. D. P. Bolton, *Aristeas of Proconnesus* (Oxford 1962) 8 for the twelve hexameters ascribed to the *Arimaspea*.

[2] For this oracle see especially Pausanias 1.17.5, and for excavations at the Nekyomanteion, where there are traces of occupation as early as Mycenaean times, Dakaris ap. Hood, *Archaeological Reports for 1958* (London 1959) 11. N. G. L. Hammond, *Epirus* (Oxford 1967) 366 n. 4.

Eumelos, the early Argonautika and related Epics

Hellenic times however the place was beside or much closer to the sea. There may well be an allusion to this locality in two lines from the *Naupaktia* (F 2 Kinkel = Herodian περὶ μον. λέξ. p. 15 [II p. 922 Lentz²]): '... but he, rich in sheep and rich in kine, did settle in dwellings upon the shore of the wide-pathed sea.'

ἀλλ' ὃ μὲν οὖν ἐπὶ θινὶ θαλάσσης εὐρυπόροιο
οἰκία ναιετάασκε πολύρρην, πουλυβοώτης.

[ἐπὶ θινὶ Cramer ἐπινευσὶ cod.]

The lines are reminiscent of a Hesiodic fragment about Hellopia, a land also in Epeiros, within the confines of which lay Zeus's oracle at Dodona (Hesiod F 134, 1–3 Rzach):

ἔστί τις Ἑλλοπίη πολυλήιος ἠδ' εὐλείμων,
ἀφνειὴ μήλοισι καὶ εἰλιπόδεσσι βόεσσιν.
ἐν δ' ἄνδρες ναίουσι πολύρρηνες, πολυβοῦται. ...

Both poets may have the same rich district of Epeiros, the Acheron valley and Hellopia in mind, with Dodona at the extremity of the kingdom

ἔνθα δὲ Δωδώνη τις ἐπ' ἐσχατιῇ πεπόλισται

(Hesiod F 134, 5 Rzach).[1]

Dodona was once part of the kingdom of Thesprotia (Aeschylus, *P.V.* 831) and from it the upland pastures lead down westwards towards the coast – Δωδώναθεν ἀρχόμενοι πρὸς Ἰόνιον πόρον (Pindar, *Nem.* 4–53). If, like the Hesiodic fragment, the two lines of the *Naupaktia* do refer to Hellopia or Thesprotia, then the subject of them will be Mermeros who died hunting on the mainland, and whose son Ilos lived at Ephyra. The subject of the fragment, ὁ μέν, is contrasted with someone else, now lost; Pheres or Jason his father may be meant. As we shall see, there was an epic centred on this very part of Epeiros – the *Thesprotis*, but the examination of it must wait till we come to Eugammon of Kyrene. As to the date of the *Naupaktia* there is no pointer in the literary evidence, but it is not likely to have taken shape before the settlement of the Eretrians in Corcyra in the mid-eighth century B.C. Of Corinthian propaganda in the fragments there is no trace, nor, since Naupaktos was not a Corinthian colony, need we expect to find any.

[1] See, for more detail, H. W. Parke, *The Oracles of Zeus* (Oxford 1967) 46.

73

To complete the chapter we now return to fragments ascribed to Eumelos which have a remote, or no, connexion with the early tale of the Argonauts. To the line of Helios at Corinth succeeded that of Sisyphos, who had a place in the *Korinthiaka*: Eumelos is said to have asserted that Neleus father of Nestor died at the Isthmos where he was buried in a secret place. When Nestor came to Sisyphos, the king refused to show him his father's monument (Pausanias 2.2.2.). The occasion of this story is lost. There is no particular reason to link it with the founding of the Isthmian games.

Sisyphos recurs in a frankly propagandist myth putting Ephyra or Corinth at the head of the dynasty of Lakedaimon. This is reported by the Scholia to Apollonios Rhodios (1.146–149a, pp. 19–20 Wendel). Glaukos, who, as in Homer (*Iliad* 6.154), was a son of Sisyphos, lost his horses and came looking for them to Lakedaimon. There he coupled with Panteidyia, who later married Thestios. So Leda her daughter, though said to be a daughter of Thestios, really sprang from a king of Corinth. The bland assurance of this patent, and anti-traditional, fiction, quite in the Eumelian manner, commands admiration. The poet followed the Spartan royal line down at least as far as the Trojan war, if we may believe Apollodoros (*Lib.* 3.11.1), according to whom Eumelos stated that Xenodamos was a son of Menelaos and a nymph Knossia. Knossia's name shows that she was a Cretan, as was the mother of Menelaos (Apollod. *Epitome* 3.3). Menelaos visited Crete for the obsequies of his mother's father Katreus at the very time when Paris was in Sparta (Apollod. *loc. cit.*). That then may well have been the occasion of the procreation of Xenodamos. The Corinthian versions of these Lakonian genealogies were not confined to Corinth; for Alkaios or Alkman, about a century after Eumelos, accepted that Leda was a daughter of Glaukos: 'them did the blessed daughter of Glaukos bring forth' said one or the other of them concerning the mother of Helen and the Dioskouroi (Adespota F 94 Page): τοὺς τέκε θυγάτηρ Γλαύκω μάκαιρα. Of Bellerophon's horse Pegasos there is no word in the fragments of Eumelos. Yet he was popular with vase painters in Corinth as early as *ca.* 675 B.C. (Dunbabin 78–79) and appears already in Hesiod (*Theogony* 281 and 325. Cf. F 7b9 Rzach). Eumelos then may well have described him, with or without wings. In a Hesiodic fragment (*P.Oxy.* 2495, F 21 iii 1-4) Pegasos is called 'very swift', ὠκύτατον. Here then he may be winged.

Less securely to be ascribed to Eumelos are three fragments of the *Europia*. Pausanias mentions an anonymous poem (9.5.8) which he calls the 'epic on Europe'; Clement writes of the composer of the *Europia* (*Strom.* 1.164=Eumelos F 11 Kinkel); and a scholium on *Iliad* 6.131 (=Eumelos F 10 Kinkel) has 'Eumelos who composed the *Europia*'. These fragments provide a poor foundation for assigning a poem on the subject of Europa to Eumelos; Europa herself is mentioned in none of them, but Thebes is; and a poem, whether by Eumelos or another, could fitly be called *Europia*, yet deal with Thebes because Kadmos was a kinsman – according to some a brother – of Europa and came as far as Delphi and Thebes in his search for her; Zeus, in the guise of a bull, had stolen her away from Phoenicia across the sea to Crete, where she became by him the mother of Minos, Sarpedon and Rhadamanthys (Hesiod F 30 Rzach).[1] Another link between Europa and Thebes is Harmonia's necklace which had first been given by Zeus to Europa and by her to Kadmos, Harmonia's husband (Pherekydes 3 F 89). A part of the legend which would have specially delighted Eumelos was the killing of the dragon at Thebes by Kadmos; for some of the dragon's teeth were given by Athena to Aietes and proved useful to him when Jason had to be put to the test in Kolchis (Ap. Rhod. *Arg.* 3.1176–1184). The poem described how Hermes taught Amphion to play the lyre (Pausanias 9.5.8), which the stones followed to fortify Thebes;[2] and if the Homeric scholium may be believed, Eumelos himself in the *Europia* dealt at length with the career of Dionysos, who was born to Zeus and Semele in Thebes (F 10 Kinkel). The scholium states that the god was purified by Rhea at Kybela in Phrygia and learned the rites of initiation (see also Apollodoros, *Lib.* 3.5.1). The association of Dionysos with Phrygia is emphasised by Euripides in the *Bacchae* (58 ff and 78 ff). That as early as 700 B.C. Eumelos dwelt upon it is possible – one may compare the importance of Zagreus in the *Alkmaionis* (F 3 Kinkel), and Phrygian influence was strong amongst the Greeks while the great

[1] Antimachos of Kolophon (F 3 Wyss), who may well follow the *Europia* here, states that Zeus hid Europa in the mountain cave at Teumesos in Boiotia.
[2] See also F. Vian, *Les Origines de Thèbes* (Paris 1963) 71.

kingdom of Midas still flourished at Gordion before the ruin brought by the Kimmerian invaders of Asia Minor laid it low. The allegedly Eumelian fragment includes the story of wicked Lykourgos king of Thrace who insulted and expelled Dionysos, a story known to Homer (*Iliad* 6.130–140) who tells how the raving ministrants of the god were chased and struck to the ground while Dionysos himself had to take refuge with Thetis in the sea. Thereafter Zeus blinded the Thracian king. Since the Eumelian fragment adds the detail that Dionysos took refuge with Thetis and *Eurynome*, it cannot come solely from the *Iliad*. The difference does not prove the ascription to Eumelos correct; but the poet may well have mentioned Eurynome because as an Okeanid she was also held, by some, to have been the mother of the Asopos river, and could therefore have been of concern to the Corinthian poet (Apollod. *Lib.* 3.12.6). We conclude that the case for ascribing the Dionysos fragment to Eumelos is not cogent, but attractive.

The two lines quoted by Clement from 'the poet of the *Europia*' present a quite different problem. Clement's way of naming the author could be simply a pedantic circumlocution for 'Eumelos'; if it is, we have no assurance that the verses come from a *Europia*. The subject is the sanctuary at Delphi: 'The poet of the *Europia*' wrote Clement 'reports that the image of Apollo at Delphi is a pillar, in these words: "That we may hang up to the god a tithe and the spoils from the holy buildings and the tall column." '

> ὄφρα θεῷ δεκάτην ἀκροθίνιά τε κρεμάσαιμεν
> σταθμῶν ἐκ ζαθέων καὶ κίονος ὑψηλοῖο.

Delphi appears in the Kadmos legend – on Apollo's instructions the hero followed a cow thence till, at the site of Thebes, she fell down for weariness (Hellanikos 4 F 51). But these verses look less like a hero's prayer for victory than the poet's own hope for Corinthian success in a contemporary war. Corinth was engaged, not without success, in hostilities with her neighbours about 700 B.C.;[1] so Eumelos, if the verses are his, would have had good reason to compose them.

The choice of a Theban subject by a Corinthian author would also require some explanation, if the poem is genuinely by Eumelos. There was an Asopos in Boiotia as well as the river in the neighbourhood of

---

[1] See my *Early Sparta* (London 1962) 35.

Eumelos, the early Argonautika and related Epics

Corinth, which flowed by Phleious and Sikyon; but the shared name is hardly enough to justify or explain the devotion of a special poem to Thebes. One point deserves note: the Bacchiads had ties with Thebes, for we are told by Aristotle (*Politics* 1274a31–1274b5) that a Bacchiad, Philolaos, departed to Thebes and legislated for the city. Eumelos, then, may have had a family interest in Thebes. The ascription to him of fragments about Theban legend is thus not absurd.

His Arkadian neighbours, too, drew his attention. Lykaon, he is said to have maintained, had a daughter Kallisto (Apollod. *Lib.* 3.8.2). Some said that she was placed amongst the stars as the Great Bear (Eratosthenes, *Katasterismoi* 1). Her son, by Zeus or Apollo, was Arkas – there may be a pun here on *Arkas* (Arkadian) and *arktos* (bear). Arkas begat Elatos and Apheidas by a nymph Chrysopeleia ('the golden dove'),[1] with whom we may compare the Peleiades who were priestesses of Zeus and Dione amongst the oaks at Dodona. According to Charon of Lampsakos (262 F 12b) Arkas, out hunting, met her just as her oak tree in which she had been born was about to be swept away by a river in spate. (The loss of her tree threatened ruin to a hamadryad.) When Arkas had diverted the stream and packed the tree with earth, Chrysopeleia bestowed her favours upon him and two sons were the result. They divided the land between them, Apheidas becoming specially associated with the neighbourhood of Tegea (Ap. Rhod. *Arg.* 1.162). The story may be a pendant to the Arkadian legend according to which the first man Pelasgos was born from the earth in the mountain forests (Hesiod F 43 Rzach with Asios F 8 Kinkel). According to a Hesiodic fragment (F 44 Rzach) Pelasgos was the father of Lykaon; but we are not informed that Eumelos declared Arkas to be a great-grandson of Pelasgos the first man.

There still remains to be considered a fragment which, if it is admitted at all, is usually placed amongst the Eumelian *dubia*. Ioannes of Lydia (*De Mensibus* 4.71 p. 123 Wuensch) states that, according to Eumelos the Corinthian, Zeus was born in Lydia; there was still in the Lydian's time (sixth century A.D.) a place west of Sardeis on the heights of Mount Tmolos which was of old called Gonai Dios Hyetiou 'The begettings of Zeus the rain god' and in his day 'of Deusios'. Iohannes adds that the

[1] Apollod. *Lib.* 3.9.1 and Tzetz. ad Lyc. 480 (= Eumelos F 15 Kinkel).

77

Kouretes guarded the god there. Excavation of a mountain sanctuary on Tmolos, if the correct place could be found, might support the tradition; discovery of a sanctuary dating from the late eighth century would confirm it. A genuine fragment of Eumelos, the *prosodion* for the Messenians, shows that the poet was interested in Zeus of another summit, Ithome. The fragment plausibly assigned to Eumelos on the story of Dionysos and Rhea at Kybela in Phrygia also suggests that the poet may have been interested in the Asiatic Rhea, the mountain mother.[1] To claim that Eumelos was therefore also concerned with the birth of Zeus to Rhea, not in Crete, but on Mount Tmolos, is to fall short of syllogistic certainty. But the reasoning has a likelihood and we must hesitate before banishing irrevocably the Lydian fragment from the remains of the poet. Eumelos was here, perhaps, deliberately contradicting the tradition reported in Hesiod's *Theogony* which placed the birth of Zeus to Rhea in Crete.

Two final details are of little significance. A comment on the words 'the sweetly breathing Muse' of Pindar (Schol. Pindar *Ol.* 13.22) remarks that 'Eumolpos' a Corinthian wrote a *Return of the Hellenes* (from Troy presumably) and implies that the said poet declared flute music to flourish especially in war. If we put, as has been proposed, 'Eumelos' for 'Eumolpos' here, then Eumelos was interested in flute playing, as well he may have been. But for the alleged *Returns of the Hellenes* there are no matching fragments. Secondly, Jerome after Eusebius (*Chronicle* at Olymp. 4.2) remarks that *Eumelus poeta qui Bugoniam et Europiam conposuit ... agnoscitur*. The reference in the title Βουγονία could perhaps be to the birth of bees and the making of honey in the carcass of an ox (cf. Verg. *Georg.* 4.554-558. Varro *De Re Rust.* 2.5.5), as in Samson's lion; but *Bougonia* may also mean the breeding of oxen, as Marcksheffel pointed out.[2] It is conceivable that Eumelos composed a work on cattle-breeding, a kind of Corinthian rival to the *Works and Days* of Hesiod. His own name means 'rich in flocks', and the wealth of the Bacchiads is as likely in the first phase of colonisation to have come from agriculture, cattle and sheep as from overseas trade.

[1] Compare Steph. Byz. s.v. Κυβέλεια ... ἔστι καὶ Κύβελα Φρυγίας καὶ Κύβελα ὄρος ἱερόν, ἀφ᾽ οὗ Κυβέλη ἡ Ῥέα λέγεται.
[2] p. 241.

Eumelos, the early Argonautika and related Epics

But this is a large hypothesis to construct on a single mention of one name, which may be simply a corruption of *Theogonia*.

The shadowy figure of Eumelos broods over all the subsequent history of Corinthian poetry. In spite of Pindar's praise of the Corinthian Muse[1] no other native-born Corinthian epic poet is named in the archaic period. (Aison, if he is not a confusion with Periander's friend Arion of Lesbos, is but a ghost.)[2] It seems that Eumelos was so successful in inventing and codifying an epichoric mythology that he killed local originality in verse. Increasingly in the seventh century Corinthians found an outlet for their creative skills in vase-making and painting; in the visual, not verbal, representation of myth and legend. We must make allowance for the enormous gaps in our knowledge, for even fifth-century Corinthian history is a still dark domain; but the scarcity of names of poets is remarkable. Eumelos gave his city a glorious, and largely fictitious, heroic past; but, it seems, he also fossilised prematurely her epic genius and stereotyped her indigenous tradition.

---

[1] *Ol. 13.22.*
[2] Simonides, F 104 Page. The date of the poet Diodoros (*F.Gr.Hist.* 452 F 1) is not known. Andreas an archaising Corinthian poet named by [Plutarch] *De Musica* 1137 F is undatable.

VI

Epimenides

More than a century after Eumelos the tale of the Argonauts was again made the subject of a poem, this time by a Cretan. Epimenides is best known for his powers of retrospective prophecy – Aristotle remarks that he explained things that had happened in the past but were not clear in the present (*Rhet.* 3.17); he was remembered, too, for his purification of Athens from a plague in the time of Solon (Aristotle *Ἀθπ.* 1 with Plutarch, *Solon* 12); and for his being accounted one of the Seven Wise Men. But he was also an epic poet, who, according to Diogenes Laertios (1.111), composed a poem in five thousand verses on the *Birth of the Kouretes and Korybantes and the Theogonia*; such a ponderous title can hardly have been original, but the fragments do show that he was concerned with Theogonies. Diogenes also ascribes to Epimenides a poem on the *Building of the Argo and the Journey of Jason to the Kolchians*, allegedly of five thousand verses. This title too cannot be genuine.

A few fragments ascribed to the Cretan prophet evidently come from the story of the *Argo*. Epimenides (D.K. 3 B 13) asserted, for example, that Aietes was a Corinthian and that his mother was Ephyra. The poem may therefore have agreed with Eumelos in bringing Aietes from Corinth to Kolchis. A fragment calling the Harpies children of Okeanos and Earth would also belong naturally to the *Argonautika* (D.K. 3 B 7). We are told also that Epimenides added a fifth son, Presbon, to the four sons of Phrixos catalogued by Hesiod (F 152 Rz.). These meagre details are, however, a poor harvest from a poem said to be 6,500 lines long, and none deals with the construction of the *Argo* which, Diogenes implies, was a significant part of the poem (yet there is no reason to dismiss the Epimenidean *Argonautika* as a fiction, invented, for example, by the forger of titles, Lobon of Argos).

An unusual variant of the Argonautic story is to be seen in Herodotos

Epimenides

(4.179). It may well have its origin in the poem of Epimenides, since it is concerned with a voyage of *Argo* immediately after she was built beneath Mount Pelion, but before she went to Kolchis. Jason put a hecatomb aboard with a bronze tripod intending to sail round Pelos ponnese to Delphi; but when he was rounding Maleia, a storm blew up which bore him to Libya. He found himself in the Tritonian shallows and was unable to escape from them, until the god Triton appeared and offered to lead him into the open sea in return for the tripod. The tripod was duly handed over, and Triton declared that the descendant of the Argonauts who obtained the tripod would found thereabouts one hundred Greek cities. The story belongs to the later seventh century B.C. when the Greeks were colonising the Libyan coast. Its concern with the first voyage of *Argo* is notable; for in the earliest tradition *Argo* went directly to the Euxine after her launching. This voyage past Crete may therefore well be an innovation of Epimenides himself. Notable too is the fact that Herodotos says nothing about the ship continuing to Delphi, without the tripod. The tale thus suggests perhaps that the possessor of the tripod has no need of Delphic sanction to ensure the success of his colonies. It is interesting therefore that the fragments of Epimenides reveal intense hostility towards Delphi's pretentions.

Two verses challenge the claim of Pytho to be the centre of the earth, the point where the omphalos or navel lay; here, said the legend reported by Plutarch (*Mor.* 409E), had met the two eagles or swans set to fly by Zeus from opposite extremities of the earth. When Epimenides received from the Pythia an ambiguous response, he said: 'For there never has been a central navel of the earth and sea; and if there is one, it is apparent to the gods, but mortals see it not';

οὔτε γὰρ ἦν γαίης μέσος ὀμφαλὸς οὔτε θαλάσσης·
εἰ δέ τις ἔστι, θεοῖς δῆλος, θνητοῖσι δ᾽ ἄφαντος.

(D.K. 3 B 11)

The enmity was mutual; Delphi too poured abuse upon the insolent Cretan seer, no doubt with a feeling of professional rivalry. The verse, expressed in Hesiodic language,

Κρῆτες ἀεὶ ψεῦσται, κακὰ θηρία, γαστέρες ἀργαί

is ascribed by St Paul (*Ad Titum* 1.12) to a Cretan prophet (the Apostle failed, however, to see the logical contradiction involved in a Cretan calling all Cretans liars). The prophet is usually thought to be Epimenides, but can he have attacked himself as a Cretan? Surely the words are a riposte to Epimenides, not, as St Paul thought, an attack by a Cretan on his fellow-countrymen – against whom, so far as we know, Epimenides had no grudge (see Jacoby on *F.Gr.Hist.* 457 F 2). The Apostle's mistake was due to the Delphic response's appearance in a collection of Epimenidean sayings (see 457 T 8a).

Of the remaining verses, whose Epimenidean authorship we need not doubt, two are theogonical and show that he wrote, as a Cretan Hesiod, on the kinships of the gods. Amongst the children of Kronos were 'golden Aphrodite of the fair tresses, and the immortal Fates and Furies with their changeful gifts':

ἐκ τοῦ καλλίκομος γένετο χρυσῆ ᾽Αφροδίτη
Μοῖραί τ᾽ ἀθάνατοι καὶ ᾽Ερινύες αἰολόδωροι.

(D.K. 3 B 19)

Which version, the Oriental or the Hellenised, of Aphrodite's birth Epimenides accepted does not appear from the fragments. Backwards in time he traced the divine genealogies to the primal entities Aër and Night (D.K. 3 B 5); forwards he traced them downwards to himself, whom he claimed to be a descendant of Selene, the Moon. This assertion is made in some exceptionally interesting verses about the Nemean Lion (Aelian, *H.A.* 12.7):

καὶ γὰρ ἐγὼ γένος εἰμὶ Σελήνης ἠυκόμοιο,
ἣ δεινὸν φρίξασ᾽ ἀπεσείσατο θῆρα λέοντα·
ἐν Νεμέᾳ δ᾽ ἄγχουσ᾽ αὐτὸν διὰ πότνιαν ῞Ηραν
⟨θείη ἲς ἐδάμασσε βίης ῾Ηρακληείης⟩.[1]

'For I too am sprung from long-tressed Selene who with dire shakings did throw off the wild lion; whom the divine strength of mighty Herakles laid low, as he throttled it in lady Hera's cause.' Epimenides, then, like the Nemean lion, had kinship with the Moon.[2] Nor was this his only tie with her; for he, like Endymion whom the Moon loved, had fallen asleep in a cave. Endymion slept, either in Elis or in a cave of Mount Latmos in Karia, for ever; Epimenides was asleep in a Cretan cave for forty years (Paus. 1.14.4) or even fifty-seven (Diog. Laert. 1.109), or so it was claimed. (If Delphi knew the tale of the long sleep,

---

[1] Suppl. Diels.   [2] See also Euphorion F 84, 4 Powell.

Epimenides

then the assertion that Cretans were liars possessed special plausibility.)
We know that Epimenides mentioned Endymion: he declared that the
prince fell in love with Hera; when Zeus objected, Endymion asked to
be allowed to sleep for ever (Schol. Ap. Rhod. *Arg.* 4.57). Epimenides
may have felt that his unusually long siesta gave him some affinity, as
a new Endymion, with the Moon; but Aiakos, not Endymion, was the
heroic name he chose for himself (Diog. Laert. 1.114), as though he
were with Rhadamanthys a keeper of the House of Hades. The Cretans
also called him a Koures, presumably because like the young Zeus (the
Kouros, or young male god of the Cretans)[1] he had spent part of his
life in a cave in their island (Diog. Laert. 1.115).

In dating Epimenides about 600 B.C. the majority of ancient writers
about him agree; but Plato (*Laws* 642 D) makes a Cretan declare that
Epimenides came to Athens ten years before the Persian wars, thus
about 500 B.C. Plato's chronology is mistaken, and it is difficult to see
how he, or his Cretan informant, came to make the error. Aristotle
ignores it in the *Constitution of the Athenians*; and in view of his remark
that the Cretan's function as a seer was to explain hidden past events,
he cannot have accepted a story in which Epimenides predicts the
coming of the Mede. A possible explanation of Plato's error is that
sayings of Epimenides, the *Katharmoi*, were consulted in Athens when
the Persian menace threatened; a text may even have been brought
from Crete.[2] Xenophanes, it is true, is said to have heard that the seer
lived for 157 years (D.K. 21 B 20), but to accept this alleged lifespan in
the hope of exonerating Plato from error would strain the faith of even
the most credulous chronologist.

Outside Athens and Crete the poet's concerns, in epic and in contemporary life, were closest with the Peloponnese. He is said to have
predicted a defeat of the Spartans in Arkadia (Theopompos 115 F 69)
and also to have declared Arkas and Pan to be twin sons of Zeus and
Kallisto (D.K. 3 B 16); and his mention of Ephyra and Korinthos

[1] On the hymn to whom, found in eastern Crete, see West, *J.H.S.* 85 (1965)
esp. 156.
[2] For a possible consultation of Epimenidean oracles in Sparta about 500 B.C.,
see Leahy, *Phoenix* 12 (1958) 155. The seer's body was said to have been kept there
(Diog. Laert. 1.115) and its skin may have been covered with writing; Suda s.v.
Ἐπιμενίδης· . . . καὶ παροιμία 'τὸ Ἐπιμενίδειον δέρμα' ἐπὶ τῶν ἀποθέτων.

suggests ties with Corinth. He was therefore, besides being prophet, purifier and politician, an international poet of renown. As such, he deserves a secure place in any work on early Greek poetry, despite the deep uncertainty about his life, writings and achievements.

VII

Kinaithon and Asios

In antiquity Sparta was reputed to have been tardy to foster the arts of epic poetry. Her slowness was shared by other Dorian states, so Maximus of Tyre believed (23.5): 'late in time did Sparta rhapsodize, late too did Crete, and the Dorian people in Libya' – the last refers to Kyrene whose local epic poet Eugammon is said to have lived in the mid-sixth century B.C.[1] The belief in Spartan neglect of epic was reinforced by the story of the bringing of the Homeric poems to Lakedaimon from Samos by Lykourgos the lawgiver; the tale implied that Sparta had no poet of her own to match Homer so early as Homer's day.[2]

Yet there was a flourishing body of local legend in Lakedaimon. It came down from the Mycenaean age, preserved and elaborated by the non-Dorian stock of the country, the Achaean survivors from the ruin of the late bronze age civilisation of Peloponnese. Still in the seventh century the Spartans were having to battle against the Achaean remnant which, in its doughty independence, became a nuisance, if not a threat, in the way of the expanding state.[3] The existence of a vigorous epic tradition amongst these isolated survivors of a once glorious kingdom which had passed into history about 1200 B.C. cannot be proved;[4] but the elegies of Tyrtaios show strong influence of epic (as well as vernacular Ionic)[5] language; and we do not have to assume that all this epic influence came from Ionia rather than from Sparta.

---

[1] See *G.R.B.S.* 3 (1960) 24 and Chapter XII below.
[2] Plutarch, *Lyk.* 4. See also Allen, *Homer. Origins and Transmission* (Oxford 1924) 48.
[3] *B.C.H.* 82 (1958) 589.
[4] Cf. J. A. Notopoulos, *Hesperia* 29 (1960) 196.
[5] For Ionisms in Tyrtaios see K. J. Dover in *Archiloque* (Entretiens Hardt 10, Geneva 1964) 193.

Greek Epic Poetry

The name of but one indigenous Lakedamonian early epic poet is recorded for us by ancient writers – Kinaithon. The *Tabula Borgiana*, as we have already noted, ascribed to him an *Oidipodia*;[1] with what justification we know not. Already in the fifth century B.C., Hellanikos asserted that Kinaithon had composed a *Little Iliad* (Schol. Eur. *Troad.* 822);[2] but this remark may entail no more than that some of Kinaithon's poetry revealed knowledge of Homer or was thought to have been composed with the *Great Iliad* in mind. The *Telegonia* of Kinaithon (p. 196 Kinkel), if it ever existed, would similarly have been an extension of the *Odyssey*, its subject being a son of Odysseus, Telegonos; but the text of Jerome (*Chron. Ol.* 4.2) who alone mentions the title may be corrupt here, and Leutsch's proposed change to *Genealogias* accords well with the extant fragments. As for the *Herakleia* alleged to be Kinaithon's by the scholiasts to Apollonios Rhodios (1.1355–1357c, p. 122 Wendel), the correct author's name here may be Konon, who is named as an author of a *Herakleia* according to the strongest manuscript evidence of the scholia at *Argonautika* 1.1165 (p. 105 Wendel. See also *F.Gr.Hist.* 26 F 2). The alleged poem of Kinaithon on Herakles is therefore best left out of account, though in favour of reading Kinaithon's name in both passages of the Apollonios scholia is the fact that the kings of Sparta traced their descent from Herakles; a *Herakleia* would therefore have been assured of an appreciative local audience in Kinaithon's own country. One of the fragments alludes to the loss of Hylas by Herakles during the voyage of the *Argo* – a possible theme for a Herakles epic; the other passage states that Kinaithon (or Konon) called the monster Aigaion, as Homer did, Briareos also, and that Poseidon threw him into the Aegean sea. This story has more in common with early *Titanomachies* than with a *Herakles* epic; and even if the ascription of it to Kinaithon is correct, the title *Herakleia* may here be mistaken. If Aigaion found a place in Kinaithon's poetry, then near the beginning of the *Genealogies* is the place for him. Indeed a genealogical poem (Pausanias 8.53.5 and 2.3.9) is the only work confidently to be associated with Kinaithon's name.

---

[1] Kinkel p. 4.

[2] Ἑλλάνικος G. Hermann, cod. μελάνικος. See Severyns 345 and cf. J. A. Davison in Wace and Stubbings, *A Companion to Homer* (London 1962) 260 n. 9.

Kinaithon and Asios

Of the four significant fragments one concerns Crete, one the Argonautika, and two the family of Menelaos. Pausanias (8.53.5) gives the Cretan genealogy: Rhadamanthys, son of Phaistos,[1] son of Talos, son of Kres. It can be inferred from this that the poet assumed Rhadamanthys to be king of Phaistos, and hence Minos to be king of Knossos. The other great Cretan prince of that generation was Sarpedon who founded Miletos in Karia (Ephoros 70 F 127); he was perhaps linked with the mother city of Miletos, Cretan Milatos or Miletos, which appears in the *Iliad* (2.647) beside Phaistos and Knossos (2.646 and 648). Remarkably, Kinaithon rejected the Hesiodic genealogy according to which Minos, Sarpedon and Rhadamanthys were all brothers, being sons of Zeus and Europa (F 30 Rzach).

The children of Jason and Medeia were according to Kinaithon a boy Medeios or Medos (Μῆδον Siebelis) and a girl Eriopis (Pausanias 2.3.9). There is no sign that the poet accepted the affiliation of Mermeros to Jason and Medeia, but we may have here a pointer to Kinaithon's date; for Medeios can hardly be other than the eponymous ancestor of the Medes; as such he may well appear also in a late addition to the *Theogony* of Hesiod. To decide when the Medes became important enough to the Hellenes to be included in their genealogies is not easy. After the great war between the Lydians and Medes *ca.* 585 B.C. the Medes were well known to the Greeks; on the other hand we have no evidence that Greek colonisation of the southeastern Euxine coasts from about 650 B.C. onwards brought Greeks and Medes into immediate association. A date about 625 B.C. for Kinaithon may not be far wrong, mid-way between Tyrtaios and Alkman, in the years after the Second Messenian War, when to remind the Spartans of their non-Dorian and non-Herakleid past had again become respectable; but a *floruit* as late as 550 B.C. is possible.

To Menelaos and Helen Kinaithon gave a son Nikostratos (F 3 Kinkel = Schol. Ven. A. *Il.* 3.175). He may not have been the first to do so, because a Hesiodic fragment (F 99 Rzach) mentions that Hermione and Nikostratos were the children of Menelaos and Helen; in Homer (*Od.* 4.12–14) Hermione is called an only child of Helen; fitly therefore

---

[1] 'Ηφαίστου and 'Ηφαιστον in the manuscripts must be corrected to Φαιστοῦ and Φαιστόν (L. Malten, *J.d.I.* 27 (1912) 264).

does the fragment of Hesiod state that Nikostratos was their youngest child:

ἣ τέκεθ' Ἑρμιόνην δουρὶ κλειτῷ Μενελάῳ·
ὁπλότατον δ' ἔτεκεν Νικόστρατον, ὄζον Ἄρηος.

The emphasis upon martial qualities in the name Nikostratos 'he whose army conquers' and the tag 'shoot of Ares' imply that the child grew up to have a valiant career; but in what circumstances we are not told. In Aglaosthenes of Naxos (499 F 1) he seems to be the founder of a Cretan city.

To Pausanias (2.18.6) we are also indebted for the statement that Kinaithon declared Orestes to have had a bastard son Penthilos, by Erigone daughter of Aigisthos. Penthilos was the eponymous ancestor of the Penthilidai, a family prominent in Lesbos about 600 B.C., who traced their descent to Agamemnon through Orestes. Penthilos according to some authors had a prominent part in the leading of the Aeolian migrants from mainland Greece to Lesbos and the coastlands of north-western Asia Minor two generations or so after the Trojan War (Strabo 582). The claim to descent from Agamemnon was made by certain noblemen of Lesbos as early as the time of Alkaios;[1] and Lesbian ties with Sparta began at least as early as the visit of Terpander of Antissa in 676 B.C. (Hellanikos 4 F 85a): so Kinaithon, amongst others, may well have connected Penthilos with the Aeolian migration. In his view Erigone was, presumably, a daughter of Aigisthos by Klytaimnestra (Apollod. *Epitome* 6.25), but Pausanias is not explicit about that. Since Penthilos is called a bastard, in the epic of Kinaithon Orestes may also have had a legitimate wife. She would be Hermione daughter of Menelaos and Helen (Pausanias 2.18.6). Thus we may

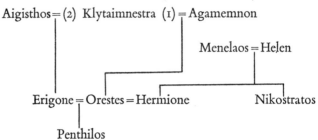

[1] F D12, 6 *Poetarum Lesbiorum Fragmenta* edd. Lobel and Page (Oxford 1955).

with some confidence assign the foregoing genealogy to Kinaithon. It is not certain that Kinaithon mentioned Megapenthes, a son of Menelaos by a slave woman (*Odyssey* 4.11–12. See also Severyns 377). The son of Orestes and Hermione was Teisamenos who fell in battle while driving Ionians out of Achaia in northern Peloponnese (Pausanias 2.18.8) and Teisamenos (or, rather, what were alleged to be his bones) had, like the bones of Orestes, an interesting role in Spartan mythological warfare of the mid-sixth century B.C.,[1] but what achievements, if any, Kinaithon assigned to him cannot be said.

One last fragment yields a further crumb of truth, if only negatively. Pausanias (4.2.1) states that he read the Hesiodic *Ehoiai*, the *Naupaktia* and the genealogical works of Kinaithon and Asios, in order to try to discover who were the children of Polykaon by Messene. The search proved unfruitful, but the periegete's words do show that he had found, or expected to find, details of Messenian myth-history in the work of Kinaithon. The poet indeed can hardly have ignored Messenian legend, living as he did in a society which Messenia supported with her crops or threatened with her arms. A poem on the Oidipous legend, too, would have found a ready audience in Sparta, where the Aigeidai, a family claiming an origin in heroic Thebes, were long prominent (Pindar, *Pyth.* 5.75. Herodotos 4.149.1). So even the unique ascription of an *Oidipodia* to Kinaithon deserves a mention. As for the Herakles epic allegedly composed by a Demodokos of Sparta (Kinkel p. 212), both poem and poet may be fictions.

More substantial is the evidence for the date and compositions of Asios of Samos, son of Amphiptolemos. Not more than one of the fragments concerns Samos, but there is no reason to doubt Pausanias (7.4.1) and Athenaios (125 B) when they call him a Samian. The name Amphiptolemos has a poetical air – we would perhaps expect Amphipolemos in Ionia; but the form Amphipolemos would not scan in epic hexameters or in elegy. So the father's name may well come from an excellent source, a *sphragis* or poetical signature of the Samian poet himself.

Asios was, within the limits imposed by the stereotyped traditional schemes he inherited, as enterprising, or as reckless, an innovator as

[1] Herodotos 1.67–68. Paus. 7.1.8. See also Leahy, *Historia* 4 (1955) 26–38.

Eumelos. His first aim was to provide his native island with a mythological prehistory to rival Crete's. To achieve it, he boldly placed the
eponymous heroine of Samos Old Town, Astypalaia, in the same
generation with Europa. Pausanias (7.4.1 = *F.Gr.Hist.* 545 F 1, 1) provides an elaborate genealogy taken from Asios, as he states:

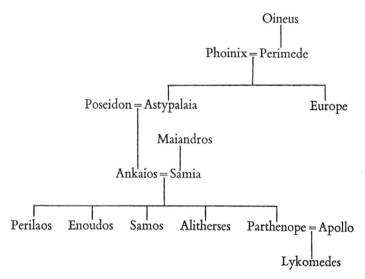

Here we may suggest that, as Zeus brought Europa (or Europe) to
Crete, so did Poseidon (perhaps in the guise of a horse, as Poseidon
Hippios) bring Astypalaia, also from Phoenicia, to Samos. Thus did
Asios effectively counter any claim that Samos had been colonised from
Crete, as, in later times at least, was believed by some persons (Hero-
doros *F.Gr.Hist.* 31 F 5).

Oineus may have provided Asios with a link to the legend of Danaos
because some held an Oineus to have been a son of Aigyptos (Apollod.
Lib. 2.1.5). Poseidon's mating took place beside the river Imbrasos in
Samos, not far from the sanctuary of Hera (Ap. Rhod. *Arg.* 2.865–867).
Ankaios his son was according to Apollonios Rhodios an Argonaut;
but we are not informed that Asios had earlier made him one too.[1]

---

[1] Ankaios died in pursuit of a boar which had been ravaging Samos; see Aristotle
ap. Schol. Ap. Rhod. 1.188 and J. P. Barron, *The Silver Coins of Samos* (London
1966) 5. Asios may well have told the story.

Kinaithon and Asios

As king in Samos, Ankaios ruled over the Leleges, Pausanias reports, following Asios. The Leleges were thought to be an indigenous people of the eastern Aegean coastlands and the adjacent islands (Pherekydes 3 F 155); so Asios would perhaps have supposed them to be already in Samos when Ankaios was born. The naming a daughter of the Meander river Samia reflects Samian interest in the Asiatic mainland on the Mykale peninsula not far from the river; this interest culminated in a series of bloody battles with the mainland Ionian city Priene for land on Mykale early in the sixth century B.C.[1] By making Samia a daughter of the great river of southern Ionia Asios was, in the Eumelian manner, asserting a claim to territory long in dispute. Samia and her child Samos also compensated a little for the neglect by Homer of Asios's native island.

The names of her children need comment. Samos, the proper name, is feminine but here he is a son. A poetical name of Samos was Parthenie because Hera spent her maidenhood in the island. But Parthenope's name does not necessarily allude to that tale; she is, rather, a pre-Hellenic maiden heroine of the islands of the southwestern Aegean. In Leros she was worshipped as Iokallis (see Jacoby on *F.Gr.Hist.* 545 F 1) and her name was given to a city founded by Rhodians (at or near the site of Naples) in Campania (Strabo 654) – though some believed this Parthenope to be a Siren. Her appearance in the mythological system of Asios reflects growing Samian interest in the Campanian coast during the sixth century B.C. This interest resulted, about 526 B.C. according to Eusebius, in the foundation of a colony at Potioloi or Dikaiarcheia (Steph. Byz. s.v. Ποτίολοι). Parthenope, some asserted, was a Samian lady who travelled far afield in search of her lost husband Anaxilaos; but the story may not have originated with Asios (Schol. Dionysios Perieget. 358). The significance of the other names, political or mythological, is lost. Lykomedes is perhaps the mythical progenitor of a Samian family. Parthenios, not Parthenope, was an alternative name of the river Imbrasos in Samos (Kallimachos F 599 Pf. cf. *P.Oxy.* 2085, F 3, 9); and the hero Samos is said to have had Parthenia as his bride (Tarrhaios ap. Schol. Ap. Rhod. 1.187), but this marriage cannot be traced back as far as Asios.

[1] Plutarch, *Greek Questions* 20 and *F.Gr.Hist.* 491 F 1.

Five fragments (1–5 Kinkel) display a concern with Boiotian and central Greek myth; five more (6 and 8–11) with Peloponnesian. Asios may well have visited both regions; he was perhaps in demand as a mythological propagandist abroad no less than at home in Samos. Let us take the Boiotian fragments first. Pausanias (2.6.4) quotes three verses from Asios which in language and content are strongly reminiscent of a Hesiodic catalogue: 'Antiope brought forth Zethos and lordly Amphion; she, the daughter of the deeply-eddying Asopos, had become with child to Zeus and Epopeus shepherd of the people.'

'Αντιόπη δ' ἔτεκε Ζῆθον καὶ 'Αμφίονα δῖον
'Ασωποῦ κούρη ποταμοῦ βαθυδινήεντος,
Ζηνί τε κυσαμένη καὶ 'Επωπέι ποιμένι λαῶν.

Epopeus is at home in Sikyon, the Asopia of Eumelos, who had declared Epopeus to be a lawless and outrageous king. There is no sign that Asios accepted the charge. His Antiope is wife of Epopeus, but in Eumelos she was his grandmother. According to Asios (Pausanias 2.6.3), when Lamedon son of Koronos became king of Sikyon after Epopeus, he gave Antiope away. She therefore was forced to leave Sikyon, and on the way to Thebes by the road at Eleutherai she brought forth her sons Amphion and Zethos. Since they were the off-spring of a double intercourse, we may conjecture that Zethos was born to Zeus and Amphion to Epopeus, just as of Alkmene's children, Herakles was son of Zeus, Iphikles of Amphitryon. In these verses Asios ingeniously ties Sikyonian myth to Theban in a manner akin to Eumelos's grafting of Corinthian myth into the Argonautika. Antiope had in her own right a place in Boiotian myth; the Hesiodic catalogue reported that she was a daughter of Boiotian Hyrie (F 132 Rzach), but Asios may not have agreed. His fragment would also suit the tale in Apollodoros (*Lib.* 3.5.5) according to which she was a daughter of Nykteus; Zeus slept with her, and when she was with child she ran away to Epopeus in Sikyon and married him. Nykteus in despair killed himself after commanding Lykos to punish Epopeus and Antiope. So Lykos marched against Sikyon and overwhelmed it. Then he killed Epopeus and took Antiope away captive.

This was the occasion when, according to Asios, Lamedon handed over Antiope to Lykos. Nykteus is known to have been mentioned by

Asios, but as father of the Arkadian heroine Kallisto, not of Antiope (Apollod. *Lib.* 3.8.2). Unfortunately more details of the Asian version of the tale are lacking.

The second Boiotian fragment deals with the eponymous hero Boiotos himself. Strabo, discussing the city of Metapontion in Italy, reports that Antiochos of Syracuse held its earlier name to have been Metabon (264–265 = Antiochos 555 F 12). Metabos was believed to be a hero of Metapontion, but Strabo is at pains to point out that the name had nothing to do with southern Italy originally, since there was a heröon of Metabos at Dion in Boiotia. He confirms this view with a quotation from Asios: 'in the halls of Dion did comely Melanippe bring him forth.'

$$\Delta\acute{\iota}ου\ \acute{\epsilon}νὶ\ μεγάροις\ τέκεν\ εὐειδὴς\ Μελανίππη.$$

The name Metabos was perhaps connected with Mount Messapios in Boiotia. It is not clear that Asios made him father of Boiotos; indeed the local Boiotian tradition recorded by Korinna (F 6 Page) seems to have been that Boiotos was a son of Poseidon.

Asios is also reported (Pausanias 9.23.6) to have declared Ptoos to be a son of Athamas and Themisto. From Ptoos Apollo Ptoios had his epithet and Mount Ptoion its name, the poet explained. Ptoos, then, is the eponymous hero of the famous oracle near Akraiphia east of Lake Kopais. Here again is local knowledge suggesting that Asios visited Boiotia. Athamas son of Aiolos had been a king of Boiotia who went mad and killed his children. In exile he married Themisto and, according to Apollodoros (*Lib.* 1.9.2), had four sons by her – of whom Ptoos was one. How much of this story Asios told we do not know.

The remark by Asios, if Pausanias correctly reports him (5.17.8), that Alkmene was a daughter of Amphiaraos and Eriphyle, implies a drastic reworking of legend; for Alkmene was traditionally the daughter of Elektryon (Hesiodic *Shield* 3), her mother being Lysidike (Hesiod p. 272 Rzach and Merkelbach p. 46, 20). The motive for the change is lost, but the fragment shows Asios to have been interested in the story of the Argive wars against Thebes.

Topographical detail is again found in the statement that Asios thought Phokos, the eponymous hero of Phokis, to have had sons called Panopeus and Krisos (Pausanias 2.29.4). The two sons, who likewise are eponyms of the towns in Phokis, appear also in a Hesiodic catalogue (*P.Oxy.* 2495, Fr. 16, 7 ff): evidently Phokos and their mother were mentioned here, but the mother's name is lost. In her womb the sons fought (Schol. Lyk. *Alex.* 930 and 939) – with the implication that they continued to do so as men. No doubt the towns of Krisa and Panopeus had their quarrels, not least at the time of the first Sacred War for Delphi, early in the sixth century B.C.

The Peloponnesian fragments offer more scope for conjecture than illumination. Pausanias ascribes to Asios ("Ἄσιος is to be put correctly here) a genealogy of the Tyndaridai (3.13.8):

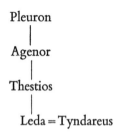

Pleuron
|
Agenor
|
Thestios
|
Leda = Tyndareus

This shows that Asios ignored, or rejected, the Eumelian genealogy (*F.Gr.Hist.* 451 F 6) in which, to the greater glory of Corinth, Leda was made a daughter of Thestios in name only, but in fact of Glaukos. Further quite extensive genealogising is implied by the fragment

κοῦραί τ' Ἰκαρίοιο Μέδη καὶ Πηνελόπεια

(Schol. Marc. ad *Od.* 4.797).

In the *Odyssey* (4.797) Iphthime is a daughter of Ikarios and a sister of Penelope, but here Mede and Penelope are his daughters. Asios almost certainly tied up this family with his list of descendants of Pleuron, because as early as Stesichoros (F 50 Page), who was in Sparta about 550 B.C.,[1] Tyndareus and Ikarios were said to be brothers, being both sons of Perieres.

Another Eumelian detail ignored, or discarded, by Asios was the ancestry of Sikyon, son of Marathon son of Epopeus. He kept the Attic association, but rejected the Corinthian's system: Sikyon was made by him a son of Metion, son of Erechtheus (Pausanias 2.6.5). The refusal to

---

[1] *Early Sparta* 64 and 71.

sever the tie with Attica suggests a desire to please Athens as well as Sikyon. Also rejected, it seems, was the Argive claim in the *Phoronis* to the first man: 'Pelasgos like to a god did black Earth give forth' asserted Asios 'in the lofty forests of the mountains, that the race of mortals might be'. The mountains are those of the Arkadians, whose claim to priority the Samian poet therefore admitted. It had already been acknowledged in Hesiodic poetry, which declared Pelasgos both Arkadian and autochthonous (F 43–44 Rzach). The Arkadian heroine Kallisto also found a place in his Peloponnesian verses (Apollod. *Lib.* 3.8.2). He made her a daughter of Nykteus, here again differing from Eumelos who held her to be a daughter of Lykaon. We do not know that Asios mentioned Lykaon, whom some believed to be a son of Pelasgos (Hesiod F 44). Nykteus, 'he of the night', alludes with his name to the catasterism of his daughter; she became the Great Bear in the sky at night. Somehow Asios would have linked her father with Pelasgos.

The problem of dating Asios cannot be definitely solved. Yet a proposal to place him early in the sixth century has much to commend it.[1] The poet worked when the oral tradition of epic tags and clichés was still alive. He perhaps alludes to Samian claims upon parts of south Ionia. He displays an interest in Spartan genealogies, Theban prehistory, and above all Sikyon. He compliments Athens and implicitly criticises many of the Corinthians' mythological claims. He rejects an Argive legend in favour of an Arkadian one. He is concerned with Phokis, and perhaps knows of trouble between Panopeus and Krisa. All these details point to a date soon after 600 B.C. in a period when Samos had been making a special effort on Mykale; Sikyon under Kleisthenes in alliance with Athens was engaged in war in Phokis over Krisa and Delphi; when Kleisthenes was at war with Argos, and expelled pro-Argive epic poets; and Corinth was unfriendly to Sikyon. Kleisthenes brought in the hero Melanippos to Sikyon; and Asios constructed an atypical genealogy for Amphiaraos who had killed Melanippos. The hypothesis of a connexion between Asios and the tyrant Kleisthenes is therefore attractive; but we cannot claim the dating of the poet to the early sixth century to be demonstrably correct. The reference by Athenaios to

[1] W. G. Forrest, *B.C.H.* 80 (1956) 43 n. 3.

Greek Epic Poetry

'Asios the Samian poet, that ancient fellow' (125 B) is unhelpful. Two more fragments ascribed to Asios are less certainly his. Douris of Samos quoted by Athenaios (*F.Gr.Hist.* 76 F 60 = Athen. 525 EF) preserved some verses, which he supposed to be by Asios; they describe the Samians in their finery walking to the shrine of Hera and illustrate the proverb 'march to the Heraion with knotted hair' – βαδίζετ᾽ ⟨εἰς⟩ Ἡραῖον ἐμπεπλεγμένον (βαδίζειν codd. fortasse ἐμπεπλεγμένοι)

οἳ δ᾽ αὔτως φοίτεσκον, ὅπως πλοκάμους κτενίσαιντο,
εἰς Ἥρας τέμενος, πεπυκασμένοι εἵμασι καλοῖς·
χιονέοισι χιτῶσι πέδον χθονὸς εὐρέος εἶχον,
χρύσειαι δὲ κόρυμβαι ἐπ᾽ αὐτῶν τέττιγες ὥς,
5 χαῖται δ᾽ ἠωρεῦντ᾽ ἀνέμῳ χρυσέοις ἐνὶ δεσμοῖς,
δαιδάλεοι δὲ χλιδῶνες ἄρ᾽ ἀμφὶ βραχίοσιν ἦσαν
]τες ὑπασπίδιον πολεμιστήν.

'Even so they used to walk, whene'er they had combed their locks, to the precinct of Hera, swathed in fair garments; with snowy tunics they swept the floor of the broad earth; and golden brooches like cicadas surmounted their topknots as their hair in its golden bands waved in the breeze; and delicately wrought bracelets encircled their arms' (Lacuna) '. . . a warrior sheltered beneath his shield'.

Some scholars have professed to detect a mocking tone, reminiscent of late fifth-century Attic comedy, in these verses e.g. (ὑπασπίδιον πολεμιστήν); others see signs of late language unsuited to epic, or Atticisms (κτενίσαιντο, ἠωρεῦντ᾽).[1] It is argued therefore that these lines are not by Asios, or that Asios is to be dated in the fifth century B.C. or even that a second Asios lived then; now we may perhaps grant that Douris, who was often irresponsible, mistakenly ascribed the verses to Asios, if they belong to the fifth century and their author is looking back to the great days of Samian luxury in the sixth. But the linguistic argument is far from cogent, because Atticisms may have been introduced as an accident of textual transmission. Nor is the argument from comic tone any stronger – the *Margites*, for example, a comic poem certainly earlier than 600 B.C. and said to have been ascribed to Homer by Archilochos (Eustrat. on Aristotle *N.E.* 6.7), is evidence of the high antiquity of mocking or comic poetry. The writer

[1] Cf. C. M. Bowra, *Hermes* 85 (1957) 391–401.

is perhaps not so much looking far back in time as looking at an event in Samos from elsewhere and describing his countrymen, not without a touch of humour, for foreigners, perhaps even with Atticisms in Attica. So we may suggest that the verses may well be by Asios; but they are unlikely to have been composed for his own near contemporaries, the dandies in Samos.

Humour, with a sense of the absurd, is also to be seen in some elegiac couplets ascribed to him. The elaborate compound words enhance the poet's feeling for a grotesque situation. The scene is the wedding feast of Homer's father, Meles: 'There came a dinner parasite – lame, a branded runaway slave, exceeding old, like to a vagabond was he – when Meles wed. Unbid came he, in need of soup. But the hero stood in the midst of them, after rising up out of the mire.' The 'hero' can hardly be the runaway slave; surely he is Meles. Since there is mud on the ground, the wedding feast seems to be held outside. κνισοκόλαξ is then perhaps a 'sacrifice – parasite'. There was a tradition in Samos about Homer's parents: in the fifth century Euagon a local historian of the island mentioned Meles (*F.Gr.Hist.* 535 F 2).[1] The tone of the verses is distinctly satirical:

χωλός, στιγματίης, πολυγήραος, ἶσος ἀλήτῃ,
ἦλθεν κνισοκόλαξ, εὖτε Μέλης ἐγάμει,
ἄκλητος, ζωμοῦ κεχρημένος. ἐν δὲ μέσοισιν
ἥρως εἱστήκει βορβόρου ἐξαναδύς (Athen. 125D).

Professional rivalry with the Homeridai, descendants through Homer of Meles, may perhaps be inferred from the lines, and the reference to the wedding is remarkable; is the poet questioning the purity of their pedigree? Meles was in some accounts the river of Smyrna or its hero – Μαίονος δὲ θυγατρὸς καὶ Μέλητος τοῦ ποταμοῦ "Ομηρον (*Contest of Homer and Hesiod* p. 227, 53 Allen): hence the reference to the hero emerging from the mud. But, the poet is perhaps saying, is not the true ancestor of the Homeridai the runaway slave who turned up at the wedding feast by the river? Had Kleisthenes of Sikyon, who drove the Homeridai from his city, known these verses, they would have delighted him.

[1] This Meles must be distinguished from Meles the father of the Kolophonian poet Polymnestos, who flourished *ca.* 625 B.C. ([Plut.] *De Mus.* 1133A).

Such then was Asios; patriot, tendentious mythologist, genealogist – perhaps wit, satirist and court poet. Out of the ruins of ancient epic poetry the gleam of his intelligence still shines faintly, enabling us to glimpse the gay and critical spirit of his times.

VIII

Earlier Epics about Herakles

In the multiplicity of tales concerning the son of Alkmene, a core consisting of three distinct elements may be seen. It comprises (1) the Theban story of the hero who frees the city from tribute to her neighbours in Orchomenos; (2) the Argive, Tirynthian or Mycenaean legend of his servitude to Hera's favourite Eurystheus follows – out of this arose the Labours, ultimately canonised into the number twelve; and finally (3) there were the adventures, such as the visit to Omphale in Lydia, the episode with Laomedon at Troy, and the sack of Oichalia, most of which brought Herakles far afield. Many of these tales, the Keyx story for example, are set in northern Greece and belong to a northern group of legends. The stories of this group culminate in the cremation of the hero on Mount Oita.

The elaborate character of the Herakles story in Homer testifies to the high antiquity of the epics about the son of Alkmene; the tales may well have originated in the Mycenaean period; and it has been suggested with some plausibility that the Peloponnesian Labours – e.g. Lernaian Hydra, Nemean lion, Erymanthian boar, stables of Augeias and the Keryneian hind – reflect the growing power of Mycenae in Peloponnese,[1] though we need not indulge ourselves in the romantic euhemerism which declares Herakles to have been a mercenary general in the service of Eurystheus.

Homer's passing allusions to Herakles display a coherent view of the hero's place in the general scheme of Greek legend. The poet knows that Herakles was born at Thebes to Zeus and Alkmene; that Hera cheated Zeus into promising precedence to Eurystheus (*Iliad* 19.95–136); that tasks were performed for Eurystheus (*Iliad* 8.363) including the fetching from Erebos of the dog of Hades (*Iliad* 8.368), whom Hesiod calls

[1] Cf. M. P. Nilsson, *The Mycenaean Origin of Greek Mythology* (Cambridge 1932) 209.

99

Kerberos (*Theogony* 311). Homer alludes to a war by Herakles against Pylos in which Hera was shot in the right breast by an arrow. Hades too was wounded (*Iliad* 5.392–397), and Nestor's eleven brothers were killed (*Iliad* 11.690–693; cf. Hesiod, *P.Oxy.* 2481, Fr. 3). He condemns, but does not explain, the killing by Herakles of his guest Iphitos (*Od.* 21.22–30); he knows that Megara daughter of Kreon was his wife (*Od.* 11.269); that Laomedon of Troy, having been delivered from a sea monster by Herakles, failed to reward the hero, who therefore sacked the city (*Iliad*. 20.144–148, 5.638–642); and that on his return from Troy Herakles was forced by winds to put in to Kos (*Iliad* 15.28). In the *Iliad* there is no sign that Herakles is a god; he did not escape his doom, though Zeus loved him, for he was laid low by fate and by the anger of Hera (*Iliad* 18.117–119). In the *Odyssey* the shade of Herakles appears, together with those of other heroes, to Odysseus in Hades, and only as an afterthought are we told of the apotheosis, how the real Herakles now delights in the company of the immortals at their feasts and has Hebe to wife (11.601–605). Herakles had a son Tlepolemos, who came from Rhodes to fight before Troy (*Iliad* 2.653–670); the mother of Tlepolemos, Astyoche, had been taken by Herakles at the sack of Ephyra beside the river Selleis – from later sources we learn that this was the Ephyra by the Acheron;[1] and from Kos and neighbouring islands there went to Troy the sons of Thessalos, himself a son of Herakles (*Iliad* 2.676–680). Thus, since Herakles had a son and grandsons at Troy, the hero himself flourished about two generations before the Trojan War, according to Homer. In view of the settlement of Herakleidai in the southeastern Aegean islands we expect to find that epics on the subject of Herakles were popular there; and indeed the earliest identifiable *Herakleia*, that of Peisandros, comes from Kameiros in Rhodes.

Ancient estimates of the date of Peisandros vary. The lowest guess, that he flourished about *ca.* 648 B.C., may not have been far wrong; we cannot check it, but Argive and Corinthian vase painters had already found the Herakles stories to be popular in the mid-seventh century,[2]

[1] Apollod. *Lib.* 2.7.6. Cf. Pindar, *Ol.* 7.23. See also P. Friedländer, *Herakles* (*P.U.* 9) [Berlin 1907] 94–95.
[2] Dunbabin 78–80.

so epic poems on him, especially amongst families claiming descent from him, as in Sparta and in Rhodes, are likely to have also been popular at that epoch. Clement of Alexandria alleged that Peisandros 'stole' from Peisinous, an epic poet of Lindos in Rhodes (*Strom.* 6.2.25), but this means no more than that Clement knew quotations from both poets in which standard epic phrases appeared; both poets would have borrowed from the traditional language of the local hexameter poetry. Peisandros has to be distinguished from Peisandros the Hellenistic mythographer (*F.Gr.Hist.* No. 16) and from Peisandros of Laranda who wrote a grandiose poem, the *Heroikai Theogoniai* in 66 books in the third century A.D. (Heitsch 2.44–47).[1] Our Peisandros, the Rhodian, is said to have been the first to have given Herakles a club (Suda, s.v. Πείσανδρος cf. Strabo 688) – in Homer he has a bow. For apparel Peisandros gave to him the skin of the Nemean lion (Eratosthenes, *Katasterismoi* 12), and the Rhodian poet was perhaps the first to provide Herakles with the cup of the Sun, ancestor of the Rhodian Heliadai, for his journey to the far West. Peisandros may indeed have been the first to send Herakles far beyond Greece in the course of the Labours, to the apples of the Hesperides at the edge of the Ocean and to the cattle of Geryon. These remote tasks perhaps reflect early Rhodian exploration of the western Mediterranean which according to Strabo (654) had begun even before the first Olympiad; in reaction against these geographical extravagances Hekataios about 500 B.C. deliberately returned to the older version of the Geryon tale, which placed the cattle in north-western Greece (*F.Gr.Hist.* 1 F 26).[2]

Peisandros was, to judge from the extant fragments, chiefly concerned in his *Herakleia* with the labours performed for Eurystheus. Indeed he may have been the first to make the number twelve for the labours canonical. An inscription in hendecasyllables for a Rhodian statue of Peisandros (Theokritos, *Ep.* 22) states that the poet described Herakles 'and all the tasks he laboured to fulfil' – χὥσσους ἐξεπόνασεν εἶπ' ἀέθλους – which presumably means 'the whole dozen'. The earliest evidence for all twelve together is however as late as about 450 B.C.,

---

[1] See also for the different Peisandroi, F. Vian, *Quintus de Smyrne. Les Posthomerica* (Paris 1959) 99–100, and cf. R. Keydell, *Hermes* 70 (1935) 301–311.

[2] See *G.R.B.S.* 8 (1967) 91.

in the metopes of the temple of Zeus at Olympia. On the western metopes were: (1) Nemean Lion; (2) Lernaian hydra; (3) Stymphalian birds; (4) Cretan bull; (5) Keryneian hind; (6) girdle of Hippolyte. The eastern metopes illustrated: (7) the Erymanthian boar; (8) Mares of Diomedes; (9) Geryon; (10) Atlas and the Hesperides; (11) Kerberos; (12) Augeian stables.[1] The Euripidean list (*Hercules Furens* 359–429) substitutes Centaurs for the Erymanthian boar, and for the Stymphalian birds, Cretan bull and Augeian stables has Kyknos, Sea-monsters and the Relief of Atlas as supporter of the heavens. The Centaurs however are simply a part of the story of the boar (see Jebb, *Sophocles. The Philoctetes* p. xi). Of the scenes in the metopes Peisandros had already described the Nemean Lion, which he made the first Labour, the Lernaian Hydra (Paus. 2.37.4), the Keryneian hind (Schol. Pind. *Ol.* 3.50a; 1. p. 119 Dr.), and the Stymphalian birds (Paus. 8.22.4). His treatment of these topics seems to have been distinguished by a capacity for ingenious innovation – a multiplication of the number of heads of the Hydra to make it more fearsome, for example. Since Herakles, as an exemplar of military prowess to Dorian heavy infantrymen could not fitly carry a bow, he could not shoot at the Stymphalian birds: so Peisandros had him drive them away from the lake with a clashing of castanets. Vase-painters from about 600 B.C. onwards depict Herakles with a club, but earlier with a bow (Bowra 124); the fashion perhaps reflects the influence of Peisandros, who would therefore be dated late in the seventh century B.C.[2]

Other fragments are less immediately concerned with the Labours. It is reported that Peisandros called the daughter of Antaios, a giant

[1] R. Ross Holloway, *G.R.B.S.* 8 (1967) 100. Pausanias (5.10) describes the metopes of the labours as he saw them. By mistake he leaves out Kerberos, who can be inserted in the eleventh place, at the east end of the temple last but one to the north. The places in which the fragments were found agree with the order given by Pausanias [B. Ashmole and N. Yalouris, *Olympia. The Sculptures of the Temple of Zeus* (London 1967) 24].

[2] The statement of Megakleides (ap. Athen. 512 F–513 A) that Stesichoros was the first poet to give Herakles his club, lionskin and bow is almost certainly mistaken. Both conceptions of him, as heavily armed soldier and as archer, may well have existed for a long time together. Xanthos, a predecessor of Stesichoros in lyric poetry, described the hero without the club, lionskin and bow as the Himeran himself is said to have reported (Xanthos F 1 [699] Page).

who ruled in Libya, Alkeis (Schol. Pind. *Pyth.* 9.185a). The context of this tale is the return of Herakles from Atlas and the Hesperides. Antaios made all who passed through Libya wrestle with him. He was invincible when touching the earth, but Herakles defeated and killed him by holding him, in a wrestler's hug, above the ground (Apollod. *Lib.* 2.5.11). This tale is likely to have been popular at athletic contests of the Rhodians and their Dorian neighbours, such as the Triopian games (Herodotos 1.144.2), though we are not told of recitations there. It perhaps reflects Rhodian interests in the Libyan coast about the time of the foundation of Kyrene (*ca.* 630 B.C.). Rhodian settlers are said to have joined Battos there (Xenagoras 240 F 10), and Rhodian pottery of the later seventh century B.C. has been found at Tocra on this coast,[1] which Rhodian traders may well have visited.

Two lines (Peisandros F 7 Kinkel) are all that survive from the *Herakleia* itself: 'for him did the grey-eyed goddess Athene create at Thermopylai warm baths by the shore.'

τῷ δ' ἐν Θερμοπύλῃσι θεὰ γλαυκῶπις Ἀθήνη
ποίει θερμὰ λοετρὰ παρὰ ῥηγμῖνι θαλάσσης.

(Schol. Rav. ad Ar. Nub. 1050)

The verses allude to the warm sulphurous springs which appear in the pass of Thermopylai, where in antiquity the sea came close to the foot of the mountain. Here Athena, by sending forth the water from the mountainside, enabled Herakles to wash after his exertions. The occasion was perhaps his encounter with the deceitful Kerkopes, the 'tailed-men'; these were monkey-like dwarfs whom Herakles carried with their heads hanging downwards from a pole. They are so represented in early Greek art and were, by some, believed to have dwelt near Thermopylai, where the pass was narrowest (Herodotos 7.216). Six epic verses describing their wickedness are extant; three are anonymous, and have no obvious connexion with Peisandros (Allen, *Homeri Op.* V 160); three, ascribed to a Diotimos (Kinkel, pp. 213–214), refer to the trouble caused by the Kerkopes to Boiotian travellers at a meeting of roads (such as at the entrance to the Thermopylai pass). We need not doubt that Peisandros described the warm springs at Thermopylai, but it is noteworthy that Herakles is also connected with warm springs in

[1] J. Boardman and J. Hayes, *Tocra. The Archaic Deposits* I (London 1966) 41.

Rhodes itself – at Thermydrai, the harbour of the Lindians (Apollod. *Lib.* 2.5.11). Zenobios (6.49) states that Peisandros told of Athena sending up warm springs for Herakles in many places; so the poet may well have mentioned the Lindian springs of his own island also. The Kerkopes at Thermopylai must have pleaded for their lives;[1] their words are perhaps preserved by Stobaios (*Floril.* 12.6): 'there is no cause of indignation in speaking even a lie to save one's life':

οὐ νέμεσις καὶ ψεῦδος ὑπὲρ ψυχῆς ἀγορεύειν.

Herakles in ridding the world of them would be a just killer; such words were used of him, though not necessarily in this context, by Peisandros – δικαιοτάτου δὲ φονῆος (F 10 Kinkel. Cf. McLeod, *Phoenix* 20 (1966) 102 n. 35).

A proverb ascribed to a Peisandros, 'there is no sense amongst Centaurs', νοῦς οὐ παρὰ Κενταύροισι (F 9 Kinkel), may have appeared in the Rhodian's account of the Erymanthian boar, because Herakles was entertained by the Centaur Pholos in an Arkadian cave before he caught the animal. Pholos had hesitated to open a jar for fear of trouble from the other Centaurs when they smelt the wine; and indeed trouble followed (Apollod. *Lib.* 2.5.4). The proverb was perhaps put in the mouth of the hesitant Pholos himself; Protocorinthian vase-painters, perhaps influenced by epics such as the *Herakleia* of Peisandros, showed a special liking for the Centauromachy (cf. Dunbabin, p. 78).

Peisandros is said to have used the word ἀέ 'always' (for ἀεί, αἰεί or αἰέν). ἀέ is a Doricism, not an epic form; but Peisandros may well have introduced an occasional local word into his verse. Neither he nor any other epic poet was required slavishly to employ at all times the epic-Ionic vocabulary of Homer. With this two-letter fragment we may take leave of Peisandros, whose fragments do not provide enough evidence to determine the scope of his work. We learn from an incidental reference in Athenaios (11.783C) that Peisandros described the campaign of Herakles against Troy. The poet said that Telamon was given by Herakles a cup (ἄλεισον) as a prize for valour, but that

---

[1] For this episode see C. O. Müller, *The Dorians* I (London 1839) 447–448, on the release of the Kerkopes by Herakles-of-the-black-buttocks, whom they recognised when suspended from the pole, and against whom an oracle μή τευ μελαμπύγου τύχοις had warned them. See also Archilochos F 110 Bergk.

is all we are told about the episode. Another fragment indicates that Peisandros mentioned Klymene (Lippold, *Philologus* 68 (1909) 153). She was a mother of Atlas and also, according to some authorities, a bride of the Sun, Helios, by whom she became mother of Phaethon. She may well have appeared in the story of Herakles' adventures in the Far West.

That Peisandros was an innovator we can see; that he was specially concerned with the Labours – not necessarily all twelve, however – is clear; that he was highly regarded in his own island is obvious from the epigram in which he is called 'first of the verse-makers of yore' (Theokr. *Ep.* 22) – πρᾶτος τῶν ἐπάνωθε μουσοποιῶν. To verify this judgement we are unable. Nor can we estimate the length of his *Herakleia*. The edition known to Athenaios (469 C), however, contained at least two books, for Book II included a description of Herakles receiving the cup of the Sun from Okeanos.

Some poets, less ambitious than Peisandros, fixed their attention on one episode or another in the life of Herakles. Such a man was Kreophylos of Samos, whose epic on the *Sack of Oichalia* was thought so good that some people assumed it to be Homer's (Kallimachos, *Ep.* 6). Others believed Kreophylos to have been Homer's host and to have been given the poem by his guest (Strabo 638); or, it was believed, Kreophylos, whom some called a Chian like Homer, was the great poet's son-in-law (Schol. Plat. *Rep.* 600 B). Kreophylos seems in fact to have been one of the earliest of a numerous class of persons, those who were accounted Homeridai without being descendants of Homer. Oichalia was usually supposed to be in Euboia. There Sophokles (*Trachiniai* 237 and 750), following Hekataios (1 F 28), placed it in the territory of Eretria, an Ionian neighbourhood. This position is the one likely to have been chosen by an Ionian such as Kreophylos, but others placed the Oichalia attacked by Herakles in Arkadia (Strabo 438). Pausanias however (4.2.3) asserts confidently that the poem of Kreophylos, which he calls a *Herakleia* and may never have seen entire, agrees with the Euboian claim to the city sacked by Herakles. Yet Homer (*Iliad* 2.730) seems to place it in Thessaly.

Herakles had defeated Eurytos, King of Oichalia, in an archery contest. He therefore claimed the promised prize, the king's daughter

Iole or Ioleia. When Eurytos refused to hand her over, Herakles sacked the city, slew Eurytos, and took Iole captive. One line survives from the poem, but without context (Allen, *Hom. Op.* V p. 146):

ὦ γύναι, αὐτὴ ταῦτα τ᾽ ἐν ὀφθαλμοῖσιν ὅρηαι.

'Lady, thyself seest these things in thy sight.' The words are spoken to Iole by Herakles.

The poem's date is not known. The linking of Kreophylos to Homer would imply a time nearer to 700 B.C. than to 600 B.C. and the alleged visit of Lykourgos of Sparta to him in Samos points to the same epoch. But certainty here is beyond reach. Kreophylos is said to have given Eurytos two sons, but a Hesiodic fragment assigns him four sons and a daughter, Iole (Schol. Laur. Soph. *Trach.* 266). The Samian poet therefore had his own views upon details of the story. We do not know that he composed poems on other subjects; the assertion that Kreophylos gave a version of the death of Medea's children in Corinth (Schol. Eurip. *Med.* 264) is unverifiable.

Two more poems, both ascribed with little likelihood to Hesiod, are concerned with single episodes in the story of Herakles. In the *Wedding of Keyx*, a distinct poem rather an than element in the Hesiodic catalogues (Schwartz 200–202), a scene is the feast at Trachis, to which Herakles has wandered from Kalydon (cf. Apollod. *Lib.* 2.7.6). The tone of the poem is set by the moral 'of their own accord are good men sent to the feasts of the good', αὐτόματοι δ᾽ ἀγαθοὶ ἀγαθῶν ἐπὶ δαῖτας ἵενται (Hesiod F 155 Rzach), words spoken by Herakles (cf. Bacchylid. F 18 Jebb). It seems that the food was laid out on three-footed tables (Hesiod F 157); that persons all sharing a common ancestor (ἀπάτωροι F 159b) were present;[1] and that wood was thrown on to the flames in the fireplace when the meal was over (F 158): here some riddling verses showed how children consumed their mother, that is to say, how the flames ate the wood which gave them birth, first drying them, then burning them.

αὐτὰρ ἐπεὶ †δ᾽ αὐτοὶ μὲν κνίσσης† ἐξ ἔρον ἔντο
μητέρα †μητρός† ἄγοντο

---

[1] For another possibility, that this means 'fatherless ones' see Merkelbach and West, *R.M.* 108 (1965) 314.

Earlier Epics about Herakles

$$\left.\begin{array}{l}\alpha\dot{\upsilon}\\ \dot{\alpha}\zeta\end{array}\right\}\alpha\lambda\acute{\epsilon}\eta\nu \ \tau\epsilon \ \kappa\alpha\grave{\iota} \ \dot{o}\pi\tau\alpha\lambda\acute{\epsilon}\eta\nu \ \sigma\phi\epsilon\tau\acute{\epsilon}\rho\sigma\iota\sigma\iota \ \tau\acute{\epsilon}\kappa\epsilon\sigma\sigma\iota$$

$$\tau\epsilon\theta\nu\acute{\alpha}\nu\alpha\iota.$$

1. δαιτὸς μὲν εἴσης M.W. F 266.

The word before ἄγοντο may be παισίν (Lobel, P.Oxy. 2495 F 37, 8 ff): so they fed the mother to her children.[1] Herakles well repaid the hospitality of Keyx by conquering the troublesome Dryopians of Mount Parnassos nearby (Apollod. Lib. 2.7.7). This Keyx should perhaps be distinguished from the wicked Keyx, also mentioned by 'Hesiod' (M.W. F 16), who was punished for calling his wife Alkyone Hera (Apollod. Lib. 1.7.4), and for being named Zeus by her.

Conversation at the feast may have ranged over earlier exploits of Herakles, including his eating contest with Lepreos (M.W. F 265) and his part in the Argonautika: one fragment alludes to his having left the Argo at Aphetai ('the place of quittance') in Magnesia (Hesiod F 154 Rzach) a tale repeated by Herodotos (7.193).[2] Keyx himself was nominally a kinsman of Herakles, being a son of one of Amphitryon's brothers (Schol. Soph. Trach. 40);[3] so the presence of Herakles at the wedding was most welcome, and the mention of kinsmen ἀπάτωροι in the poem was apt.

A second Hesiodic epic, concentrated on a single episode in the Herakleian tales, was the Aigimios. This poem is likely to have been popular in Dorian states where Herakleidai were prominent, for it related how the Dorians of the canton of Doris near Parnassos were aided by Herakles in a boundary war with the wild Lapiths (Schwartz 261). Not all the fragments said to come from a poem called Aigimios are strictly relevant to this theme. There were, too, differences of opinion about the authorship, some ascribing it to Hesiod, others to a Kerkops of Miletos (Athenaios 503 D). It was supposed that there had been a rivalry between Hesiod and Kerkops (Diogenes Laert. 2.46), a story which at least implies the existence of competing poems

[1] The elaborate interpretation of these verses by M. L. West, C.Q. 11 (1961) 142–145 may be compared. He suggests that the feasters roast acorns. See also R.M. 108, 310 f.

[2] Pherekydes (3 F 111a) and Antimachos (F 58 Wyss) add the detail, which may be early, that Herakles was discharged because he was too heavy for the ship.

[3] See Marcksheffel 155.

attributed to each of them on the same themes. One such theme was, it seems, the story of Aigimios. Diogenes supposed the poets to be contemporaries, but others held Kerkops to be a Pythagorean and much later than Hesiod.[1]

One fragment mentions a shady place of refreshment or rest: Herakles may be saying to Aigimios after the victory over the Lapiths 'here betimes shall be my cool resting place, leader of men', ἔνθα ποτ' ἔσται ἐμὸν ψυκτήριον, ὄρχαμε λαῶν (Hesiod F 190 Rzach); but the context is not secure. An excursus may have been devoted to the precept that lovers' oaths are not binding and do not draw down the anger of the gods. Io was perhaps given as an example (Hesiod F 186–189 Rzach); Zeus had sworn, falsely, to Hera that he had not touched Io; 'wherefore Zeus freed from penalty for mankind an oath concerning the private deeds of Kypris' (F 187 Rzach):[2]

ἐκ τοῦ δ' ὅρκον ἔθηκεν ἀποίνιμον ἀνθρώποισι
νοσφιδίων ἔργων πέρι Κύπριδος.

The poem or poems explained that Zeus named Euboia after the *bous* or cow into which Io had been turned – formerly the island had been called Abantis (F 186 Rzach); and there was a vivid description of Argos, the watcher set by Hera to look over the cow (F 188): 'she sent great and mighty Argos to oversee her with his four-eyed gaze looking this way and that; the goddess gave rise to unwearying strength in him, no sleep fell upon his eyelids, but ever did he keep an unceasing guard':

καί οἱ ἐπίσκοπον Ἄργον ἵει κρατερόν τε μέγαν τε,
τέτρασιν ὀφθαλμοῖσιν ὁρώμενον ἔνθα καὶ ἔνθα,
ἀκάματον δέ οἱ ὦρσε θεὰ μένος, οὐδέ οἱ ὕπνος
πῖπτεν ἐπὶ βλεφάροις, φυλακὴν δ' ἔχεν ἔμπεδον αἰεί.

ἐπὶ σκοπὸν M.W. (= M.W. F 294)

Io's distant wanderings may well have found a mention, too, in the poem (M.W. F 295). The precept that lovers' oaths could be broken with impunity is, without mention of the *Aigimios*, also ascribed to Kerkops, who related that Theseus had broken his troth to Ariadne for the sake of Aigle (Athenaios 557 A). Another fragment of the

---

[1] See e.g. Suda s.v. Ὀρφεύς (3.564.27 Adler).

[2] M.W. F 124, however, doubt that these verses come from the *Aigimios*.

Earlier Epics about Herakles

Aigimios told of the taking of the golden fleece; here the context may be another lover who broke his vows – Jason who ultimately abandoned Medea (F 184 Rzach). In the *Aigimios* (F 185 Rzach) the story of Thetis casting her children into a cauldron of water – to see if they were mortal – was told; one may compare Medea's treatment of her children. Peleus objected when many had died and stopped the throwing of Achilles into the cauldron. The consequences of this were that Achilles was not made immortal and Thetis, in anger abandoning her husband and son, departed to the Nereids (Apollod. *Lib.* 3.13.6 cf. *Iliad* 18.434 ff). Here, then, the theme of broken vows may have recurred in the poem.

In return for his help, Herakles was given by Aigimios one third of the land in the kingdom of Doris: this may be the ψυκτήριον or refuge mentioned in the poem. The Dorians kept the portion for the descendants of Herakles in trust when he went off to fight Kyknos (Diodoros 4.37); included in the gift may well have been the town of Erineos, whence Dorians and Herakleidai later set out to conquer Peloponnese (Tyrtaios F 2 Diehl³).

Pindar, who mentions Aigimios, may well have known the epic about him. Once he alludes to him as a maker of ordinances for the Dorians (*Pythian* 1.64); and in *Pythian* 5 (69–72) Argos, Pylos and Lakedaimon are said to have been conquered by the descendants of Herakles and Aigimios, as though the true Dorians are hardly of less importance than the line of Herakles himself. In this context it is proper to consider some Hesiodic verses (F 191 Rzach) which are often ascribed to the *Aigimios*, though they may never have belonged to the poem. The Dorians, says the poet, 'are all called triply divided' (if that is the meaning of τριχάϊκες) 'because far from their homeland they portioned out the land in three.'

πάντες δὲ τριχάϊκες καλέονται
οὕνεκα τρισσὴν γαῖαν ἑκὰς πάτρης ἐδάσαντο.

(= M.W. F 233)

The meaning of τριχάϊκες was disputed in antiquity. Homer uses the word of the Dorians of Crete (*Od.* 19.177), perhaps in allusion to the three Dorian tribes. Here the reference may be, instead, to the triple division of Peloponnese, described by Pindar in *Pythian* 5. If so, the verses are not likely to come from the *Aigimios*, which was concerned with an episode several generations earlier. The change from πάτρης to πάτρης is attractive; the reference would perhaps then be to the division of land, separately *for their families*, in Doris at Erineos, Kytinion and Boion.[1]

If, as we may, we reject the ascription of the *Aigimios* to Hesiod the poem is not datable. The verse

$$\delta\epsilon\iota\nu\grave{o}s \ \gamma\acute{a}\rho \ \mu\iota\nu \ \check{\epsilon}\tau\epsilon\iota\rho\epsilon\nu \ \check{\epsilon}\rho os \ \Pi a\nu o\pi\eta\hat{\iota}\delta os \ A\check{\iota}\gamma\lambda\eta s$$

is said to have been expelled from the Hesiodic corpus by the Athenian tyrant Peisistratos (Plutarch, *Theseus* 20). The line refers to the love of Theseus for Aigle, and, by implication, to his abandonment of Ariadne, a topic treated by Kerkops. The verses may therefore come from an *Aigimios*. It would follow that a version of the poem was composed before the time of Peisistratos, who flourished in the third quarter of the sixth century B.C.

From Aigimios, Herakles went to fight with Kyknos. A poem on this topic survives in the form of the Hesiodic *Shield*, of which the beginning (lines 1–56) is said to have stood in the fourth book of the *Catalogues of Women* or *Eoiai* (Hesiod F 136 Rzach); and indeed the start of the *Shield*, which introduces the poem on Kyknos, is an account of Alkmene in the Hesiodic manner, even introducing her with ἤ οἵη (M.W. F 195) as the first words. The core of the poem (vv. 139–320) is the description of the shield worn by Alkmene's son Herakles in the combat with Kyknos, son-in-law of Keyx. The shield, being a literary construct, is not easily dated, and attempts to make archaeological comparisons with early Greek shields are, though enterprising, inconclusive.[2] A suitable historical occasion for the composition would be the years before the First Sacred War, when (or better, *if*) about 600 B.C., Boiotian attempts at control of southern Thessaly were becoming overt;[3] for the contest between Kyknos and the Theban hero was fought at Pagasai (*Shield* 70) and the tomb of Kyknos was blotted out by the river Anauros which flows into the Pagasitic gulf. Kyknos was killed

[1] Müller, *Dorians* 2.13.

[2] Cf. R. M. Cook, *C.Q.* 31 (1937) 204–214, who would date the *Shield* early in the sixth century B.C. and suggests that the author drew both on the Homeric Shield of Achilles and on contemporary art.

[3] Cf. P. Guillon, *Études béotiennes* (Aix-en-Provence 1963) and Forrest, *J.H.S.* 86 (1966) 173.

by Herakles because he had plundered pilgrims on their way to Apollo's shrine at Pytho, and so the killing had Apollo's approval (*Shield* 477–480). Here perhaps is presupposed an alliance between Boiotia and Phokis with Delphic backing against southern Thessaly. Similarly the *Kerkopes* (in which Herakles again comes to the help of wayfarers, and specifically Boiotians) may reflect opposition to Boiotian aspirations to control Thermopylai, an essential base for an advance into Thessaly. Such Boiotian ambitions would have been checked by the victory of the Thessalians and their allies in the First Sacred War;[1] so the *Shield* and the *Kerkopes* may well belong before *ca.* 590 B.C. but not long before; and since the *Shield* is developed from the *Catalogues of Women*, that poem (or at least its fourth book) cannot have been composed later than about 600 B.C. It is thus most unlikely that the Hypothesis A to the *Shield* (p. 101, 11 Rzach) is correct in stating that Stesichoros, who lived soon afterwards, about 550 B.C., ascribed the poem to Hesiod. Stesichoros, it is true, composed, perhaps with the *Shield* in mind, a poem on Kyknos (F 30 Page), but this fact does not explain the assertion in the *Shield's* hypothesis. The assertion is perhaps to be regarded as an outgrowth of the strangely mistaken theory which claimed Stesichoros as a son of Hesiod (cf. Marcksheffel 32–33). Just possibly Stesichoros used the name 'Hesiod' to mean the Hesiodic school without intending to attribute the poem to Hesiod himself.[2]

Thanks to the author of the *Shield* and to Stesichoros the battle with Kyknos became a popular theme with Attic and other vase painters from about 550 B.C. onwards, and it also appeared on the Amyklaian throne (Pausanias 3.18.10 Bowra 122). Stesichoros introduced to the story a temple; there is no temple in the *Shield* which describes only an altar and Apollo's sanctuary at Pagasai (lines 70 and 99). A painting of the Kyknos episode on a Late Corinthian amphora includes a structure which may well be a temple;[3] so here at least the artist followed the Stesichorean version. Indeed, if the Hesiodic poem is to be dated about 600 B.C., then it had little immediate effect upon vase painters; that is perhaps to be expected if the poem's purpose was mainly to please local Boiotian patriots.

---

[1] Forrest, *B.C.H.* 80 (1956) 33 ff.   [2] J. A. Davison, *Eranos* 63 (1956) 135 ff.
[3] H. Payne, *Necrocorinthia* (Oxford 1931) 131.

Other elements in the Herakles story would have lent themselves to special treatment: the Nessos incident for example, which was also known to vase painters in Attica from about 650 B.C. onwards (*J.H.S.* 32 (1912) plates 10–12) and in Argos from a little earlier (*A.B.S.A.* 35 (1934/5) plate 52); we are not told of epics entirely devoted to such themes, but their existence is perhaps to be inferred from epic titles of poems by the lyric poet Stesichoros. The *Kyknos* has already been noted; the *Garyonais* is another peculiarly Herakleian theme; and the *Kerberos* (Stesichoros F 29 Page) a third. There was, however, a limit to the scope of such poems, whose authors therefore were tempted to include much matter not strictly relevant; and when Panyassis chose to give to the Herakles legends their fullest expression he naturally returned to a continuous treatment in the manner of Peisandros, and wrote a *Herakleia* or *Herakleias*.

IX

Epic Poetry in Attica
and the *Theseis*

The Athenians maintained that their city was exceptional in having been continuously occupied from heroic until historical times. In the early Hellenic age they believed that even in the midst of the disasters traditionally associated with the Dorian invasion their ancestors had held on, thus bequeathing to the state the right to claim autochthony. In view of this alleged continuity we would expect to find in Attica a strong tradition of heroic poetry of Mycenaean origin giving rise to local epics with local authors; yet in the record there is no mention of an Attic Hesiod or Homer, and named epic poems on purely Athenian subjects – notably the Theseus legends – emerge late, in comparison with the poetry of Boiotia, Corinth and the Argolis. Athens came late to the creation of her own epics; and those epics were soon, by about 500 B.C., overtaken by a new, and to the Athenians more congenial, poetical expression of heroic ideals, tragedy.

Yet there are early indications of Athenian interest in epic poetry. Before 700 B.C. the Pylian story of the Molione is almost certainly to be recognised in Attic Geometric vase painting;[1] and the brothers are, as in Hesiod (F 13 Rzach), depicted as Siamese twins, a feature ignored by Homer. There are also Attic representations of Centaur battles of about the same date, *ca.* 725 B.C.[2] Moreover the earliest Athenian inscription – on an Attic Geometric oenochoe – is a hexameter, though it may not have been written by an Athenian.[3]

$$\text{ℎος νυν ορχ}\overline{\epsilon}\text{στ}\overline{ο}\text{ν παντον αταλ}\overline{ο}\text{τατα παιζει}$$

The Homeric *Hymn to Demeter* reveals close local knowledge of

[1] Johansen 25. Brann 65–66, following Hampe. I am not quite convinced that she has identified the death of Astyanax on another sherd (p. 15).

[2] Dunbabin 77 with references.

[3] Jeffery 68.

Eleusis, its topography and cult; so we may perhaps infer the existence of a hymnic tradition in that part of Attica, and the local poets may have composed hexametric poetry on heroic as well as divine themes.[1] Pausanias (4.1.5) also hints at a local poetical tradition there: he mentions a hymn to Demeter composed by 'Mousaios' for an Attic family, the Lykomidai; in the hymn it was said that Kaukon, son of Kelainos, son of Phlyos (evidently the eponymous hero of Phlya in Attica), son of Earth brought the rites of the Great Gods from Eleusis to Messene. The poem thus seems to have been genealogical as well as cultic, in the manner, perhaps, of Hesiod's *Theogony*. A large body of hymnic, purificatory, oracular and theogonical poetry passed under the title of Mousaios (D.K. No. 2), whose name became attached to many anonymous, for the most part Attic, hexameters. Pausanias (1.22.7) believed that the only genuine work of Mousaios was the hymn for the Lykomidai, but talk of authenticity is here pointless. The poem was no more than an oral heirloom of the family. The 'Mousaian' poetry does not bear the marks of a high antiquity. Some of it may have originated no earlier than the period of literary activity under the Athenian tyrants, which included the forgery by Onomakritos of 'Mousaian' oracles (Herodotos 7.6).

If Eleusis welcomed poets in western Attica, in the east of the country Brauron may also have offered shelter, for we learn of singing or recitation of the *Iliad* by rhapsodes at a Brauronian festival; but as to the period in which the festival was held nothing is reported; nor are its sponsors known.[2] There is evidence too that all kinds of poems were recited in competition by children at the great Athenian festival of kinsmen, the Apatouria (Plato, *Tim.* 21 B). In Athens itself musical competitions were held at the Panathenaia, a small annual festival expanded at four year intervals into the Great Panathenaia, in which athletic contests were included about 565 B.C.;[3] Plato (*Ion* 530 B)

[1] The fragment Εὔμολπος Δόλιχός τε καὶ ⟨Ἱπποθόων⟩ μεγάθυμος (M.W. F 227) may well be Eleusinian in origin. There is no good reason to ascribe this line to the *Mopsopia* of Euphorion (F 35(c) Powell), simply because that poem dealt with Attic antiquities. The fragment is extracted from Herodian π. μον. λέξ. 10.

[2] Hesychios s.v. Βραυρωνίοις. τὴν Ἰλιάδα ᾖδον ῥαψῳδοὶ ἐν Βραυρῶνι τῆς Ἀττικῆς.

[3] For the date Eusebius, *Chronicle*. Armenian Version (ed. Karst, 1911) 188 and

reports that there were contests for rhapsodes in the fifth century at the Panathenaia, but we do not know that such *contests* had already been included in the mid-sixth century festival. However, *recitations* by rhapsodes of successive parts of the Homeric poems are said to have been introduced to the Panathenaia by Hipparchos, son of the tyrant Peisistratos ([Plato] *Hipparch.* 228 B), and it is surely no coincidence that Attic vase painters of the last quarter of the sixth century B.C. became exceptionally interested in epic scenes from the Iliad.[1] This growing interest may well be linked with rhapsodic recitations (as distinct from competitions), such as those alleged to have occurred at Brauron. Here it is proper to recall that, like Hipparchos, the early sixth-century lawgiver of Athens, Solon, is said to have arranged for the recitation of Homer 'from a cue (ἐξ ὑποβολῆς), so that where the first poet ceased, at that point the next should begin' (Diog. Laert. 1.27). This interesting tale perhaps presupposes the existence of a text of Homer (to provide the cues and control the order of episodes); as such, the story is quite plausible, but it is important to note that we have no evidence here for the preparation in Athens of a special Athenian *edition* of the poet.

In the Platonic *Hipparchos* (228 B) it is alleged that Hipparchos son of Peisistratos first brought the poems of Homer to Attica; this may mean no more than that he obtained an authorised text from the Homeridai in Chios with which to guide the rhapsodic recitations at the Panathenaia.[2] The change may be regarded as an attempt to regularise the informal recitations earlier arranged by Solon. The regularisation of rhapsodic *competitions* may be no earlier than Perikles' Panathenaic Law.[3]

Neither the *Ion* nor the *Hipparchos* passage permits any secure inference about the preparation of an Athenian text of Homer, but both agree with the evidence of vases in showing that epic stories were popular in late sixth-century Athens. Evidently the insignificance of Athens in the *Iliad* and the *Odyssey* did not lessen the popularity of those poems amongst Athenian audiences; and despite the rarity of Athenians

---

Pherekydes 3 F 2. Cf. J. A. Davison, *J.H.S.* 78 (1958) 27.
[1] Johansen 226–227.   [2] Johansen 239 n. 334.
[3] Plutarch, *Perikles* 13.11. See also Wade-Gery 30.

in the *Iliad,* Athens had been quite ready to use the poem as political propaganda against the Aeolians in the Troad early in the sixth century B.C.: the Aeolians were not mentioned in the *Iliad* at all whereas it was undeniable that Menestheus of Athens went to Troy (Herodotos 5.94.2 and *Iliad* 2.552).

For Solon, or whoever introduced the 'Solonian' law about recitations, 'Homer' may have included more than the *Iliad* and the *Odyssey.* Like Kallinos, Solon may well have regarded the *Thebais* as Homeric. About 500 B.C. an Attic vase painter, the Kleophrades painter, showed a rhapsode reciting: the words he utters are part of an epic hexameter about Tiryns ὧδέ ποτ᾽ ἐν Τίρυνθι (*A.R.V.* 2.1632). The words do not come from the *Iliad* or the *Odyssey,* as we have them, but would suit the *Thebais,* a version of the Io story, or a Herakles epic. Such stories may have found attentive audiences in Athens as elsewhere, but to patriotic Athenians the legends about Theseus, the unifier of Attica and the local rival to Herakles, were especially welcome.

Yet specific literary evidence for Athenian Theseus epics is jejune and the names of their composers were lost early (see H. Herter, *R.M.* 88 (1939) 283). Aristotle (*Poetics* 8) criticised the poets of the *Theseides* because like the authors of *Herakleides* they assumed that because there was a single hero there was also a single theme; but there were really several loosely connected stories. In the Heraklean poetry the episodes sometimes were treated in distinct poems, e.g. *Oichalia's Sack,* but Attic epics dealing with special topics in the Theseus legends – the Minotaur for example – are not mentioned. Herakles and Theseus appear as equals in the late archaic reliefs of the Athenian treasury at Delphi and a similar attempt was made in epic to link Theseus with Herakles as his peer; thus, when Herakles attacked the Amazons Theseus joined him and wed the Amazon Antiope. Later the Amazons with Antiope attacked Athens when the marriage of Theseus with Phaidra daughter of Deukalion the Cretan was being celebrated, and Herakles helped to defend the city, according to 'the author of the *Theseis*', as Plutarch calls him.[1] Theseus and Antiope appear together on several Attic Black and early Red Figure vases; the local epic theme was evidently popular in sixth-century Athens. (Bothmer 124–125.)

[1] *Theseus* 28. Cf. Apollod. *Epit.* 1.16.

Conversely Theseus may have been made to help Herakles in some of his labours: hence, perhaps, the statement that according to 'the author of the *Theseis*', the Keryneian hind had golden antlers. The reindeer is said to be the only species of female deer with antlers, but we do not have to suppose that Herakles and Theseus therefore went in this version of the tale to the far north in search of the hind:[1] surely a special hind sacred to Artemis is not bound by ordinary rules of genetics.

In Homer, Theseus, who lived a generation or more before the Trojan war, is but a pale memory. Once the poet names Theseus in connexion with Peirithoos and Kaineus with whom the hero battled against the Centaurs (*Iliad* 1.263–5). Theseus and Peirithoos also appear together, uneasily and unexpectedly, in the *Nekyomanteia* (*Od.* 11.631); the Megarian who objected to this verse as an Athenian interpolation due to Peisistratos was biased, but he had a case (Hereas *F.Gr.Hist.* 486 F 1). In the *Nekyomanteia* too Theseus, Ariadne and Phaidra appear together (*Od.* 11.321–325) in a passage which does the hero more justice than the Hesiodic tale according to which Theseus abandoned Ariadne for Aigle (F 105 Rzach) – hence the Megarian charge that Peisistratos tampered with the Hesiodic text.[2] Homer here remarks that Theseus once 'led Ariadne daughter of baneful Minos from Crete towards the lap of holy Athens, but had no joy of her because Artemis killed her beforehand in sea-girt Dia at the instigation of Dionysos'. Since the motive of Dionysos is left unexplained, there is something to be said for the alternative reading by Aristophanes in line 324 ἔσχεν for ἔκτα: 'Artemis retained her.' The version would then tie in with the story according to which Dionysos fell in love with Ariadne and carried her off to Lemnos (Apollodoros, *Epitome* 1.9).

The killing of the Minotaur by Theseus in Crete was the outstanding success of the hero's career; it was a tale specially pleasing to Athenian

---

[1] Cf. Frazer, *Apollodorus* pp. 190–191.

[2] It may well be that poets of Theseides were patronised, not by Peisistratos, but by the ancestors of the great Kimon; Kimon *ca.* 475 claimed to be bringing the bones of Theseus back from Skyros in triumph (Plut. *Kimon* 8.5–7). This event at least suggests a family interest in the Theseus tales. Ion of Chios, who belonged to the Kimonian circle, even made the Chian hero Oinopion a son of Theseus (Plut., *Theseus* 20.2).

patriots because with the creature's death the annual tribute of seven youths and seven maidens from Athens ceased. Hesiodic fragments suggest that the detailed story, which surely featured prominently in the *Theseis*, developed early: Eurygyes (or Androgeos) whose violent death at Athens led to the payment of the human tribute to his father Minos appears in a single verse:

$$Εὐρυγύης \ δ' \ ἔτι \ κοῦρος \ †'Aθηναίων \ ἱεράων.†$$

(Hesiod F 105 Rzach)

[Εὐρυγύῃ δ'ἔτι κοῦροι 'Aθηναίων ⟨∗∗∗'Aθηνάων⟩ ἱεράων West M.W. F 146].

Here Athens is again called 'holy' as in the Homeric passage about Ariadne. According to some (Apollod. *Lib.* 3.15.7) Eurygyes had defeated all comers at the Panathenaia; this development of the story may not be earlier than the institution of the athletic contests at the festival about 565, but may yet have appeared in the *Theseis* if the poem was composed late in the sixth century. The Minotaur is not essential to the story, because the tribute was payable to Minos alone as father of the dead Androgeos. However, the monstrous offspring of Pasiphae, with human body and bull's head, appears already in a Hesiodic text (M.W. F 145), and the bull-man is in fact very ancient since he already appears on a Late Minoan sealstone (*A.R.* 1958, 24). As for the human tribute, that may well recall the period of Minoan naval dominance in the Aegean before 1400 B.C. when Crete was powerful enough to tax parts of the Greek mainland.

There is no merit in ascribing to the *Theseis* other parts of the Theseus-cycle of legends, unless they can be matched by fragments. To conjecture whether, for example, the seizure of Helen or the hero's birth and sojourn in Troizen appeared in the epic is profitless, even if the stories are of high antiquity.[1] Theseus can however be seen to have had a prominent part in another epic, the *Minyas*. The name of this poem is unexplained; the fragments do not support Welcker's conjecture (1.253 ff) that it was concerned with the defeat by Herakles of the Minyans of Orchomenos. Analogy with the name *Naupaktia* suggests that the poem may have been composed, or recited, at Orchomenos, where, local lore asserted, the bones of Hesiod had been

---

[1] For the Troizenians' beliefs about Theseus see especially W. S. Barrett, *Euripides. Hippolytos* (Oxford 1964) 2–3.

piously reburied (Pausanias 9.38.4); so people in Orchomenos, who evidently valued poets, may have had a local epic of their own.

All the notices of the *Minyas* concern persons in Hades. Taking Theseus with him, Peirithoos visited Hades in an attempt to recover Persephone and make her his bride. While there they made no use of Charon's boat: Pausanias (10.28.2) quotes two lines from the poem and states his belief that the *Minyas* was the source for a painting of Hades by Polygnotos at Delphi. The poem was, therefore, probably earlier than the mid-fifth century.

ἔνθ' ἤτοι νέα μὲν νεκυάμβατον, ἣν ὁ γεραιὸς
πορθμεὺς ἦγε Χάρων, οὐκ ἔλαβον ἔνδοθεν ὅρμου.

'There they took not from within its mooring place the corpse-conveying bark which the aged ferryman Charon used to row.' When in Hades Peirithoos and Theseus met Meleager. Pausanias (10.31.3) states that Meleager appeared in the *Minyas* and in the *Ehoiai*; a papyrus text which may well come from the *Ehoiai* (Merkelbach pp. 52–54) reveals Meleager explaining to Theseus how doom and Apollo killed him in the war against the Kouretes. In the *Minyas* also Apollo, not, as in Homer, the Fury, was said to have caused his death. Other heroes described in Hades in the poem were Amphion (Paus. 9.5.9) and Thamyris (Paus. 4.33.7); the one was punished for his taunting of Leto, the other for his boast against the Muses (*Iliad* 2.595–600). The *Minyas* seems therefore to have much in common with the Odyssean scenes in Hades where ghosts, some sinners, some not, are seen by Odysseus. This impression is strengthened by the appearance of Orion in both poems (Philodemos περὶ εὐσεβ. p. 7 Gomperz and *Od.* 11.572). The visit of Theseus and Peirithoos to Hades ended in disaster: the two heroes were tricked by Hades into seating themselves in the chairs of forgetfulness, to which they grew; Peirithoos was held fast but Theseus was rescued by Herakles and sent to Athens. Polygnotos painted the two heroes seated in the chairs (Pausanias 10.29.9) and here too may have followed the *Minyas*. Panyassis (F 9 Kinkel) about the time of Polygnotos's work at Delphi vividly described the heroes' flesh growing to the stone of the seats; in another version the heroes were tied down by snakes. The rescue of Theseus would have formed a dramatic conclusion to an epic, which, to judge by the extant fragments, may have been exceptional in being set for the most part in the House of Hades.

When Theseus was in Hades with Peirithoos, the Dioskouroi took advantage of his absence to recover Helen from Aphidnai in Attica, to which Theseus had forcibly taken her. Kastor and Polydeukes marched against the place, took it, got possession of Helen and led Aithra, the mother of Theseus, away captive (Apollod. *Lib.* 3.10.8). Later when Helen fled from Lakedaimon with Paris, Aithra went with her: hence her appearance in the *Iliad* amongst the attendants of Helen at Troy (3.144). By then she would have been of advanced years, though Homer does not say so.

The loss of Helen and of Aithra could be excused by the preoccupation of Theseus elsewhere; but one version was less favourable to Athenian sentiment. Predictably Hereas the Megarian, that dedicated hypercritic of Attic mythological pretentions, seized upon it (*F.Gr.Hist.* 486 F 2), because, it seems, a defeat of Theseus at Aphidnai by the Dioskouroi was part of the story. Halykos, son of the Megarian Skeiron, was killed by Theseus himself when he came to help the Dioskouroi at Aphidnai – or so Hereas asserted, quoting some hexameters:

τὸν ἐν εὐρυχόρῳ ποτ᾽ Ἀφίδνῃ
μαρνάμενον Θησεὺς Ἑλένης ἕνεκ᾽ ηὐκόμοιο
κτεῖνεν.

'... Halykos, whom Theseus slew fighting in spacious Aphidna for the sake of Helen of the lovely tresses.' These lines are unlikely to come from an official Athenian *Theseis*, but Hereas may have found them in a Hesiodic poem; the rather unflattering line on Theseus's passion for Aigle was similarly exploited by Hereas (Hesiod F 105 Rzach). Hesiodic poets had no motive, and no wish, to consider Attic sensibilities.

If the *Minyas* was an Orchomenian, not – in spite of the prominence of Theseus in it – an Athenian, poem, then the principal claimant to authorship must be Chersias, whom Plutarch believed to have lived in the age of the Seven Wise Men, early in the sixth century B.C. (*Moralia* 156 E). Pausanias, who knew of the poetry of Chersias only through quotations in a book by a certain Kallippos of Corinth on the Orchomenians (9.38.9 = *F.Gr.Hist.* 385 F 2), quotes two lines showing that Aspledon, the eponymous hero of the Boiotian town, was a son of

Poseidon and Mideia (who gets her name from the Boiotian, not the Argolic, place of that name: *Iliad* 2.507):[1]

ἐκ δὲ Ποσειδάωνος ἀγακλειτῆς τε Μιδείης
'Ασπληδὼν γένεθ' υἱὸς ἀν' εὐρύχορον πτολίεθρον.

Kallippos evidently had access to a number of rare local epics; according to Pausanias (9.29.1 = *F.Gr.Hist.* 385 F 1) the work of Kallippos on Orchomenos also quoted four lines of an otherwise unknown poem, the *Atthis* of a Hegesinous. The title *Atthis* would lead us to expect an Attic subject, but here too Poseidon appears in a Boiotian genealogy: 'Poseidon the earthshaker lay with Askre, and she with the passing of the seasons bore a son to him Oioklos, who first did settle Askre by the springs at the foot of Helikon with the sons of Aloeus.'

"Ασκρῃ δ' αὖ παρέλεκτο Ποσειδάων ἐνοσίχθων
ἣ δή οἱ τέκε παῖδα περιπλομένων ἐνιαυτῶν
Οἴοκλον, ὃς πρῶτος μετ' 'Αλωέος ἔκτισε παίδων
"Ασκρην, ἥ θ' 'Ελικῶνος ἔχει πόδα πιδακόεντα.

In the Eumelian genealogy the principal son of Aloeus was Epopeus who ruled over the Asopia, the land of Sikyon. Here in Hegesinous his kingdom may have been the Asopos of Boiotia; the streams from Helikon join to flow close to the headwaters of that river, not far from Eutresis. The reason why the sons of Aloeus appear with Askre in a poem called *Atthis* would thus be that Marathon, the eponymous hero of the Attic state, was a son of one of them, Epopeus. Indeed the genealogy Aloeus – Epopeus – Marathon may have originally belonged to the Attic-Boiotian borderlands, and have been shifted thence to Corinth and Sikyon by Eumelos.

When the tenuous evidence is surveyed it is clear that Attica contributed comparatively little to the sum of epic (the lost 'Mousaian' and Onomakritean hymns are a distinct problem, and do not concern us here). Few fragments of indigenous poetry survive and even they are for the most part derivative from epics about Herakles. Theseus stands out as the prime local hero, but we cannot form a coherent notion of

---

[1] Steph. Byz. s.v. 'Ασπληδών quotes a line from a quite different local tradition which held Aspledon to be a son of Orchomenos and to have brothers Klymenos and Amphidokos: ... 'Ορχομενοῦ δὲ υἱεῖς "Ασπληδὼν Κλύμενός τε καὶ 'Αμφίδοκος θεοειδής".

the lost *Theseides*. Attica's role was rather in the fostering of existing poetry than in the creation of new epics. In particular, as the vase paintings suggest, the *Iliad* and the *Odyssey*, substantially as we know them now, found enthusiastic audiences at Athens from about 525 onwards. So the Athenians may well have obtained or prepared texts of Homer for themselves by that time.[1] So much and no more, despite the charges of editorial malpractice energetically brought by Megarians and their Pergamene successors, need lie behind the story of the Peisistratean recension of the Homeric texts.

[1] The evidence for the Peisistratean recension is gathered by T. W. Allen, *Homer* (Oxford 1924) 225–248 and (with rather different inferences from it) by Merkelbach in *R.M.* 95 (1952) 23–47.

X

The *Kypria*

There survive in Photios and less fully elsewhere summaries of the *Chrestomathy* of a Proklos. Included in the Photian summary is a précis of the poems of the Trojan cycle which dealt with those parts of the tale of Troy not embraced by the *Iliad* and the *Odyssey*. The summary begins with the plan of Zeus to stir up the Trojan war and ends with the marriages of Penelope to Telegonos and of Kirke to Telemachos after the death of Odysseus.

It is by no means agreed who Proklos was and whether he had the texts of all the lost epics about the Trojan War before him when he summarised them. However, according to Photios, Proklos did say that the poems of the epic cycle were preserved, and were studied not so much for their merit as for the succession of events in them (Allen, *Hom. Op.* v 97, lines 8–11); and the Patriarch did maintain that Proklos had read the cycle.[1] If, as is sometimes assumed, the author of the *Chrestomathy* was a grammarian of the Antonine age, some at least of the poems may well have been available to him in their entirety. If on the other hand he was the immensely learned and industrious Neoplatonist who died in A.D. 485, he was still writing earlier than the Mohammedan invasions and the decline of interest in ancient literature. This later Proklos wrote about Homer and may well have seen fit to summarise poems which, if they existed at all, must have been quite rare in his day. A little later John Philoponos stated that the poems in the Cycles could no longer be found.[2] A further problem is to decide how far the summaries represent the contents of the poems and how far they have been adjusted to provide a continuous sequence of events. Examination of the fragments suggests, as we shall see, that the

[1] A point emphasised by T. W. Allen, *Homer* (Oxford 1924) 56. Cf. (for objections) M. Sicherl, *Gnomon* 28 (1956) 210 n. 1.

[2] See *F.Gr.Hist.* I² *10 (16 T 2).

summaries and the fragments correspond well; from this one may infer that the original poems were, as Proklos himself implies, composed when the *Iliad* and the *Odyssey* were already in existence. Like the *Iliad* and the *Odyssey* the epics of the Trojan Cycle – *Kypria, Aithiopis, Little Iliad* (whose title presupposes the existence of the *Iliad*), *Sack of Ilios, Nostoi* or *Returns* of the heroes from Troy, and *Telegoneia* – drew on traditional tales, many of them very ancient; they differ from the *Iliad* and the *Odyssey*, as Aristotle pointed out, in their failure to concentrate on a single theme; they were therefore diffuse and without dramatic unity, being a series of episodes.[1] The ancients, unlike some moderns,[2] were sure that the authors of the Trojan cyclic poems were younger than Homer; thus Arktinos, to whom Proklos ascribes the *Aithiopis*, was declared to be a pupil of Homer (Artemon 443 F 2); Lesches, the presumed poet of a *Little Iliad*, is alleged to have competed with Arktinos and defeated him (Phainias of Eresos ap. Clem. Alex. *Strom.* 1.131); Stasinos, one of the supposed authors of the *Kypria*, was asserted to be Homer's son-in-law (Tzetzes, *Chil.* 13.636); and Eugammon, the author of the *Telegoneia*, is dated by Eusebios about 568/5 B.C. (53rd Olympiad). The upper limit for dating these poets depends on the dating of Homer and Hesiod; that is a problem we must now tackle.

Herodotos (2.53.1) believed that Homer and Hesiod lived four hundred years, and no more, before his own time. The poets alleged to be earlier than Homer and Hesiod were, he thought, in fact later in time (2.53.3) – in so far as works ascribed to remote personages such as Orpheus and Mousaios may have been invented in the sixth century B.C. at Athens by Onomakritos, that was a thoroughly sound opinion. Four hundred years may be the historian's way of saying 'ten 40-year generations'; such generations of Homer's descendants could be, and were, counted. In the fifth century they were given by Akousilaos

[1] They thus provided an abundance of plots for tragic dramatists, notably for Euripides, whose use of the *Kypria* is discussed by F. Jouan, *Euripide et les Légendes des Chants cypriens* (Paris 1966).

[2] The thesis of W. Kullmann in his *Die Quellen der Ilias* (*Hermes* Einzelschriften 14, Wiesbaden 1960) maintains that much of the Cycle as we now know it antedates the *Iliad*. I find his view paradoxical. For comment see D. L. Page, *C.R.* 11 (1961) 205–209.

The *Kypria*

(2 F 2) and by Hellanikos in his *Atlantis* (4 F 20) – according to some Homer was a descendant of Atlas (Wade-Gery 91). Ten generations at a more normal average of three to a century would give a date some three hundred years before Herodotos, who seems to have regarded Homer and Hesiod as contemporaries. This belief was not unique to Herodotos; it stems from the tradition of their having competed, which is already explicit in a Hesiodic fragment (F 265 Rzach) wherein they are said by Hesiod or someone impersonating him, to have sung together in Delos.[1] Hesiod's date is well attested; he carries Homer's date with him. Hesiod remarks that he took part in the funeral games of Amphidamas at Chalkis (*Opera* 654–659). This Euboian nobleman or prince was killed in a sea battle during the Lelantine War (Plut. *Mor.* 153 F), a conflict in which horsemen took part (Aristotle, *Pol.* 1289b 36–39) before hoplite fighting became standard military practice. The Lelantine war is best regarded as one part of the early colonial struggles of the late eighth century B.C. in which Chalkis fought Eretria in the plain between them; they and their respective allies competed intermittently elsewhere, Corinth gaining successes in the West, notably in Corcyra from which Eretrians were expelled about 734 B.C., and Miletos (Eretria's ally) in the East.[2] Hesiod, then, would have been at the funeral games for Amphidamas sometime between 725 and 700 B.C. Homer his contemporary would have flourished in the same period, about ten generations before Herodotos. Nor may the tradition of a contest between them be ignored. It was attested in a papyrus as early as the third century B.C. (Flinders Petrie Papyrus ap. Allen. *Hom. Op.* V p. 225) and was almost certainly known to the sophist Alkidamas early in the fourth century.[3] In character the Contest, if we may judge by the extant *Certamen* which is fabricated out of hexameter verses and riddles, some obviously old, was not unlike the ancient tests of wit and skill between mantic heroes such as Mopsos and Kalchas (Hesiod F 160 Rzach).

If Homer lived late in the eighth century, then his successors who

---

[1] The tradition of a competition between them, though not at Delos, may go back as far as Lesches (Plut. *Mor.* 153 F where we can keep 'as Lesches says', ὡς φησι Λέσχης: the poet reported the contest of his seniors).

[2] Forrest, *Historia* 6 (1957) 161–4. West, 43–44.

[3] T. W. Allen, *Homer* (Oxford 1924) 20.

took account of his work (even to the extent of excluding Odysseus almost entirely from the *Nostoi*, if we may trust the summary of that poem by Proklos), cannot have been active earlier than about 700 B.C. Early in the seventh century B.C. writing was becoming a widespread skill in Greece; the poets of the Trojan cycle may well therefore have written down (or dictated) their epics themselves, though we cannot prove that they did. At the same time it is clear from the verse fragments that the poems of the Trojan cycle, like other early epics, drew heavily upon the common and ancient fund of oral tradition and language.

The *Kypria* forms a long preface to the Iliad. The poem's name is still unexplained; it may mean 'the poem composed in Cyprus' – the variant *Kypriaka* is known – or the title may allude to the prominent part taken by the Cyprian goddess Aphrodite. Proklos alleged that there were eleven books; compared with the five of the *Aithiopis*, four of the *Little Iliad*, two of the *Sack of Ilios*, five of the *Nostoi*, and two of the *Telegoneia*, this, then, was a substantial poem. There is no reason to think these divisions into books earlier than the Alexandrine era of scholarship.

It will be convenient to give a translation of the summary of the *Kypria*, according to the text of Severyns, and then to place the identifiable fragments in their contexts. The opening presumably refers back to the *Epigonoi*, some of the heroes in which also fought at Troy.

'This is continued by the poem called the *Kypria* which is handed down in eleven books. . . . Zeus takes counsel with Themis about the Trojan war. Strife arrives when the gods are feasting at the wedding of Peleus and stirs up a dispute between Athena, Hera and Aphrodite about their beauty. They are led by Hermes at the order of Zeus to Alexandros on Mount Ida for his judgement; and Alexandros, excited by the prospect of the marriage with Helen, decides in Aphrodite's favour. Then at Aphrodite's suggestion he builds a fleet, and Helenos prophesies to them concerning the future, and Aphrodite commands Aineias to sail with Alexandros. Kassandra foretells future events. After landing in the country of Lakedaimon Alexandros is welcomed by the Tyndaridai, and after that in Sparta by Menelaos; and Alexandros gives presents to Helen during a feast. Next Menelaos sails off to Crete after bidding Helen provide the guests with all their needs until they depart. Meanwhile Aphrodite brings Helen and Alexandros together, and after their mating they put a mass of treasure on board and sail away by night.

'Hera stirs up a storm against them, and they are driven to Sidon where Alexandros sacks the city. Then he sailed away to Troy and celebrated his marriage to Helen.

'Meanwhile Kastor and Polydeukes were caught in the act of driving off the cows of Idas and Lynkeus. Kastor is slain by Idas, but Lynkeus and Idas are killed by Polydeukes. Zeus gave them (Kastor and Polydeukes) immortality on alternate days.

'Afterwards Iris reports to Menelaos what has happened at his home. He comes back and takes counsel with his brother about the expedition against Ilios, and then goes on to visit Nestor.

'In a digression Nestor describes to him how Epopeus was utterly destroyed after seducing the daughter of Lykourgos, and the tale of Oidipous, the madness of Herakles, and the story of Theseus and Ariadne.

'Then they journey over Hellas and assemble the leaders. They caught Odysseus out when he pretended to be mad, since he was unwilling to join the expedition, by kidnapping his son Telemachos for punishment, at the suggestion of Palamedes.

'After that the princes meet together at Aulis and sacrifice. The portent of the snake and the sparrows is revealed and Kalchas foretells to them what the outcome will be. Then they put out to sea and land in Teuthrania and, taking it for Ilios, sack it. But Telephos rushes out in defence and kills Thersandros, son of Polyneikes, and is wounded himself by Achilles. A storm falls on them as they sail away from Mysia and they are scattered. Achilles puts in to Skyros and marries Deidameia, daughter of Lykomedes. Next he heals Telephos who, prompted by an oracle, had come to Argos, so that he might become their leader on the voyage to Ilios.

'When the fleet had gathered a second time at Aulis, Agamemnon while hunting shot a stag and boasted that he was better than Artemis. So the goddess was angry and sent storms to hold them back from sailing. Kalchas explained the anger of the goddess and ordered the sacrifice of Iphigeneia to Artemis. This they undertake to do, and send for her as though she were to be a bride for Achilles. But Artemis snatches her away and conveys her to the Tauroi and makes her immortal, and sets a stag in place of the maiden beside the altar.

'Next they sail to Tenedos and while they are feasting Philoktetes is bitten by a water-snake and is abandoned on Lemnos owing to the evil stench of the wound. Achilles is given a late invitation and quarrels with Agamemnon. Then they go ashore at Ilios but the Trojans hem them in and Protesilaos is killed by Hektor. Then Achilles drives them off and slays Kyknos son of Poseidon. Next they take up their dead and send an embassy to the Trojans to demand back Helen and the treasure. But when the Trojans heed them not, they attack the city wall, and next go out against the countryside and sack the cities round about also. Afterwards Achilles desires to behold Helen, and Aphrodite and Thetis conduct them to a meeting. Next, when the Achaeans are eager to return home Achilles checks them. Thereafter he drives off the cows of Aineias and lays waste Lyrnessos and Pedasos and many of the nearby cities, and kills Troilos. Patroklos takes Lykaon to Lemnos and sells him into slavery. Achilles takes Briseis as a prize out of the spoils, and Agamemnon Chryseis. The death of Palamedes follows, and the plan of Zeus to relieve the Trojans by withdrawing Achilles from the alliance of the Hellenes, and a catalogue of the Trojan allies.'

The first point to be remarked in this summary is the sharing by *Kypria* and *Iliad* of a common epic tradition; the second is the manner in which the *Kypria* presupposes the *Iliad* and is composed with the *Iliad* in mind. To distinguish between (*a*) a tradition appearing in both poems and (*b*) the imitation of the *Iliad* in the *Kypria*, is however rarely possible. The *Iliad* recalls a version of the Judgement of Paris (24.28–30). Does the *Kypria* follow the *Iliad* or do both poems take the tale from very ancient lore? When the *Kypria* declared that Zeus had a plan to withdraw Achilles from the battle, did its author have the plan alluded to in *Iliad* 1.5 in mind? Or is Zeus's plan here in Homer not simply the withdrawal of Achilles, but the overall plan, mentioned at the beginning of the *Kypria*, to reduce the population of the world by stirring up the Trojan War? Homer in the *Iliad* makes Alexandros sail from Lakedaimon with Helen to Troy by way of Sidon (6.290–292), so does the *Kypria* according to Proklos. Is the *Kypria* deliberately deferring to the Homeric version of Paris' flight with Helen? These

The *Kypria*

questions may be posed but none of them can be answered confidently. What is significant is that, according to Proklos, the *Kypria* ends where the *Iliad* begins, and the *Aithiopis* begins where the *Iliad* ends. Either then the *Iliad* was composed to fill the gap between the *Kypria* and the *Aithiopis*, or *Kypria* and *Aithiopis* were composed to introduce and to continue the *Iliad*. The former alternative conflicts with the clear ancient testimony that the authors of the cyclic poems were Homer's followers, and must surely be rejected, if any credence is to be given to the Proklan summaries.

Fragments of the *Kypria* may now be examined and related to the summary of the version known to Proklos. According to some the Plan of Zeus to lighten the burden of population on earth included the Theban war (Schol. *Iliad* 1.5), but the summary of the *Kypria* puts the plan after the Theban war and begins with the marriage of Peleus and Thetis. The lightening of Earth's burden is foretold in some beautiful verses ascribed to 'Stasinos the poet of the *Kypria*': 'Once upon a time when the countless tribes of men were widely dispersed and weighed down the face of the deep-breasted earth, Zeus beheld and had pity and in his wise heart proposed to lighten the all-nurturing earth's burden of men by fanning the great contest of the Iliac war, that the weight of death might empty the world. So the heroes were slaughtered in Troy, and the plan of Zeus was accomplished.'

> ἦν ὅτε μυρία φῦλα κατὰ χθόνα πλαζόμεν' ἀνδρῶν
> ⟨ἐκπάγλως ἐβάρυνε⟩ βαθυστέρνου πλάτος αἴης.
> Ζεὺς δὲ ἰδὼν ἐλέησε καὶ ἐν πυκιναῖς πραπίδεσσι
> σύνθετο κουφίσαι ἀνθρώπων παμβώτορα γαῖαν,
> 5 ῥιπίσσας πολέμου μεγάλην ἔριν Ἰλιακοῖο,
> ὄφρα κενώσειεν θανάτου βάρος· οἱ δ' ἐνὶ Τροίῃ
> ἥρωες κτείνοντο· Διὸς δ' ἐτελείετο βουλή.

2. ἐκπάγλως Schneidewin, ἐβάρυνε Boissonade.

The language of this fragment has some remarkable neoterisms: for example, the scansion ἐνὶ Τροίῃ as ∪ ∪ – – and the form Ἰλιακοῖο, which is absent from the *Iliad*.   (*Kypria* F 1 Allen)

The marriage of Peleus and Thetis provided an opportunity to put the plan into effect; it was not originally part of the plan itself, but had been brought about because, to please Hera, Thetis had avoided wedlock with Zeus; the god therefore was angry and swore that she would cohabit with a mortal (*Kypria* F 2 Allen). This tale ties on to the Prometheus legend; for Prometheus knew that if Thetis had a son by Zeus that son would overthrow him (Aeschylus F 321b Mette), and Thetis fled from Zeus's attentions in that tale. One of the wedding presents was the great spear, later used by Achilles at Troy (*Iliad* 16.140–144). This ashen shaft had been cut by Cheiron, polished by Athena and fitted with a point by Hephaistos (*Kypria* F 3 Allen). No verse fragment from the *Kypria* refers to the strife of the goddesses at the marriage feast; so we cannot be certain that the golden apple inscribed 'To the fairest' was the occasion of the quarrel in the earliest form of the *Kypria*.

In the text known to Athenaios, Aphrodite's preparations for the beauty contest on Mount Ida appeared in the first book of the *Kypria* (Athen. 682 DF). Here the poet excels himself in verses of the highest merit: 'She clothed herself with garments which the Graces and Hours had made for her and dyed with the flowers of spring – such flowers as the Hours do wear – in crocus and hyacinth and blossoming violet and the fair bloom of the rose, so sweet and full of nectar, and the divine buds, flowers of narcissus and lily. In such fragrant garments is Aphrodite clothed at all seasons. . . . Then with her handmaidens did laughter-loving Aphrodite weave sweetly scented chaplets, the flowers of the earth, and place them upon their heads – those goddesses with their shining headbands, the Nymphs and Graces, and with them golden Aphrodite, as they sweetly chanted on the Mount of Ida with its many springs.'

A   εἵματα μὲν χροῒ ἕστο τά οἱ Χάριτές τε καὶ Ὧραι
        ποίησαν καὶ ἔβαψαν ἐν ἄνθεσιν εἰαρινοῖσι,
        οἷα φοροῦσ' Ὧραι, ἔν τε κρόκῳ ἔν θ' ὑακίνθῳ
        ἔν τε ἴῳ θαλέθοντι ῥόδου τ' ἐνὶ ἄνθεϊ καλῷ
5   ἡδέι νεκταρέῳ, ἔν τ' ἀμβροσίαις καλύκεσσι,
        ἄνθεσι ναρκίσσου καὶ λειρίου· τοῖ' Ἀφροδίτη
        ὥραις παντοίαις τεθυωμένα εἵματα ἕστο.

        A6   καλλιροου codd. καὶ λειρίου Meineke. δ' οια codd. τοῖ' Koechly.

B   ἣ δὲ σὺν ἀμφιπόλοισι φιλομμειδὴς Ἀφροδίτη . . .
        πλεξάμεναι στεφάνους εὐώδεας, ἄνθεα γαίης,

ἂν κεφαλαῖσιν ἔθεντο θεαὶ λιπαροκρήδεμνοι,
Νύμφαι καὶ Χάριτες, ἅμα δὲ χρυσῆ Ἀφροδίτη,
5   καλὸν ἀείδουσαι κατ' ὄρος πολυπιδάκου Ἴδης.

Aphrodite was no stranger to Ida. To Anchises in his homestead on the mountain had she come in her transcendent beauty, pretending to be a Phrygian princess. The most elegant of the Homeric Hymns told, in language reminiscent of the *Kypria*, how she approached the hero and filled his heart with love, that she might become by him the mother of Aineias. Now at Skepsis on Ida there lived in the eighth and seventh centuries B.C. a family claiming descent from Aineias (Strabo 608)[1] and hence from Aphrodite; the *Hymn to Aphrodite* may well have been composed in their honour, and the story of the Judgement of Paris, which was set on their home ground, would surely have been of deep interest to them. So would the tradition that Aineias accompanied Paris to Sparta. It is worth asking therefore in what historical circumstances the Judgement story arose. We know that the Aeolians of the north-east Aegean islands held beauty contests of their womenfolk; such competitions are attested in Lesbos (Alkaios G 2.32 Page/Lobel) and in Tenedos (Myrsilos 477 F 4).[2] We may conjecture that the Aeolians who from 750 B.C. onwards settled in the Troad also held such gatherings, perhaps even at Skepsis. It was a short step for a poet from a Judgement of mortals to a Judgement of goddesses; indeed the human competitors at the Aeolian contests may well have been entertained by epic recitals on this very theme. It is clear that the story early became popular. Homer alludes cryptically to the ἄτη, doom, involved in the contest and says that Paris chose Aphrodite who offered him 'grievous lust' (*Iliad* 24.30), which entailed the power to seduce Helen. The poet remarks that Paris 'upbraided the goddesses' (24.29) – the losers Hera and Athena presumably, thereby reinforcing their implacable hatred – when they came to his homestead.

Ἀλεξάνδρου ἔνεκ' ἄτης
ὃς νείκεσσε θεάς, ὅτε οἱ μέσσαυλον ἵκοντο,
30   τὴν δ' ἤνησ' ἥ οἱ πόρε μαχλοσύνην ἀλεγεινήν.

The variant reading ἀρχῆς in line 28 recurs in *Iliad* 3.100. Here in Book

---

[1] Homer alludes to them in *Iliad* 20.307–308.
[2] See also T. C. W. Stinton, *Euripides and the Judgement of Paris* (London 1965) 10.

24 it perhaps alludes to the promise from Hera to Paris of dominion over Asia if he would choose her. The judgement story had reached Sparta by the mid-seventh century B.C., because it is shown on an ivory comb of that time, from the sanctuary of Orthia; and its widespread popularity in the early Hellenic epoch is shown by its appearance on the throne of Apollo at Amyklai near Sparta and on the chest of Kypselos at Olympia (Pausanias 3.18.12 and 5.19.5). Its importance in the Trojan epics would have been enough to justify the naming of the *Kypria* after Aphrodite's success in the fatal contest.

The prominent part given to Kastor and Polydeukes in the Proklan summary is in harmony with the fragments of the *Kypria*. Their immortality on alternate days is perhaps alluded to in the words 'Kastor was mortal and a portion of death was destined for him, but Polydeukes, scion of Ares, was immortal' (*Kypria* F 6 Allen):

Κάστωρ μὲν θνητός, θανάτου δέ οἱ αἶσα πέπρωται.
αὐτὰρ ὅ γ' ἀθάνατος Πολυδεύκης, ὄζος Ἄρηος.

Kastor, then, was mortal at a time when Polydeukes was immortal. Apollodoros (*Lib.* 3.11.2) explains the context: 'Polydeukes was carried up to heaven, but refused to accept immortality while his brother Kastor was dead. So Zeus allowed them to be every other day among the gods and among mortals.' The *Kypria* fragment presumably refers to a time before Zeus made the concession. The *Odyssey* (11.303–304) shares with the *Kypria* a belief in the heroes' immortality on alternate days; ἄλλοτε μὲν ζώουσ' ἑτερήμεροι, ἄλλοτε δ' αὖτε | τεθνᾶσιν.

The seizure of the Leukippides, Ilaeira and Phoibe, by the Dioskouroi is said to have been mentioned in the *Kypria* (F 8 Allen), but if so, the Proklan summary ignores it. The brothers' battle with Idas and Lynkeus is, however, well attested. A verse fragment describes the episode, in which Lynkeus, the keen sighted, spied Polydeukes and Kastor seated in a hollow tree trunk: 'At once Lynkeus, relying on his swift feet, made for Taygetos. He climbed its highest peak and gazed all over the isle of Pelops, son of Tantalos; soon the renowned hero saw with his sharp eyes both horse-taming Kastor and Polydeukes the prize-athlete within the hollow oak tree. Standing nearby he thrust at them . . .' (*Kypria* F 11 Allen).

The *Kypria*

αἶψα δὲ Λυγκεὺς
Ταΰγετον προσέβαινε ποσὶν ταχέεσσι πεποιθώς.
ἀκρότατον δ' ἀναβὰς διεδέρκετο νῆσον ἅπασαν
Τανταλίδου Πέλοπος, τάχα δ' εἴσιδε κύδιμος ἥρως
δεινοῖς ὀφθαλμοῖσιν ἔσω δρυὸς ἄμφω κοίλης
Κάστορά θ' ἱππόδαμον καὶ ἀεθλοφόρον Πολυδεύκεα·
νύξε δ' ἄρ' ἄγχι στὰς μεγάλην δρῦν.

The consequence of this fight was the death, and later revival, of Kastor, whose attention had been, with his brother's, given to the cattle raid while Paris was seducing Helen.

Helen's ancestry was of moment to the *Kypria* which dwelt upon it at length. Kastor and Polydeukes were born to Leda, and so nominally was Helen, though some, including the author of the *Kypria*, believed her to be the child of Nemesis with whom, when she had turned herself into a goose, Zeus in the form of a swan mated (Apollod. *Lib.* 3.10.7). The endeavours of Nemesis to escape from the persistent attentions of Zeus are described in a twelve-line fragment: 'And after them (the Dioskouroi) she (Leda) brought forth (from the egg laid by Nemesis) a third child, Helen, a wonder to mortals. Rich-tressed Nemesis had once given her birth after mating in love with Zeus king of the gods 'neath harsh violence. For she fled from him and desired not to mingle in love with father Zeus, son of Kronos, because shame and resentment troubled her heart. So she fled over land and the unharvested dark water, and Zeus pursued, longing in his heart to catch her. Now in the form of a fish did she hasten out over the wide sea, along the wave of the surging main, now over Ocean's river and the limits of the earth, now over loamy continent. Again and again did she become all manner of dread creatures such as the land nourishes, that she might escape him.'

τοὺς δὲ μέτα τριτάτην Ἑλένην τέκε θαῦμα βροτοῖσι
τήν ποτε καλλίκομος Νέμεσις φιλότητι μιγεῖσα
Ζηνὶ θεῶν βασιλῆϊ τέκε κρατερῆς ὑπ' ἀνάγκης
φεῦγε γάρ, οὐδ' ἔθελεν μιχθήμεναι ἐν φιλότητι
5   πατρὶ Διὶ Κρονίωνι· ἐτείρετο γὰρ φρένας αἰδοῖ
καὶ νεμέσει· κατὰ γῆν δὲ καὶ ἀτρύγετον μέλαν ὕδωρ
φεῦγε, Ζεὺς δ' ἐδίωκε· λαβεῖν δ' ἐλιλαίετο θυμῷ·
ἄλλοτε μὲν κατὰ κῦμα πολυφλοίσβοιο θαλάσσης

ἰχθύϊ εἰδομένη πόντον πολὺν ἐξορόθυνεν,
10   ἄλλοτ' ἀν' ὠκεανὸν ποταμὸν καὶ πείρατα γαίης,
     ἄλλοτ' ἀν' ἤπειρον πολυβώλακα· γίγνετο δ' αἰεὶ
     θηρί', ὅσ' ἤπειρος αἰνὰ τρέφει, ὄφρα φύγοι νιν.

(Athenaios 334 B = *Kypria* F 7 Allen). Welcker thought that there was
a lacuna after the first line but there is no need to assume one; the
subject of τέκε in line 1 need not be the same as that of τέκε in line 3.
The awkwardness is due to τέκε having to mean 'bring forth', and
'hatch', the egg of Nemesis.[1] The swift changes of shape by the goddess
recall the rapid metamorphoses of the Old Man of the Sea in the *Odyssey*
(4.455–459) and of the Neleid Periklymenos in his combat with Herakles
(*P.Oxy.* 2485 and 2486, 13–18); and her flight reminds us of the
successful escape of Thetis from Zeus, which also was described in
the *Kypria* (F 2 Allen).[2]

When Helen fled with Paris they sailed, according to Homer and the
Proklan summary, to Sidon. Herodotos (2.117) however believed that
the *Kypria* could not have been by Homer because in the version
known to him the lovers went straight to Troy 'with a smooth sea and
a fair wind': the historian's words recall a hexameter πνεύματί τ' εὐαεῖ
λείῃ τε θαλάσσῃ vel sim., as Welcker saw (2.515). There must therefore
have been another version of the *Kypria* from which the voyage to
Sidon was excluded. It so happens that one of the authors claimed for
the *Kypria* was a Halikarnassian, from the home town of Herodotos
(Demodamas 428 F 1); Herodotos, then, may well have known a
local, divergent, poem on the subject of the *Kypria* [see also *G.R.B.S.*
8 (1967) 25–27].

The visit to Sidon almost certainly involved a visit to Cyprus. Helen
is said to have had a son Pleisthenes whom she took to Cyprus, and
another son Aganos whom she bore to Alexandros (Schol. Eur.
Androm. 828). Moreover Apollodoros (*Epit.* 3.3–4) states that Alexandros
stayed with Helen for some time in Phoenicia and Cyprus to avoid
pursuit. The Paphian goddess Aphrodite may well have featured in the

[1] On the confusion between Leda and Nemesis see, however, B. C. Dietrich,
Death, Fate and the Gods (London 1965) 158.

[2] See also E. Bethe 2.155. According to Philodemos (περὶ εὐσεβ. ap. Bethe
2.158) Nemesis produced (τεκεῖν) the egg when she was in the form of a goose,
as the *Kypria* stated; but Leda was pursued by Zeus who appeared as a swan.

The *Kypria*

Cypriote and Levantine episodes, and can hardly have been absent from any version that may have been composed by the Cypriote poet Stasinos, one of the alleged authors of the *Kypria*. Here we may note fitly that Aphrodite of Cyprus was, like the Muse, regarded as a patroness of song; δὸς δ' ἱμερόεσσαν ἀοιδήν, begs a poet who knows her as queen of Salamis in Cyprus (Hom. *Hymn* 10.5), and another who asks her for victory in what is evidently a Cyprian competition (Hom. *Hymn* 6.19–20) says δὸς δ' ἐν ἀγῶνι | νίκην τῷδε φέρεσθαι. The ancient notion therefore that the *Kypria* was composed by a Cypriote has considerable merit.

When Menelaos had agreed with Agamemnon that Helen must be recovered by force of arms, he went to consult Nestor, who, reports the summary, told him stories of heroes in earlier generations and their dealings with women. The entertainment is the most likely context for verses in praise of wine, which may well have been spoken by Nestor: 'Menelaos, you must know that the gods made wine as the best thing for mortal men to scatter their cares' (Athen. 35 C).

οἶνόν τοι, Μενέλαε, θεοὶ ποίησαν ἄριστον
θνητοῖς ἀνθρώποισιν ἀποσκεδάσαι μελεδῶνας.

Afterwards Nestor and Menelaos went on a tour of Greece; this tour served in place of the Catalogue of Ships which had already been preempted by the *Iliad*; the Catalogue's traditional place in the epic scheme was in the muster at Aulis (Wade-Gery 53). Consistently the Proklan summary omits the Achaean catalogue from the muster at Aulis, and reserves the Catalogue of the Trojan allies for the aftermath of the Great Foray of Achilles, prior to which Priam's allies were not concerned in the defence of Ilios. The recruiting tour was itself an early part of the tradition; Nestor himself in the *Iliad* mentions his arrival at Phthia to summon troops to the muster (11.767–784), but on this occasion he was accompanied by Odysseus, not Menelaos. Since Menelaos was the obvious person to recruit the avenging army, the *Iliad*'s version is likely to be secondary.[1]

The portent of the snake and sparrows at Aulis had already appeared in the *Iliad* before its inclusion in the *Kypria*. Its significance was explained by Kalchas, that the nine sparrows were the nine years of

[1] Johansen 114 n. 184.

war to come: 'For that number of years ... from now shall we campaign but in the tenth shall we take the city of the broad streets' (*Iliad* 2.328–329).

ὣς ἡμεῖς τοσσαῦτ' ἔτεα πτολεμίξομεν αὖθι,
τῷ δεκάτῳ δὲ πόλιν αἱρήσομεν εὐρυάγυιαν.

αὖθι here means 'forthwith'. So the ten years of the war were counted from the first muster at Aulis before the mistaken attack on Teuthrania and the regrouping again at Aulis. It follows that the time spent by the Achaean force continuously beneath the walls of Troy was considerably less than ten years. The visit of Achilles to Skyros and his wedding to Deidameia followed the Teuthranian campaign. A consequence of the visit was the birth of Neoptolemos, whose name was given by Phoenix, according to the *Kypria* (Pausanias 10.26.4).

The second muster at Aulis was marked by the attempted sacrifice of Iphigeneia to secure favourable winds. Homer knows of three daughters of Agamemnon; the *Kypria* mentioned Iphigeneia as a fourth (F 15 Allen. Cf. *P.Oxy.* 2513, 14); her appearance in the story looks to be a recent innovation, as is her melodramatic rescue by Artemis. Yet even here the notion of substitution of victims at a sacrifice must be admitted to be ancient, as the story of Abraham and Isaac shows. The carrying of Iphigeneia to the Tauroi perhaps reflects early Hellenic knowledge of the north Black Sea shores; the story is unlikely therefore to have been current long before about 700 B.C. Homer, on the other hand, shares with the *Kypria* summary the story of Philoktetes' abandonment on Lemnos (*Iliad* 2.721–724), and this may be a very early element in the tale of Troy.

The theme of Achilles' dispute with Agamemnon over the late invitation to the feast at Tenedos is less certainly Homeric. Demodokos sings in the *Odyssey* (8.73–82) of a famous quarrel of Achilles and Odysseus at a feast of the gods. This quarrel pleased Agamemnon because, Homer implies, Apollo in Pytho had predicted success when the best of the Achaeans should fall out: 'for then rolled on the beginning of trouble for the Trojans and Danaans, through the counsels of great Zeus.' The *beginning* of trouble surely refers to an early stage in the war, and the Odyssean Scholiasts can hardly be correct in seeing here an allusion to an otherwise unattested dispute between Achilles and Odysseus after Hector's death, late in the war. Nor would Agamemnon cheerfully recall such an oracle after the disastrous quarrel between himself and Achilles, which was the core of the *Iliad*.[1] A feast and sacrifice in Tenedos would suit Homer's words θεῶν ἐν δαιτὶ θαλείῃ (*Od.* 8.76); but a quarrel between Achilles and Agamemnon is less apt, for Homer says that the dispute was between Achilles and Odysseus. The feast in Tenedos was the subject of the *Syndeipnoi* of Sophokles; in this play a dispute between Agamemnon and Achilles was followed by abuse between Odysseus and Achilles (Sophokles F 566 and 567 Pearson); here, verily, was a dispute between leaders of the Achaeans – three of them. I incline therefore to the view that Demodokos sang of the feast at Tenedos; but no doubt Apollo had carefully failed to define who were the 'best' of the Achaeans.

Two verses, not explicitly assigned to the *Kypria*, perhaps belong to the context of the feast in Tenedos. Agamemnon says:

οὐκ ἐφάμην ᾿Αχιλῆι χολωσέμεν ἄλκιμον ἦτορ
ὧδε μάλ᾿ ἐκπάγλως, ἐπεὶ ἦ μάλα μοι φίλος ἦεν.

(*Kypria* F 16 Allen)

'I never thought to anger so dreadfully the doughty heart of Achilles, for dearly beloved was he to me.' If these words are correctly placed – they hardly suit the bitterness of the *Iliad*, then the failure to invite Achilles on time was not deliberate.

At the landing in the Troad, says Proklos in his summary, Protesilaos was killed by Hektor. Here too the *Kypria* enlarges upon the *Ilia* which is content to remark that a Dardanian man slew him (2.701). His widow in Phylake is mentioned by Homer (*Iliad* 2.700), but he does not name her; again enlarging upon the *Iliad*, the *Kypria* reported that she was Polydora, daughter of Meleager (Pausanias 4.2.7).

After the death of Protesilaos and the routing of the Trojans by Achilles there came the embassy to demand the return of Helen. As we learn from the *Iliad* (3.205-224), the Achaean emissaries, Menelaos and Odysseus, were welcomed by Antenor in Troy. He befriended them and even saved their lives when the Trojan Antimachos had demanded

[1] Cf. W. B. Stanford, *The Odyssey of Homer* Vol. I (London 1959) 333.

in the assembly that the two heroes should be put to death (cf. *Iliad* 11.138–141).[1] Later, when Troy was sacked, Antenor's house was spared in recognition of his loyalty to his distinguished Achaean guests.

No fragment alludes to the great battle at the wall, but this was an important part of the story, as can be seen in the *Iliad* which mentions it several times. Its place in legend was perhaps assured by the visible remains of the great fortification walls of Troy VI which must have been remarked by epic poets or their Aeolian informants from the mid-eighth century B.C. onwards, if indeed memories of it were not handed down in oral tradition from the Mycenaean age.[2] Pindar (*Ol.* 8.30) states that Aiakos helped Poseidon and Apollo to build the wall, and a scholiast commenting on the passage explains that the gods had to be helped by a mortal in order that the entire city should not be impregnable. Homer knew of a place by a fig tree where the wall could be stormed and alludes to the battle there, in which the two Aiante, Idomeneus, Agamemnon and Menelaos, and Diomedes thrice led the assault on the city at its weakest point (*Iliad* 6.433–437):

$$\pi\alpha\rho' \ \dot{\epsilon}\rho\iota\nu\epsilon\acute{o}\nu, \ \ddot{\epsilon}\nu\theta\alpha \ \mu\acute{\alpha}\lambda\iota\sigma\tau\alpha$$
$$\dot{\alpha}\mu\beta\alpha\tau\acute{o}\varsigma \ \dot{\epsilon}\sigma\tau\iota \ \pi\acute{o}\lambda\iota\varsigma \ \kappa\alpha\grave{\iota} \ \dot{\epsilon}\pi\acute{\iota}\delta\rho\omega\mu\omega\nu \ \ddot{\epsilon}\pi\lambda\epsilon\tau\omega \ \tau\epsilon\hat{\iota}\chi\omega\varsigma.$$

The Great Foray in the *Kypria* included attacks on Lyrnessos, Pedasos and other cities as well as the driving off of the cattle of Aineias. In the *Iliad* Briseis (whose name simply means 'the girl from Brisa' in Lesbos) is taken from Lyrnessos (2.689–690) and Chryseis from Thebe beneath Mount Plakie (1.366–369). The poets of the *Kypria* however differed from Homer as to Briseis; for they said that she was taken from Pedasos (*Kypria* F 18 Allen). Amongst the other places attacked in the Great Foray were Lesbos (*Iliad* 9.129), Skyros (9.668), and Tenedos (11.625)[3] – though this island may have been attacked on the way to Troy; the cattle raid of Achilles on Ida is also mentioned by Homer (*Iliad* 20.89–96), who makes Aineias recall how he had run away with the help of Zeus – at exceptional speed, no doubt, since Achilles was noted for his swiftness of foot.

[1] See also Jebb, *Bacchylides* p. 219 on *Ode* xiv; Bacchylides seems to have known this episode in the *Kypria*.

[2] C. M. Bowra, *J.H.S.* 80 (1960) 17 and 21.

[3] W. Leaf, *Troy* (London 1912) 397–399.

The *Kypria*

One problem which exercised the poets of the *Kypria* was the feeding of so vast a host at Troy. In the poem, Anios king of Delos is said to have told the Achaeans that if they were to wait with him for nine years they would take Troy in the tenth; this story, which was repeated by Pherekydes (3 F 140), depends on the prophecy of Kalchas at Aulis. The suggestion of Anios, whose daughters, the Oinotropoi, could have supplied the host, was ignored at the time. But later in the war, as Simonides, who may well have followed the *Kypria* here, reported (F 32 Page), Menelaos and Odysseus were sent to Delos to enlist the aid of the Oinotropoi;[1] these ladies – Oino, Spermo, and Elais – had the valuable power of producing unlimited wine, corn and olive oil from the earth (Apollod. *Epit.* 3.10). Rationalising historians, such as Hellanikos and Thucydides, could not accept such a tale into their narratives; so they tried to explain it away. Hellanikos (4 F 27) in writing about Krithote 'Barley-town', may well have had his Achaeans farm the Thracian Chersonese,[2] as Thucydides (1.11.1), who perhaps followed the *Troika* of Hellanikos, says they did so, to feed the army. The *Troika* of the Lesbian historian may well have drawn heavily on the *Kypria*; in turn the Hellanikan view of the Trojan War is perhaps reflected in the *Epitome* of Apollodoros, where there are some divergences from the Homeric Catalogue – in the sizes of contingents in the Catalogue of Ships, for example. Thus he, or the authors of the *Kypria*, reduced the Boiotian force by giving them forty instead of fifty ships (Apollod. *Epit.* 3.11).

The death of Palamedes was an outcome of that hero's stratagem to force the malingering Odysseus to go to Troy. Palamedes was killed by Menelaos and Odysseus; they drowned him while he was fishing (Paus. 10.31.2). Here too is a sign of independence in the *Kypria*. In the *Iliad*, as the ancients noted, fishing is essentially unheroic.

Other fragments ascribed to the *Kypria* are not to be placed with confidence. The wife of Aineias is said to be Eurydike (*Kypria* F 22 Allen: Paus. 10.26.1); in what context she was mentioned we do not know. Aineias was prominent in at least two parts of the poem, the

---

[1] Odysseus had also visited Delos on the way to Troy, as he tells Nausikaa (*Od.* 6.164).

[2] See also Jacoby on Hellanikos F 27.

Greek Epic Poetry

voyage of Paris to Lakedaimon and the cattle raid on Ida. Two moralising verses are ascribed to the *Kypria* by a Scholiast to Plato (*Euthyphro* 12 A): 'You do not like to say that it is Zeus who has done this and caused all these things to be; for where fear is there too is shame.'

> Ζῆνα δὲ τόν θ' ἔρξαντα καὶ ὃς τάδε πάντ' ἐφύτευσεν
> οὐκ ἐθέλεις εἰπεῖν· ἵνα γὰρ δέος ἔνθα καὶ αἰδώς.
> 1. ῥέξαντα Stobaios.   2. ἐθέλει νεικεῖν Burnet.

Here perhaps is more advice from Nestor to an indignant Menelaos, but 'shame' suggests the possibility of a conversation between Paris and Helen. It seems that whoever composed these verses knew of the story of Zeus's plan.

The ascription of a fragment about remotest Ocean to the *Kypria* surprises (F 24 Allen). A likely context is the flight of Thetis from Zeus. Herodian (περὶ μον. λέξ. 9) states that the island Sarpedon lay in Ocean and was the dwelling place of the Gorgons. Then he quotes these lines:

> τῷ δ' ὑποκυσαμένη τέκε Γοργόνας αἰνὰ πέλωρα,
> αἳ Σαρπηδόνα ναῖον ἐπ' ὠκεανῷ βαθυδίνῃ,
> νῆσον πετρήεσσαν.

'Becoming with child by him she bore the Gorgons, dread monsters who dwelt in Sarpedon, a rocky island in deeply whirling Ocean.' The passage refers to Phorkos and Keto, parents of the Gorgons; their genealogy had already been given by Hesiod (*Theogony* 270 ff). Phorkos and Keto were brother and sister. Their eldest brother was Nereus, whose daughter Thetis was. It would have been understandable therefore if Thetis had fled from Zeus to her kinsfolk living at the extremities of the world. The dread Gorgons may even have afforded her some defence against the father of the gods.

Homer was loth to omit a traditional document, the catalogue of Trojan allies, from his poem; so he placed it after the muster of the Achaeans near the beginning of the *Iliad*. The *Kypria* returned it to its proper place in the traditional order of events, after the vexatious Foray of Achilles which incited the neighbouring peoples, and some more distant nations, to ally themselves with Priam. There are signs that the Trojan Catalogue may have been slightly enlarged in the Kyprian version. Three lines in the Paphlagonian section (*Iliad* 2.853–855) were not read by Eratosthenes and by Apollodoros of Athens (Strabo 298 and 553);[1] and a text known to Kallisthenes introduced Kaukones, who indeed do appear amongst Trojan allies in the *Iliad*, after the Paphlagonians (Strabo 542). Some added a hero Pelegonos to the contingent from the land through which the Axios flowed (*Iliad* 2.848a). Apollodoros the mythographer (*Epitome* 3.34–35) adds a few more names, which perhaps come through the *Troika* of Hellanikos from the catalogue in the *Kypria*.[2] As in the Proklan summary, the Trojan allies are listed in the *Epitome* before the beginning of the *Iliad* proper. The detailed listing of Aeolian and north Ionian place names in the Apollodoran account of the Great Foray also points to Hellanikos of Lesbos as an intermediate source between the *Kypria* and the *Epitome* (3.32–33). One version of the *Kypria* synopsis omits the Trojan catalogue, perhaps out of deference to the *Iliad*.[3]

The chief aim of the poets of the *Kypria* was, we may be sure, to give the succession of events. These were taken from the tradition and, with some form of the *Iliad* in mind, augmented. The poem compensated for its lack of structural unity by offering much variety and great excitement, occasionally even melodrama. The story is dominated by Zeus, whose supremacy the poets were at pains to emphasise, and follows logically from the disastrous but inevitable decision of Paris to choose Aphrodite. The *Kypria* lacked the moral greatness of the *Iliad*; but we cannot declare that it deserved to be lost, for it was read and valued throughout antiquity. At the very least it offered tragedians abundant scope for the construction of ingenious plots. But it was of greater worth than a literary storehouse; parts of it expressed in elevated diction moments of supreme beauty, as in the robing of Aphrodite, or principles of genuinely philosophical and moral significance, such as the groaning of Earth, a goddess more aged and so more venerable than Zeus himself, at the weight of mankind's myriads. The

[1] T. W. Allen, *The Homeric Catalogue of Ships* (Oxford 1921) 156 f.

[2] Wade-Gery 85. The painter of a fragmentary Corinthian krater in the Louvre (E 638 (1)) where a number of Trojans and their allies are depicted with Achilles slaying Troilos on the altar of Apollo may well have been influenced by the Trojan catalogue in the *Kypria*, especially since the death of Troilos was told in that poem (Johansen 83–84).

[3] A. Severyns, *Mélanges Henri Grégoire* 2 (Brussels 1950) 578.

author of the *Kypria*, and those who imitated or repeated his poem, were capable of excellence; and Homer himself would surely have welcomed Stasinos as a son-in-law if the Cypriote had indeed, as ancients asserted, proved himself able to compose a comprehensive epic of such complexity and vision.

One story from the preliminaries to the *Iliad* is assigned not to the *Kypria* but to 'the authors who arranged the *Troika*' (οἱ συντεταχότες τὰ Τρωικά: Schol. Eur. *Androm.* 1139). It is said that when Achilles landed at Troy a spring flowed at his feet; and some believed (a little illogically) that he was the *last* to land from his ship, because an oracle had declared that the *first* to land would die first (Schol. Lyk. *Alex.* 246). The Lykophron scholia quote some hexameters to illustrate this tale and ascribe them to an Antimachos.[1] The ascription and the alleged context are both questionable, and we should resist the temptation to emend the verses to suit a landing by Achilles from a ship,[2] for the hero is clearly stated to leap from the ground. 'Fleetly leaping on high from the dark land did the son of Peleus start up like a hawk; and before his feet there welled up an ever flowing spring.'

ῥίμφα δ' ἀπ' ἠπείροιο μελαίνης ὑψόσ' ἀερθεὶς
Πηλείδης ἀνόρουσεν ἐλαφρῶς ἠύτε κίρκος·
τοῦ δ' ἔμπροσθε ποδῶν κρήνη γένετ' ἀενάουσα.

These verses evidently provide an *aition* for one of the places called Achilles' Fount or Achilles' Leap. One such was the *Achilleion* at Miletos (Aristoboulos 139 F 6), a spring in which Achilles took a shower after he had killed Trambelos, king of the Leleges. An attack on Miletos in the Great Foray would help to explain the presence of troops from as far away as Miletos amongst the allies of Priam (*Iliad* 2.868).[3]

So long as the Achaean host faced Troy with the certainty that the city was alone, there was some hope of early success. But the need for food led to the cattle raids of the Great Foray; the Asiatics rallied and so Priam's strength grew formidably. Homer was aware of the significance of the allies in altering the balance of power; until the other

[1] [Antimachos] F 84 Wyss.
[2] Cf. P. Maas ap. *F.Gr. Hist.* I², 48 bis F 1, Komm.
[3] For a different view see West, *Philologus* 110 (1966) 157.

The *Kypria*

Asiatics came to Troy there were more than ten times as many Achaeans in the field as defending Trojans, he believed (*Iliad* 2.123–133). Zeus's second plan was thus doubly effective; for at the end of the *Kypria* he had arranged to eliminate Achilles from the campaign at the very moment when the arrival of the allies was changing the defence from a beleaguered and outnumbered garrison into a numerous and capable foe, eager to hurl the Achaeans back against their ships. The poet of the *Kypria* like Homer himself, was, we may be sure, determined to emphasise the growing plight of Agamemnon's troops at the opening of the *Iliad* by drawing attention to the enlarged host now ready to fight for Troy's survival.

XI

The Aftermath of the *Iliad*

In the *Chrestomathy* of Proklos the Trojan story from the death of Hektor to the departure of the Achaeans from Troy extends through eleven books – about the length of the *Kypria* therefore. But these eleven books are said there to comprise three distinct poems. The *Aithiopis* of Arktinos the Milesian, the *Little Iliad* of Lesches of Pyrrha or of Mytilene in Lesbos, and the *Sack of Troy*, also by Arktinos. Both authors may have composed or even written down poems with those titles; but the fragments assigned to Arktinos and Lesches suggest that at some time both of them must also have treated the entire tale from the death of Hektor to the end of Troy. It will be convenient therefore to give first a translation of the summaries of all three poems in the *Chrestomathy* before attempting to place the fragments in their contexts. If, as we have suggested, the two poets were contemporaries, and if both composed poems overlapping in subject matter, then a contest between them was to be expected. Contemporary opinion was said to have judged Lesches to be the better poet (Phainias of Eresos ap. Clem. Alex. *Strom.* 1.131). There was a local tradition in Lesbos that Lesches was earlier than Terpander, who flourished about 676 B.C. when he performed at Sparta (Hellanikos 4 F 32a, b with Phainias *loc. cit.*).[1] Lesches and Arktinos, then, can reasonably be supposed to have competed about 700 B.C. So Artemon's estimate in his book on Homer that Homer's pupil Arktinos was born (if that is what γέγονε means in the context[2]) in the ninth Olympiad (744/1 B.C.) was close to the truth (*F.Gr.Hist.* 443 F 2).

The summary of the second book of the *Chrestomathy* begins with the *Iliad*: 'upon the *Kypria* there follows the *Iliad* of Homer. After this

[1] Terpander is usually accounted a melic poet; but he is also called ἐπῶν ποιητής by [Plutarch] *De. Mus.* 1132C.

[2] Cf. E. Rohde, *R.M.* 33 (1878) 161–220.

come the five books of the *Aithiopis* by Arktinos of Miletos, with the following contents. An Amazon Penthesileia joins the Trojans as an ally. A Thracian by descent, she was a daughter of Ares. While fighting valiantly she is killed by Achilles and the Trojans bury her. Next Achilles kills Thersites for insulting and reviling him because of his alleged passion for Penthesileia. Consequently a dispute arises amongst the Achaeans over the murder of Thersites.

'Achilles then sails to Lesbos and after sacrificing to Apollo, Artemis and Leto, is purified from the murder by Odysseus. Then Memnon, son of Eos (the Dawn), bringing with him a panoply made by Hephaistos comes to the aid of the Trojans, and Thetis tells her son about the coming fate of Memnon. When a battle takes place, Antilochos is killed by Memnon, and Memnon by Achilles. Thereupon Eos begs of Zeus immortality for her son and bestows it upon him.

'Achilles puts the Trojans to flight and pursuing them into the city is killed by Paris and Apollo. There ensues a great battle over the corpse, which Aias picks up and carries to the ships while Odysseus fights off the Trojans behind. Then the Achaeans bury Antilochos and lay out the corpse of Achilles.

'Thetis, coming with the Muses and her sisters, laments for her son. Next she snatches him away from the pyre and conveys him to the White Island. After that the Achaeans pile a burial mound for him and hold games. A quarrel arises between Odysseus and Aias over the arms of Achilles.

'There follow the four books of the *Little Iliad* by Lesches of Mytilene, comprising the following events. The adjudging of the arms is held and Odysseus, through the devising of Athena, wins them. But Aias becomes mad and slaughters the cattle taken by the Achaeans and kills himself.

'After that Odysseus captures in an ambush Helenos, who foretells how Troy must be taken; so Diomedes brings Philoktetes from Lemnos. Philoktetes is healed by Machaon and kills Alexandros in a duel; the corpse is mutilated by Menelaos before the Trojans recover and bury it. Next Deïphobos married Helen.

'Odysseus fetches Neoptolemos from Skyros and gives him his father's arms; and the ghost of Achilles appears to him. Eurypylos son of Telephos comes to help the Trojans and shows great courage but is killed by Neoptolemos. The Trojans are now besieged and Epeios, on Athena's set purpose, constructs the wooden horse. Odysseus then disfigures himself and enters Ilios as a spy. Being recognised by Helen he concerts plans with her for the taking of the city and, after killing some of the Trojans, returns to the ships. After that he carries the Palladion out of Ilios with the help of Diomedes.[1] Then, having placed their best warriors inside the wooden horse and burned their tents, the rest of the Hellenes sail to Tenedos. The Trojans, supposing that they were now rid of their troubles, take down part of their wall and accept the wooden horse into the city. They now feast, as though they had defeated the Hellenes.

'Two books of the *Sack of Ilios* by Arktinos of Miletos follow with these contents. Being suspicious of the circumstances of the horse the Trojans stood around it and deliberated what to do. Some advised the throwing of it down from the rocks, others the burning of it, but some said that it ought to be dedicated to Athena. In the end this last opinion prevailed.

'They now turn to good cheer and banqueting, believing themselves to be quit of the war, but in the midst of this there appeared two snakes which destroyed Laokoon and one of his two sons. At this portent, Aineias and his followers in their dismay departed secretly for Mount Ida.

'Sinon, who had earlier entered the city by pretence, now raises the fire-signals to the Achaeans, who sailed over from Tenedos, while the men from the wooden horse fall upon the enemy and after killing many of them take the city by force.

'Neoptolemos kills Priam who had fled to the altar of Zeus Herkeios; and Menelaos finds Helen and leads her down to the ships, after killing Deiphobos; but Aias son of Ileus, in trying to drag Kassandra away violently, pulls over with her the image of Athena. The Hellenes are so incensed at this that they determine to stone Aias. But he escapes to the altar of Athena and saves himself from the imminent danger.

'The Hellenes now sail away and Athena plans to wreck them at sea.

---

[1] Rylands Papyrus 22 gives a different summary of these events, in which the Palladion is captured before the arrival of Eurypylos.

The Aftermath of the *Iliad*

When Odysseus had murdered Astyanax, Neoptolemos took Andro-mache as a prize, and the remaining spoils are distributed. Demophon and Akamas who had found Aithra take her with them. After firing the city the Greeks sacrifice Polyxena at the tomb of Achilles.'

The *Tabula Iliaca* (Kinkel p. 3) agrees with Proklos in distinguishing the *Aithiopis* of Arktinos from the *Little Iliad* of Lesches the Pyrrhaian,[1] and from the *Sack*; the *Sack* is given by the Tabula to Stesichoros, though how far this monument, which was found by the Via Appia near Bovillae, represents the truly Stesichorean version is open to question (Stesichoros F 28 Page). In pre-Alexandrian times the expression *Little Iliad* seems to have covered nearly all the events at Troy subsequent to the *Iliad* of Homer. Thus Aristotle (*Poetics* 23) states that more than eight tragedies may be constructed from the *Little Iliad*, of which one is the *Sack of Troy*. In his view therefore the *Sack* was part of the *Little Iliad*, not as in Proklos a separate poem. Proklos in producing a continuous narrative of the *Posthomerica* chooses from versions ascribed to Lesches and Arktinos. These versions were, as we shall see, in places inconsistent, but Proklos, to preserve the succession of events, has selectively smoothed over or ignored contradictions.

We can now turn to the fragments. Two verses quoted by a Scholium to the last line of the *Iliad* show how that poem was linked, by a cue, to the story of Penthesileia. Here the linkings of the end of Hesiod's *Theogony* to the *Catalogues of Women*, of *Catalogues* Book iv to the *Shield* and of the *Days* to the *Ornithomanteia* are analogous.

$$\text{ὡς οἵ γ' ἀμφίεπον τάφον }\text{"Εκτορος}\begin{cases}\cdot\text{ἦλθε δ' }\text{'Αμαζών}\\ \text{ἱπποδάμοιο.}\end{cases}$$

$$\text{"Αρηος θυγάτηρ μεγαλήτορος ἀνδροφόνοιο}$$

(Aithiopis F 1 Allen)

'So were they busy about the tomb of Hektor. But there came an Amazon, a daughter of great-hearted Ares, slayer of men.' The verses

---

[1] The 'Homeric bowl' from Anthedon also gives a *Little Iliad* to Lesches (F. Courby, *Vases grecs à reliefs* [1922] 286, no. 8). These bowls were made about 275 B.C. (see H. A. Thompson, *Hesperia* 3 [1934] 457). Another bowl, unfortunately damaged, may ascribe a *Nostoi* to Agias the Troizenian (Severyns 403). The ascriptions are valuable, because they prove that the poems' authorship was not conjectured by Proklos but was generally believed many centuries earlier than his epoch.

are not ascribed to the *Aithiopis* of Arktinos, but they clearly belong to the immediate aftermath of the *Iliad*. The fragment agrees with Proklos in making the Amazon a daughter of Ares. Amazons already appear in Subgeometric art, for example on a terracotta votive shield from Tiryns soon after 700 B.C.,[1] about the time Arktinos was composing poetry about them. Penthesileia, according to Proklos, came from Thrace, but in the *Iliad* the Amazons are active in Asia Minor; Priam had seen a host of them by the river Sangarios when he fought as an ally of the Phrygians (3.189), and the third of Bellerophon's tasks was to campaign from Lykia against the Amazons, 'a match for men' (6.186). The change by Arktinos from Asia Minor to Thrace perhaps reflects increasing Ionian interest in the northern Aegean coasts and the Thraceward regions about 700 B.C., but a little later Magnes of Smyrna, a favourite of king Gyges of Lydia, composed a heroic poem on a war between Lydians and Amazons, which was evidently set in Asia Minor (Nikolaos of Damascus 90 F 62). Achilles and Penthesileia are first certainly represented together on a bronze shield strip from Delphi about 600 B.C. (Bothmer No. I, 10).

No fragment from the *Aithiopis* describes Memnon. As son of Dawn, Eos, he is likely to have come from the East. Proklos does not claim that Arktinos called him an Aithiopian, but the title of the poem *Aithiopis* shows that Memnon is likely to have been so named in it. The idea that Aithiopians lived in eastern parts as well as in the far south may well lie at the origin of the Herodotean theory that Kolchians, Egyptians and Aithiopians were all related (Herod. 2.104). From the *Tabula Iliaca* we learn that Achilles killed Memnon at the Skaian gates (*Hom. Op.* V 126 Allen). This may have happened immediately before Achilles, having thrown back the Trojans, was slain within the city by Paris. Memnon's killing of Antilochos was already known to the *Odyssey* (4.187–8); here too he is called a son of Dawn, so the affiliation may not be an extravagant innovation by Arktinos.

Proklos says nothing about a weighing of the souls of Achilles and Memnon by Zeus, while each mother, Thetis and Eos respectively, prayed that her son be saved. But a form of this *psychostasia* was popular in art from the seventh century onwards and the theme was

---

[1] Von Bothmer 1–2.

developed by Aeschylus (F 205 Mette); it had already appeared in the *Iliad* where the fates of Hektor and Achilles were weighed (22.208–213). There is thus a strong likelihood that the fates of Achilles and Memnon were said to have been weighed in the *Aithiopis* (Johansen 261).

It is remarkable that Aristotle in the *Poetics* does not include an *Amazonis* or *Aithiopis* in the themes to be subsumed under the *Little Iliad*. Perhaps therefore he regarded the *Aithiopis* as a distinct poem following the *Iliad* and preceding the *Little Iliad*. That there was disagreement about the point in the tradition at which the *Aithiopis* ended can be seen from the statement that the 'writer of the *Aithiopis*' declared Aias to have killed himself at dawn (*Aithiopis* F 2 Allen).[1] The suicide of Aias is given by Proklos to the *Little Iliad*, and so may not have been properly part of the *Aithiopis*. On the other hand 'the writer of the *Aithiopis*' may be a loose way of saying 'Arktinos'. The White Island to which Thetis conveyed her son lay off the mouth of the Danube, a river known to Hesiod but ignored by Homer; the allusion indicates Milesian interest in Pontic exploration as early as 700 B.C. As a Milesian, Arktinos can hardly have ignored growing Ionian geographical knowledge, which we saw also reflected in the Pontic expansions of the Trojan Catalogue in the *Kypria*. The lamenting for Achilles by the Muses, which Proklos reports in the *Aithiopis*, recurs in the supplementary twenty-fourth book of the *Odyssey* (24.60 ff), to which the idea perhaps came from Arktinos; but in the *Odyssey* the bones of Achilles and Patroklos are gathered together in a golden amphora (24.74) and there is no mention of Thetis conveying her son to the White Island from the pyre by the Hellespont.

When Achilles died, his arms were to be assigned to the best of the Achaeans. The dispute between the finalists, Aias and Odysseus, was resolved by a suggestion of Nestor, who recommended the sending of persons beneath the battlements of Troy to overhear Trojan comments on the heroes. This quaint story is ascribed to the *Little Iliad* by a scholiast on Aristophanes (*Knights* 1056); in it the spies hear two Trojan maidens conversing. One held Aias to be the superior and said: 'For

[1] The suicide was known at Corinth already early in the seventh century, for it appears on a Protocorinthian aryballos (Johansen 30 and Fig. 4).

Aias took up and carried out of the battle the hero, Peleus' son; but lordly Odysseus cared not to do that.'

Αἴας μὲν γὰρ ἄειρε καὶ ἔκφερε δηιοτῆτος
ἥρω Πηλείδην οὐδ' ἤθελε δῖος 'Οδυσσεύς.

To this the other replied, prompted by Athena: 'How can you have asserted that? What you have said is against sense and false. . . . Even a woman could carry a load once a man had put it on her shoulder.'

πῶς ἐπεφώνησω; πῶς οὐ κατὰ κόσμον ἔειπες
ψεῦδος; . . .
καί κε γυνὴ φέροι ἄχθος ἐπεί κεν ἀνὴρ ἀναθείη.

ψεῦδος may be intrusive, in which case we have a couplet in reply to a couplet. The concluding phrase quoted by the scholiast

ἀλλ' οὐκ ἂν μαχέσαιτο· [χέσαιτο γὰρ εἰ μαχέσαιτο]

is to be rejected as unbecoming to epic dignity.

The story of the carrying of Achilles from the battle is early; it appears already before the end of the eighth century B.C. in the Euboian colony in the island of Pithekoussai off Naples, in the impression of a sealstone[1] and was presumably well known in eastern Greece in Miletos or Lesbos quite as early. Representations of the same scene have been found also at Perachora near Corinth on an ivory signet and in Samos in a terracotta relief; both are as early as 700 B.C.[2] There were however differing opinions as to the carrier of the body. In the Trojan conversation and in the Proklan *Chrestomathy* the corpse is taken up by Aias; but a scholiast on *Odyssey* 5.310 states that Odysseus carried it, and in a papyrus fragment of an early epic it appears that Odysseus not only proposed to carry the corpse but also did take it up (*P.Oxy.* 2510, 13 and 21). It is tempting to ascribe one view to Lesches, its opposite to his rival Arktinos; but the reported existence of other *Little Iliads* – by Thestorides of Phokaia, Kinaithon, and Diodoros of Erythrai (Schol. Eur. *Troad.* 822) – warns us against this over-neat explanation.

The awarding of the arms to Odysseus made Aias insane. His madness was first recognised by the physician Podaleirios, who was as successful in diagnosis as Machaon was excellent in surgery. Some verses ascribed to 'Arktinos in the *Sacking of Troy*' emphasise the contrast in their abilities: 'For their father, the renowned Earth-Shaker, endowed both of them and made each more glorious than the other. To one he gave hands more gentle to withdraw or cut out shafts from the flesh and to heal all kinds of wounds; to the other he gave accurate knowledge of all things in his heart and to perceive hidden things and to heal festering diseases. He it was who first perceived the flashing eyes and burdened mind of Aias in his rage.'

αὐτὸς γάρ σφιν ἔδωκε πατὴρ κλυτὸς Ἐννοσίγαιος
ἀμφοτέροις, ἕτερον δ᾽ ἑτέρου κυδίον᾽ ἔθηκε·
τῷ μὲν κουφοτέρας χεῖρας πόρεν ἔκ τε βέλεμνα
σαρκὸς ἑλεῖν τμῆξαί τε καὶ ἕλκεα πάντ᾽ ἀκέσασθαι,
5   τῷ δ᾽ ἄρ᾽ ἀκριβέα πάντα ἐνὶ στήθεσσιν ἔθηκεν
ἄσκοπά τε γνῶναι καὶ ἀναλθέα ἰήσασθαι·
ὅς ῥα καὶ Αἴαντος πρῶτος μάθε χωομένοιο
ὄμματά τ᾽ ἀστράπτοντα βαρυνόμενόν τε νόημα.

        1. κλ. Ἐν. Heyne. Ἐνοσίγαιος πεσεῖν cod. Eustath.

In the *Little Iliad* (F 3 Allen) Aias was not cremated in the usual way owing to Agamemnon's anger at the slaughter of the cattle. Instead he was buried in a coffin. His grave was at Rhoiteion (Apollod. *Epit.* 5.7). Sophokles, perhaps out of deference to the Athenians or the Salaminians, states in his *Ajax* that a ban on burial was rescinded, but this was not the early form of the story.

According to the Pseudo-Herodotean *Life* of Homer, which contains a number of early details, the '*Lesser Iliad*' began: 'I sing of Ilion and Dardania of the fine horses, where the Danaoi, attendants of Ares, did suffer many things' (*Little Iliad* F 1 Allen).

Ἴλιον ἀείδω καὶ Δαρδανίην εὔπωλον
ἧς πέρι πολλὰ πάθον Δαναοὶ θεράποντες Ἄρηος.

We may imagine Homer, pen in hand, praying to the Muse to sing for him of the wrath of Achilles, or, staff in hand, singing of the wrath himself; Hesiod too may be imagined writing down his reproofs to Perses, since a succession of post-Hesiodic oral poets are not likely to have recited instructions to a Perses long since dead; but can a poet who says or sings 'I sing of Ilion' be doing anything but singing? We may conceive of a Hellenistic poet writing ἀείδω or Virgil writing *cano*; but in the still largely oral tradition of early Greece ἀείδω surely implies that the poet is singing or speaking. The writer of the Pseudo-Herodotean *Life* sensed this, and so made his 'Homer' dictate the *Little Iliad* to Thestorides, 'a teacher of letters'. The introduction to the *Little Iliad* could well be a dictated oral text, such as Lord has postulated the originals of *Iliad* and the *Odyssey* to have been;[1] but that it *was* dictated seems to me beyond proof. Similarly, a poet who in the Homeric *Hymn to Demeter* (2.1) says 'I begin to sing of long-haired Demeter, dread goddess . . .' is perhaps less likely to be writing than a poet who says 'Tell me, Muse . . .' (*Od.* 1.1). But here too proof is lacking, because we have no canon to measure the probability or likelihood of such inferences.

If a *Little Iliad* really was set down by Lesches in writing as early as 700 B.C., then there must have existed in Lesbos an adequate supply of writing materials; but that is a factor about which we have as yet no certain knowledge. On the other hand, we must not suppose that because a poem or fragment is expressed in strongly traditional language, it must therefore have been composed orally or dictated by its author. M. Parry's great contribution to Homeric scholarship is to have demonstrated the high antiquity of repeated expressions appearing ubiquitously in the poems; but we must beware of the false reasonings, (1) 'oral' entails 'formulaic' and (2) 'formulaic' entails 'oral'. For epic tags are found in some of the earliest Hellenic inscriptions, and poets with good memories could, no doubt, compose or get by heart long oral poems containing little traditional language. We have to bear in mind too, when identifying 'formulae', that the surviving corpus of early hexameters is but a small part of the whole tradition, so that we have no firm criterion of anti-traditional or non-formulaic language.

Such early autograph or dictated texts as may have been prepared would have been valuable for one purpose above all; as heirlooms they could have been used to check or correct the recitations of rhapsodes who had memorised the words of a poem composed much earlier. For example, they could have been used to control performances by Homeridai of the *Iliad*. Such perhaps was the Solonian or Hipparchian

[1] *T.A.P.A.* 84 (1953) 124–134.

arrangement, according to which rhapsodes could be checked as they recited in succession the works of Homer and took their cues at determinable points in the poems.[1]

But this is not a book on the Homeric question. We must return to the Trojan cycle. The contest for the arms required that the arms be worth having; and the *Little Iliad* left no doubt about their value. The great spear which Cheiron had given to Peleus and taught him to use was described in detail: 'about the shaft was a hoop of flashing gold, and a point was fitted to it at either end.'

$$\text{ἀμφὶ δὲ πόρκης}$$
$$\text{χρύσεος ἀστράπτει καὶ ἐπ' αὐτῷ δίκροος} \begin{cases} \text{αἰχμή.} \\ \text{ἄρδις.} \end{cases}$$

ἄρδις Scaliger (*Little Iliad* F 5 Allen)

The arms did not remain with Odysseus, but were given by him to Neoptolemos when the young hero arrived in Troy. The fetching of Neoptolemos from Skyros is noted in the *Chrestomathy*, and that it was indeed described in a *Little Iliad* is shown by a fragment in which it is explained how Achilles had come to Skyros in the first place: 'the storm carried Achilles, son of Peleus, to Skyros, and he came to a grievous harbour there in the same night.' The occasion was the return, described also in the *Kypria*, to Greece from the battle with Telephos in Mysia.

$$\text{Πηλεΐδην δ' Ἀχιλῆα φέρε Σκυρόνδε θύελλα,}$$
$$\text{ἔνθ' ὅ γ' ἐς ἀργαλέον λιμέν' ἵκετο νυκτὸς ἐκείνης.}$$

2. νυκτὸς ἀμολγῷ Schneidewin. (*Little Iliad* F 4, Allen)

We miss any comparable fragment connected with the bringing of Philoktetes from his loneliness in Lemnos. The coming of Eurypylos, son of Telephos, to Troy as an ally of Priam seems to have been told in some detail: it is already known to the *Odyssey* (11.519–521), where Homer makes Odysseus recall how he fetched from Skyros Neoptolemos (11.509), who fought doughtily and killed Eurypylos: 'and many Keteioi[2] died about him for the sake of a woman's gifts' (11.521). The woman here mentioned is Astyoche, mother of Eurypylos, who

---

[1] See also Appendix *infra*, 'Some Irish Analogies'.

[2] There is a variant reading *Cheteioi*, who may be Hittites: see my *Achaeans and Hittites* (Oxford 1960) 40.

at first would not let him go to the Trojan war; but Priam won her over by the gift of a golden vine. This object was described in the *Little Iliad* as 'the vine which the son of Kronos gave him in return for his son' – gave, that is, to Laomedon as a recompense for Ganymedes. 'It abounded with soft golden leaves and grape clusters which Hephaistos finished carefully and gave to father Zeus; and Zeus bestowed it upon Laomedon as payment for Ganymedes.' Eurypylos had fought valiantly, killing Machaon amongst others (Paus. 3.26.9: *Little Iliad* F 7, Allen), but to no avail.

The next principal episode was the construction on Mount Ida of the wooden horse, but no fragment describes the work of Epeios, its creator. There followed the visit to Troy by Odysseus in disguise. Helen, who met him in Troy, recalls his beggarly and disfigured appearance in the *Odyssey* (4.242–264). Odysseus had already been mauled[1] before he left the Achaean camp, to add to the disguise, and Helen says that she washed and anointed him (*Od.* 4.252). Proklos states that Helen made a compact with Odysseus about the capture of the city: in this point too the *Little Iliad* seems to have agreed with the *Odyssey*, in which Helen says that at the time she was once again longing to escape from Troy and return home. In his second visit (which Apollodoros, *Epit.* 5.13 combines with the first) Odysseus entered the city with Diomedes to capture the Palladion. The possessor of this image held the key to Troy. If Dionysios of Halikarnassos is to be trusted, Arktinos gave an extensive account of the history of the object, telling how it was given by Zeus to Dardanos and how the real image was hidden in Troy, a substitute being exposed. When Aineias fled from Troy he took the real Palladion, but Odysseus and Diomedes made off with the copy (*Ant. Rom.* 1.68–69). The story may have been pleasing to the Romans of Dionysios's day; to the contemporaries of Arktinos, if the poet told it, the significance would have lain in the claim of the Aineidai in Skepsis to the heritage of Priam.

On the way back to the Achaean camp Diomedes carried the Palladion. An account of the episode is found in Konon (26 F 1, 34) who reports that Odysseus thought of killing Diomedes and so

[1] The *Little Iliad* made Thoas responsible for the rough treatment of Odysseus: Schol. Lyk. *Alex.* 780.

becoming master of the image; but Diomedes noticed him drawing his sword in the moonlight. So the Argive hero, also drawing his sword drove Odysseus before him and hit his back with the flat of his sword. Hence there arose the proverb 'the compulsion of Diomedes' (Hesychios: Διομήδειος ἀνάγκη = Little Iliad F 9, Allen).

In Proklos the capture of the Palladion precedes the manning of the wooden horse. According to Apollodoros (*Epit.* 5.14) the horse had a hollow interior with an opening in the sides, with room for fifty men inside, or for three thousand, as the *Little Iliad* is said to have asserted. In Quintus of Smyrna (*Posthomerica* 12.314-335) thirty heroes are named as having entered the horse, and others too are said to have gone in. Inside the horse Neoptolemos firmly grasped the hilt of his sword, being eager for the fray, but the other heroes trembled with fear (*Od.* 11.526-532). Other occupants of the horse were Menelaos, Tydeus, Odysseus and Antiklos (*Od.* 4.280-286), but Antiklos was excluded from the list by the Homeric critic Aristarchos on the grounds that he is not mentioned in the *Iliad* and belongs to the Cycle (*Little Iliad* F 10, Allen). A splendid horse with wheels and portholes in its sides is illustrated in relief on the large amphora found in Mykonos, which was made sometime in the seventh century B.C.[1] The artist who made this magnificent horse with heroes emerging from it may well have had a poem on the sack of Troy in mind.

When the horse had been brought within the city, the traitor Sinon lit the beacon to recall the Achaean fleet from Tenedos. There was a bright moon that night: 'it was midnight and clear the moon was rising,' said Lesches (*Little Iliad* F 12), as the beacon flashed:

νὺξ μὲν ἔην μέσση, λαμπρὰ δ' ἐπέτελλε σελήνη.

This line is also quoted in the somewhat more Aeolic form ... μεσάτα, λαμπρὰ δ' ἐπέτελλε σελάνα, but we cannot be sure that this version was due to Lesches the Aeolian.

Pausanias claimed to have noticed close correspondences between paintings by Polygnotos of the *Sack* at Delphi and the poetry of 'Lesches, son of Aischylinos of Pyrrha in his *Sack of Ilios*' (10.25.5). He therefore believed that Polygnotos had made use of the poem of

---

[1] M. Ervin, Ἀρχαιολογικὸν Δελτίον 18 (1963) 37 ff. For other early representations of the Horse, from Tenos and Boiotia, see Johansen 28-29.

Lesches, for example, in painting the wounding of Meges in the shoulder during the battle at night. Since neither the paintings nor the poems survive it is impossible to check the remarks of Pausanias. The *Little Iliad* was, however, clearly much concerned with who killed whom, and with the manner of each hero's dying. For the details of this slaughter as it may have been described by Lesches, Pausanias is the prime authority (10.25.5–27.1). He shows that Neoptolemos proved himself a merciless butcher: he it was who dispatched Priam at the doors of the palace (*Little Iliad* F 16, Allen); he, too, killed the child Astyanax, by throwing him from a bastion – a story illustrated in one of the panels of the great Mykonos vase: 'Then the brilliant son of brave Achilles led to the hollow ships the wife of Hektor; but her son he seized from the bosom of the fair-tressed nurse and taking him by the foot threw him from a tower.[1] And at his fall dark death and a violent doom did take him. But Neoptolemos chose out the well-girdled wife of Hektor, and the leaders of all the Achaeans gave her to him to keep, recompensing him with a prize. And he put the famous son of horse-taming Anchises, Aineias in his sea-going ships, a prize excelling those of all the Achaeans.'

αὐτὰρ Ἀχιλλῆος μεγαθύμου φαίδιμος υἱὸς
Ἑκτορέην ἄλοχον κάταγεν κοίλας ἐπὶ νῆας.
παῖδα δ᾽ ἑλὼν ἐκ κόλπου ἐϋπλοκάμοιο τιθήνης
ῥῖψε ποδὸς τεταγὼν ἀπὸ πύργου, τὸν δὲ πεσόντα
5   ἔλλαβε πορφύρεος θάνατος καὶ μοῖρα κραταιή.
ἐκ δ᾽ ἕλεν Ἀνδρομάχην, ἠΰζωνον παράκοιτιν
Ἕκτορος, ἥντε οἱ αὐτῷ ἀριστῆες Παναχαιῶν
δῶκαν ἔχειν ἐπίηρον ἀμειβόμενοι γέρας ἀνδρί,
αὐτόν τ᾽ Ἀγχίσαο κλυτὸν γόνον ἱπποδάμοιο
10 Αἰνείην ἐν νηυσὶν †ἐβήσατο ποντοπόροισιν
ἐκ πάντων Δαναῶν ἀγέμεν γέρας ἔξοχον ἄλλων.

(*Little Iliad* F 19, Allen)

10. ἐμήσατο ποντοπόροιειν Bethe.

The distribution of spoils took place in Tenedos (*Od.* 3.153–160), after

---

[1] This was the earliest attested version of the tale; but some later authorities held that the prophecy of the child's fall to his death (*Iliad* 24.734–735) was not fulfilled. See Xanthos of Lydia 765 F 21 and Lysimachos of Alexandria 382 F 9. The words of line 4 recall the casting of Hephaistos by Zeus out of Olympos (*Iliad* 1.591):

the Greeks had sailed from Troy, leaving some of their number behind. There are striking differences here between the *Chrestomathy* which is alleged to depend from Arktinos and the fragments ascribed to Lesches. In the version of Arktinos, Priam is killed by Neoptolemos, but at the altar of Zeus Herkeios, not at the doors of the palace. Odysseus, not Neoptolemos, kills Astyanax. In the long fragment quoted above, Aineias is taken as a captive by Neoptolemos to the homeland of Achilles; but in the version adopted by Virgil (who may have followed Arktinos) Aineias escaped from the city, even as the sack was happening. The escape of Aineias (or the survival of his progeny) is also implied by the prophecy in the *Iliad* concerning the greatness of the descendants of Aineias. The words of Dionysios of Halikarnassos (*Ant. Rom.* 1.69) on the Palladion in Arktinos do not quite prove that the Milesian poet made Aineias escape with the image during the sack; according to Proklos Aineias withdrew even before the sack, when he had seen the snakes attack Laokoon. Proklos claimed to give the version of Arktinos here; certainly he gave one which contradicts that attributed to Lesches.

Amongst the captives was Aithra, the mother of Theseus, who had attended Helen at Troy (*Iliad* 3.53). She was granted, with Helen's approval, to Demophon and Akamas, the sons of Theseus, because for her sake they had come with Menestheus to Ilios (*Paus.* 10.25.8, Schol. Eur. *Troad.* 31). Two verses ascribed to an author of a *Sack* suggest that they were given other spoils too: 'Lord Agamemnon bestowed gifts upon the sons of Theseus and upon bold Menestheus, shepherd of armies.'

Θησείδαις δ' ἔπορεν δῶρα κρείων 'Αγαμέμνων
ἠδὲ Μενεσθῆι μεγαλήτορι ποιμένι λαῶν.

(*Persis* F 3, Allen)

Theseidai have no part to play in the *Iliad*, and the role of Menestheus is of little significance in the poem. Only amongst the successors of Homer does the Athenian contingent assume some importance.

The other notable Greek lady in Troy, Helen, the object of the entire expedition, was, of course, assigned to Menelaos. It is said that,

---

ῥῖψε ποδὸς τεταγὼν ἀπὸ βηλοῦ θεσπεσίοιο.

βηλός here means threshold. Panyassis however may have thought the allusion to be to the god's sandal or βηλόν (F 23 Kinkel).

according to Lesches, the hero caught sight of her with breasts unclad (presumably in the disorder of the sack) and, overwhelmed by her beauty, cast away his sword (Schol. Aristoph, *Lysistr.* 155). No verse fragment refers to the dragging of Kassandra by the lesser Aias, and none to the sacrifice of Polyxena. But the former theme was popular in archaic Greek art,[1] and it is likely that Arktinos included both Trojan women in his poem, as Proklos asserts. If Kassandra became Agamemnon's concubine in the *Persis*, than it is unlikely that Aias had raped her beforehand.

Belief in the historical fact of Aias's impiety to Athena's image was so strong amongst the Lokrians that, prompted perhaps by a plague, they sent selected daughters of their noblemen to serve the goddess at Troy in harsh circumstances to expiate the sin. This custom continued for many centuries; it was an enduring testimony to the potency of legend in Hellenic society.[2]

Two unattached fragments suggest that Stasinos or a poet of the *Kypria* may also have composed a poem about the sack of Troy. The line 'a fool is he who killing the father leaves the sons to live'

$$\nu\eta\pi\iota\circ\varsigma \ \delta\varsigma \ \pi\alpha\tau\epsilon\rho\alpha \ \kappa\tau\epsilon\iota\nu\omega\nu \ (\text{or} \ \kappa\tau\epsilon\iota\nu\alpha\varsigma) \ \pi\alpha\iota\delta\alpha\varsigma \ \kappa\alpha\tau\alpha\lambda\epsilon\iota\pi\epsilon\iota$$

(*Kypria* F 25, Allen)

is quoted by several writers. A likely context for this gnomic remark, which Clement (*Strom.* 6.19) ascribes to Stasinos, would be the justification of the murder of Astyanax; Achilles had killed Hektor, but had not been able to kill Hektor's son. Neoptolemos completes the task for his father. The second fragment states that according to the *Kypriaka* Polyxena was wounded by Odysseus and Diomedes in the sack but was buried by Neoptolemos (Schol. Eur. *Hec.* 41).[3] If this ascription is correct we must infer that Stasinos, or another Cypriote poet, carried the story of Troy well beyond the end of the *Kypria* as we know it from Proklos and from the other fragments.

In conclusion, we can see that because Proklos selects from various accounts of the aftermath of the *Iliad*, the outlines of the poems by

---

[1] See 'Troy VIII and the Lokrian Maidens' in *Studies Presented to Victor Ehrenberg* (Oxford 1966) ed. E. Badian, 148.

[2] See *Studies Ehrenberg* 147–164.

[3] The Scholiast takes this statement from a Glaukos, most likely the late fifth century B.C. literary historian, of Rhegion.

The Aftermath of the *Iliad*

Lesches and Arktinos cannot be reconstructed; their contents we glimpse, but, in contrast, the *Little Iliads* ascribed to other poets such as Diodoros and Kinaithon are utterly obscure. It can be shown that fragments concerned with distinct episodes, the fate of Aineias for example, are inconsistent with each other. There were therefore differing, or rival, treatments of the tale of Troy's fall, even as early as the time of Lesches and Arktinos. The tradition of their competition together has, therefore, some verisimilitude.

Before we leave Arktinos, an isolated fragment alleged to be his by a Latin student of metre deserves notice (Diomedes in Gramm. Lat. i.477 Keil = *Iliu Persis* F 6, Allen): 'Iambos a short while stood astride with one foot forward so that his limbs, being strained, might gain strength and have a vigorous aspect.'

[ὁ] Ἴαμβος
ἐξ ὀλίγου διαβὰς προφόρῳ ποδὶ ὄφρ' οἱ γυῖα
τεινόμενα ῥώοιτο καὶ εὐσθενὲς εἶδος ἔχῃσι.

ofra oi gya (gria) codd. ὄφρ'οἱ Keil.

Diomedes quotes the verses as evidence that Arktinos was the originator of the iambic metre. The claim could similarly, and with as little right, be made for the author of the Homeric *Hymn to Demeter* because there is an Iambe in that poem (2.195 and 202). The iambic metre almost certainly originated long before the time of Arktinos, who may however have used it, just as Homer is said, as author of the *Margites*, to have alternated hexameters and iambic trimeters. The name *iambos* (the iambic foot, ∪ −)[1] is of non-Greek, perhaps Anatolian,[2] origin, and may mean a 'one-step' dance, as *thriambos* perhaps meant 'three-step' (Latin, *triumphus*) and *dithyrambos* or *dithyramphos* 'four-step'. In the Arktinos fragment Iambos perhaps acts consistently with his name, taking a firm single-step forward, but what Archilochos a little later meant by οὔτ' ἰάμβων οὔτε τερπωλέων (F 20 Diehl[3]) is obscure.

A last point concerning Lesches must be noted. Plutarch in his account of the supposed contest of Homer and Hesiod at Chalkis (*Moralia* 153 F) gives a question by Homer and Hesiod's answer to it. 'And Homer' says Plutarch 'put forward the following verses, as Lesches

[1] ἴαμβος may also have meant a trochee, − ∪, originally.
[2] Hesychios gives Ἴαμβος as the name of a town near Troy.

states; "Muse, tell me of those things which neither happened before nor shall be hereafter."' Evelyn-White[1] supposed that the words 'as Leschès says' seem to indicate that the verse and a half assigned to Homer by Plutarch came from the *Little Iliad*. 'It is possible,' he continues, 'they may have introduced some unusually striking incident, such as the actual fall of Troy.' But we should beware of assuming that Plutarch has preserved a fragment of Leschès here; the Pyrrhaian poet is being given as Plutarch's authority for the contest. He is not being quoted by 'Homer' in the Contest. The point of the puzzle or *griphos* is to reduce the opposing rhapsode to silence. 'Hesiod' however replies by describing something that never has, and can never, happen – a chariot race at the funeral of immortal Zeus. In the *Certamen Homeri et Hesiodi* (97–101 Allen) a similar question and answer are included, but it is 'Hesiod' who puts the question. The *Certamen* is in its present form a work of the Antonine Age, but it depends upon much earlier sources. One authority quoted in it is the *Mouseion* of Alkidamas the sophist of Elaia in the Aeolis, who lived early in the fourth century B.C. Alkidamas is now known to have written a work called *On Homer*, a substantial fragment of which survives.[2] This turns out to be a source of at least the conclusion of the *Certamen* (326 ff p. 238 Allen). The question receiving the answer about Zeus' tomb occurs as part of the contest as early as the third century B.C. in a papyrus (Allen, *Hom. Op.* V 225). It is quite possible that the original authority of Alkidamas and the writer of the papyrus was none other than Leschès himself, since Plutarch's words suggest that the poet had spoken about the contest.[3]

A discussion of the historical facts out of which these early poems on the Sack of Troy grew would take us far beyond the limits of this book. That there was a historical Troy, excavations by Schliemann, Dörpfeld and Blegen have proved. That Troy VII A was sacked and burned is an indubitable fact. That Troy VII A fell sometime in the second half of the thirteenth century is a hypothesis in accord with current knowledge.[4]

[1] *Hesiod, The Homeric Hymns and Homerica* (London/Cambridge, Mass. 1950) 515 n. 1.

[2] J. G. Winter, *T.A.P.A.* 56 (1925) 120 ff.

[3] *Mor* 153 F. καὶ προὔβαλ' Ὅμηρος, ὥς φησι Λέσχης· κτλ. See also G. S. Kirk, *C.Q.* 44 (1950) 150 n. 1.

[4] C. W. Blegen and Others, *Troy* IV (Princeton 1958) 12.

The Aftermath of the *Iliad*

A study of Homer's epithets for Troy reveals that he had some knowledge of the place, almost certainly due to autopsy. But he also knew architectural facts about Troy VI and VII A which are likely to have entered poetical tradition within living memory of the Trojan War. Such facts, that Troy had good streets, walls, towers and gates, and crowded houses, that horses were bred there, and that, as excavation has shown, the structure of the western fortifications was faulty, became part of the common stock of late- and post-Mycenaean epic tradition.[1] The tradition was shared to a greater or less extent by Arktinos in Ionia, Lesches in the Aeolis, Hesiod in Boeotia, and even perhaps Kinaithon in Lakedaimon. So the author of a *Little Iliad* began his poem with an allusion to the horses of Dardania

$$\mathring{I}\lambda\iota o\nu\ \mathring{a}\epsilon\acute{\iota}\delta\omega\ \kappa a\grave{\iota}\ \varDelta a\rho\delta a\nu\acute{\iota}\eta\nu\ \epsilon\mathring{v}\pi\omega\lambda o\nu$$

because he knew as well as Homer that Dardania was renowned for its mares (even before Ilios was founded, cf. *Iliad* 20.216 ff). It is remarkable that the people who built Troy VI seem to have been the first to introduce the domesticated horse to Troy. Bones of horses from Troy VII A also are numerous. Achaeans besieging Troy cannot have failed to note the important place of horse-rearing in the Trojan economy. Hence the epithets $\epsilon\mathring{v}\pi\omega\lambda o\varsigma$ and $\mathring{\iota}\pi\pi\acute{o}\delta a\mu o\iota$, of the place and the people respectively, are likely to have entered the poetical tradition early. Interestingly, the expression $\varDelta a\rho\delta a\nu\acute{\iota}\eta\nu\ \epsilon\mathring{v}\pi\omega\lambda o\nu$ is not used by Homer; but the idea is traditional, even if the tag is not demonstrably pre-Homeric. We see, then, that the poets of the Trojan cycle were, like Homer, the inheritors of a very ancient oral tradition, whose origins lie far back in the Mycenaean age. As for the wooden horse, it is conceivable that it is the vague memory of a Mycenaean siege engine; but there is absolutely no cogent evidence about the origins of the story and speculation is fruitless. The *Chrestomathy* states clearly that the Trojans themselves took part of the wall down to enable the horse to be drawn into the city; the evidence of the Cycle therefore offers no support for the view that the Achaeans entered the city by storming it where the wall was weakest or by taking advantage of damage caused by an earthquake.

[1] C. M. Bowra, *J.H.S.* 80 (1960) 16–23.

G.E.P.   L

XII

The Returns of the Heroes from Troy

The most striking feature of the summary of the *Nostoi* or *Returns* in the *Chrestomathy* is the neglect of Odysseus, who is mentioned only as having met Neoptolemos at Maroneia in Thrace. The omission of the hero of the *Odyssey* looks to be deliberate; Odysseus, it seems, had already received his due meed of praise in the *Odyssey* when the *Nostoi* summarised by Proklos was composed. The *Nostoi* therefore heeded the adventures of the other heroes and left the tale of Odysseus alone. Proklos ascribes the *Nostoi* to a Troizenian poet, Agias, who is a mere name. Others supposed a poem on this theme to have been composed by a Kolophonian (Allen, *Hom. Op.* v. 142); and a *Nostoi* was also assigned to an Antimachos, perhaps the early Teian poet of that name.[1]

Elements of the story appear already in the *Odyssey*, which pre-supposes much traditional knowledge of the adventures of heroes returning from Troy. Nestor (3.130 ff) describes how after the sack a dispute arose between the Atreidai, since Agamemnon desired to wait in Troy to placate the anger of Athena (who had been offended by the impiety of the Lokrian Aias). Half the army, therefore, stayed at Troy and half sailed for Tenedos, where another dispute arose, as a result of which Odysseus returned to Agamemnon. Diomedes and Nestor however sailed on to Lesbos, where they were joined by Menelaos just as they were deliberating whether to sail homewards above Chios by Pseira island or below Chios past the windy promontory of Mimas (3.165 ff). In the end a portent instructed them to sail straight for Euboia; so they crossed directly to Geraistos by night. Diomedes and Nestor soon were safely at home (3.180–183), but Menelaos was blown off course near Cape Maleia, and part of his fleet was wrecked near Phaistos in Crete. Not for seven years did he and Helen return, laden

---

[1] [Antimachos of Kolophon] F 150 Wyss, where for †*in Thenito* read ἐν θ' Νόστων.

with treasure, to the Peloponnese; they came at the very time when the young Orestes murdered Aigisthos, the slayer of his father Agamemnon and his hateful mother (3.306–312). Philoktetes and Idomeneus reached their respective homes safely (3.190–192), but the Lokrian Aias, hated for his boasting and impiety by Poseidon not less than by Athena, was drowned in a wreck at the Gyraian rock (near Mykonos), as Menelaos reported to Telemachos (4.499 ff).

When Menelaos stopped in Lesbos on the way home, Odysseus joined him there and distinguished himself in a wrestling match with Philomeleides; that, presumably, was the last Menelaos had seen of Odysseus before both were blown off course and all news of them ceased (4.341–344). Homer does not say that Agamemnon came with Odysseus from Troy to Lesbos, but a local tradition reported by Sappho suggests – if the relevant fragment has been correctly supplemented – that Agamemnon and Menelaos, having been delayed together in Lesbos during their *Nostoi*, both prayed for a favourable wind.[1]

All these details show that, as in the rest of the Trojan cycle, the authors of poems on the *Returns* had an elaborate tradition to relate, or to modify by selection or expansion, as they saw fit. Even in the Proklan summary the complexity of the tales is manifest. 'To the events of the *Sack*' reports the summary 'are joined the five books of the *Returns*, a work by Agias of Troizen with the following contents. Athena causes Agamemnon and Menelaos to quarrel about the voyage from Troy. Agamemnon stays on to placate the anger of Athena, but Diomedes and Nestor put out to sea and reach home safely. Menelaos sails away after them and arrives in Egypt with five ships after the rest of his fleet has been wrecked at sea. The men accompanying Kalchas, Leonteus and Polypoites march overland to Kolophon and there bury Teiresias who died there. As Agamemnon and his party are sailing away, the ghost of Achilles appears and tries to restrain them by predicting events to come.

'Then are described the storm at the Kapherides rocks and the ruin of Aias the Lokrian. Neoptolemos at the prompting of Thetis makes the journey homewards on foot; and arriving in Thrace he meets Odysseus at Maroneia. He completes the rest of his journey and buries Phoinix,

[1] Page, *Sappho and Alcaeus* (Oxford 1955) 60.

who had died. He then travels to the Molossoi and is recognised by Peleus. Then Agamemnon is murdered by Aigisthos and Klytaimestra. The murder is avenged by Orestes and Pylades. Menelaos voyages back to his homeland.'

The close ties of this summary with the *Odyssey*'s account of the returns of Agamemnon, Nestor, Diomedes, Aias, and Menelaos are clear. Menelaos, as in the *Odyssey* (3.299), reaches Egypt with five ships. In Homer Agamemnon seems to have made for Lakedaimon by way of Maleia, not straight for Mycenae (*Od.* 4.514–515); but the summary has nothing to say about that. The poem adds the notable detail that Aigisthos, and before him Thyestes, held land (ναῖε 4.517) somewhere near Maleia at the extremity of the joint kingdom of the Atreidai. Later writers identified this holding with the island of Kythera (Andron 10 F 11); the theory is at least consistent with the omission of Kythera in the Homeric Catalogue of Ships from the domains of Agamemnon and Menelaos. The murder of Agamemnon early became a popular theme with archaic Greek artists: it appears already, for example, in Crete in the second quarter of the seventh century B.C. in a clay relief from Gortyn (Schefold, Plate 33).

Kolophon was evidently of importance in the tradition of the *Nostoi*; hence, perhaps, the ascription of the poem by some authorities to a Kolophonian author (*Nostoi* F 9 Allen). Kalchas died at Kolophon after being defeated by the local hero Mopsos in a contest of divination there (Hesiod F 160 Rzach) but there is no need to change 'Teiresias' to 'Kalchas' in the Proklan summary; for it is quite likely that in one version of the *Thebais* Teiresias came with his daughter Manto, the mother of Mopsos, to Kolophon, there to die in extreme old age after the Trojan war had ended. In the party of Kalchas was another seer, Amphilochos (Strabo 642). He later continued overland to Pamphylia in southern Asia Minor (Herodot. 7.91) and onwards to the borderlands of Kilikia and Syria, where, it was said, he founded a city, Posideion (Herodot. 3.91). Yet another of these heroic migrants into Asia Minor after the fall of Troy was Podaleirios, who settled in the Karian Chersonese in the southwest (Steph. Byz. s.v. Σύρνα. [Antimachos] F 150 Wyss).

The burial of Teiresias in the *Nostoi* is significant, in view of his

The Returns of the Heroes from Troy

importance in the *Nekyomanteia* in the *Odyssey*. For there was almost certainly a similar consultation of the dead in the *Nostoi*, including apparitions of deceased heroines, as in the *Odyssey*. Pausanias clearly states that Hades and the terrors therein were mentioned in the *Odyssey*, the *Minyas* and the *Nostoi* (10.28.7). Elsewhere he remarks that the heroine Klymene (who belonged to a generation long before the Trojan war) was named in the *Nostoi* (10.29.6); and in his account of the Delphian painting of the underworld he mentions Maira, who died a maiden (10.30.5). Both heroines may be supposed to have appeared in an underworld scene, perhaps with Teiresias, in the *Nostoi*. The Amazon Antiope may also have featured in the poem since Pausanias states that Hegias the Troizenian (who may well be the same as Agias the Troizenian) described her (1.2.1).

Three verses said to come from a poem on the *Nostoi* concern yet another heroine from a time long before the Trojan War – Medea. The Argument to the *Medea* of Euripides quotes them and, like the Scholiast to Aristophanes, *Knights* 1321, states that they were composed by 'the poet of the *Nostoi*': 'At once Medea made Aison a dear young boy and, with her cunning skills, wiped away his old age, after she had brewed many herbs in her golden cauldrons.'

αὐτίκα δ᾽ Αἴσονα θῆκε φίλον κόρον ἡβώοντα
γῆρας ἀποξύσασα ἰδυίῃσι πραπίδεσσι,
φάρμακα πόλλ᾽ ἕψουσ᾽ ἐπὶ χρυσείοισι λέβησι.

3. ἕψουσα ἐνὶ Schneidewin.

This experiment on her father-in-law recalls those on her children, but was, it seems, more successful. It was, presumably, conducted at Iolkos after the voyage from Kolchis and before her dispute with Jason. Here again a *Nekyomanteia* is a likely context for a mention of Medea in the *Nostoi*.

The expression 'storm at the Kapherides rocks' in the *Chrestomathy* alludes to the deliberate wrecking of ships on the Euboian coast by Nauplios, who employed misleading fire-signals for the purpose (Apollod. *Epit.* 6.11). Nauplios was avenging the murder of Palamedes his son, having failed to obtain compensation from the Achaeans. In the *Nostoi* he was mentioned together with his wife Philyra, the mother of Palamedes (Apollod. *Lib.* 2.1.5).

Greek Epic Poetry

The story of the meeting in Thrace of Odysseus and Neoptolemos is a development of an episode in the *Odyssey*. In his account of the events in the cave of Polyphemos, Odysseus says that he had been given sweet dark wine by Maron, a priest of Apollo, who lived at Ismaros (9.196–198). Ismaric wine from Thrace was already well-known amongst the Greeks in the time of Archilochos (*ca.* 650 B.C.) who mentions it (F 2 Diehl[3]); Homer too enlarges upon its superb qualities (*Od.* 9.203 ff), but does not name the city of Maroneia, which was not settled by the Chians before the mid-seventh century B.C. The naming of Maroneia in the *Nostoi* is however a possible indication of the poem's date – after 650 B.C., later than the *Odyssey* by at least half a century. Neoptolemos had travelled no further than Tenedos when Thetis warned him of the dangers of a sea-voyage. From there he could easily make his way to the Thracian coast before continuing to Phthia, and thence to Molossia, on foot. Apollodoros (*Epit.* 6.12) mentions the stay of the young hero in Tenedos, the warning by Thetis, and the burial of old Phoinix; he adds that the Trojan seer Helenos accompanied them, but has nothing to say about the encounter with Odysseus. Some reason must have been given for the move of Neoptolemos from his father's home to Molossia, at the other side of Mount Pindos; the journey is unexplained in the bare, selective summary in Proklos. Apollodoros (*Epit.* 6.12) gives no help here, beyond reporting that Neoptolemos conquered the Molossians and begat Molossos on Andromache; Euripides, however, says that while Neoptolemos was still at Troy he heard that his grandfather Peleus had been expelled by Akastos (*Troades* 1126–1130). Thus in the *Nostoi* Peleus may have been said to have fled westwards to Molossia, where his grandson met him. Ties of the family with the neighbourhood are implied by Homer, who described Achilles praying specifically to Zeus of Dodona (*Iliad* 16.233).

The ascription of a poem on the *Nostoi* to a Troizenian is remarkable. Agias is the first mainland Greek said to have treated the Tale of Troy (if we neglect the doubtful ascription of a *Returns* to Eumelos). The choice of his name and place can hardly be fortuitous, for the Muses were worshipped at Troizen, where they were given the title Ardalides because an Ardalos, alleged to be an inventor of the flute, had founded their cult in the place (Plutarch, *Mor.* 150 A. Pausanias 2.31.3). As an

The Returns of the Heroes from Troy

aoidos with his phorminx or a rhapsode with his staff, an epic poet such as Agias is not likely to have been a flute player too; but Troizen with its local Muses was a fit place to foster epic composition. Agias, it seems, composed his *Nostoi* with the *Odyssey* in mind, completing his poem with the return of Menelaos and ignoring the exciting adventures of Odysseus, who, as Homer had already insisted, was the last of the surviving heroes to return home (*Od.* 1.12).[1] The *Nostoi* thus embraced a period slightly longer than the seven years during which Aigisthos reigned at Mycenae: it extended from the quarrel of Agamemnon and Menelaos at Troy to the murder of the usurpers at Mycenae by Orestes who came from Athens in the eighth year of their reign (*Od.* 3.306–310 and 4.82). In the *Nostoi* embroidery upon the plainer cloth of the *Odyssey* was so detailed that even the name of the slave woman who bore Megapenthes to Menelaos was supplied (*Od.* 4.10–12 with Schol.), but the marriages of Megapenthes to a girl from Sparta and of Hermione to Neoptolemos (*Od.* 4.5) are not likely to have been described in the poem, since they occurred within the traditional sequence of events already included in the *Odyssey*.[2] In the *Chrestomathy* Orestes is helped by Pylades in the murder of Aigisthos and Klytaimestra. This detail is also a sign of relative lateness; the *Odyssey* ignores the Phokian hero, who, however, was already an essential part of the story by the time of Asios of Samos (Paus. 2.29.4). It was to Phokis that the young Orestes has been secretly conveyed after the murder of Agamemnon, as Pindar explains in his eleventh *Pythian*.

Because the Atreidai were the most princely of the heroes who left Troy for home, their *Returns* were of special interest; that is why a part of the *Nostoi* developed into a poem chiefly concerned with them, *The Return of the Atreidai*, Ἀτρειδῶν κάθοδος. Athenaios knew of at least three books of a poem with this title but gives no author's name. From it he quotes a verse and a half:

---

[1] Allen, *Homer* 74 emphasises this argument.

[2] The elaboration and modification of the story was continued in lyric poetry. Stesichoros gave the name of Orestes' nurse as Laodameia (F 41 Page), and even shifted Agamemnon's palace from Mycenae to Lakedaimon, to please his Spartan hosts (F 39). According to a forerunner of Stesichoros, the melic poet Xanthos, Orestes' sister Elektra was originally called Laodike, but her name was changed because she grew old un-wed (ἄλεκτρον οὖσαν F 2 [700] Page).

Greek Epic Poetry

Ἴσον δ' Ἑρμιονεὺς ποσὶ καρπαλίμοισι μετασπών
ψύας ἔγχεϊ νύξε.

(Athen. 399 A)

'Hermioneus with his swift feet following hard on Isos thrust with his spear at the muscles of his loins.' The context of this duel is lost.[1] A second fragment, also in Athenaios (281 B, C), describes the punishment of Tantalos, whom Zeus condemned never to enjoy the delights set before him because a heavy stone had been suspended above his head. Archilochos knows of this punishment of Tantalos (F 55 Diehl[3]); but in the *Odyssey's Nekyomanteia* Tantalos stands in a pond; whenever he tries to drink, the water retreats from him; whenever he reaches out to the delightful fruits growing about him the wind wafts them away to the clouds (11.582–592). It is impossible to decide which of these versions is the earlier, but the Athenaios passage strongly suggests that, as in the *Odyssey* and the *Nostoi*, there was an underworld scene in the *Return of the Atreidai*. Tantalos, as grandfather of Atreus, was an appropriate person to appear in the poem.

In the last poem of the epic cycle an elaborate answer was given to the question 'What happened to Odysseus after the slaughter of the suitors?' The poem, the *Telegoneia*, is ascribed by Proklos to Eugamon or Eugammon of Kyrene, who according to the Eusebian chronology flourished in Olympiad 53 (566/3 B.C.). Clement of Alexandria accused Eugammon of stealing a whole book from the work of 'Mousaios' *On the Thesprotians* (*Strom.* 6.2.25.1 See Allen, *Hom. Op.* V. 143), but this means no more than that Eugammon treated subjects also found in an independent poem on Thesprotia. A poem called *Thesprotis* is in fact attested; in it Odysseus was said to have had a son Ptoliporthes by Penelope (Paus. 8.12.5–6). Ptoliporthes is not the same person as the 'Polypoites son of Odysseus' who is mentioned in the Proklan *Chrestomathy*, since the latter was a son of the Thesprotian princess Kallidike and Odysseus (Apollod. *Epit.* 7.35).

After the events of the *Nostoi*, states the *Chrestomathy*, comes the *Odyssey* of Homer. 'Then there are the two books by Eugammon a Kyreneian with the following contents: "The suitors are buried by

---

[1] In *Iliad* 11.101 Isos is a bastard son of Priam. The name Isos or Issos is perhaps an eponym of the Lesbian town Issa: cf. E. Maass, *Hermes* 24 (1889) 645–647.

The Returns of the Heroes from Troy

their kinsfolk, and Odysseus after sacrificing to the Nymphs sails away to Elis to inspect the herds of cattle and is welcomed by Polyxenos. He receives as a gift a bowl upon which is shown the tale of Trophonios, Agamedes and Augeias.

' "Then he sails back to Ithaka and performs the sacrifices ordained by Teiresias. Next he arrives amongst the Thesprotians and marries Kallidike, queen of the Thesprotians. Then the Thesprotians are engaged in a war with the Brygians, with Odysseus in command; thereupon Ares puts to flight the companions of Odysseus, and Athena opposes the god in battle. Then Apollo separates them. After the death of Kallidike Polypoites, the son of Odysseus, succeeds to the kingdom and Odysseus himself comes back to Ithaka.

' "Meanwhile Telegonos sailing in search of his father lands on Ithaka and plunders the island. Odysseus runs out to the defence but is killed by his son unwittingly. Telegonos recognises his mistake and conveys his father's body with Telemachos and Penelope to his mother, who makes them immortal. Telegonos marries Penelope, and Telemachos Kirke" '

Eugammon had, apart from the *Thesprotis*, one suggestive source for the plot of his poem in the *Odyssey* itself. This was the speech of the shade of Teiresias to Odysseus (*Od.* 11.119–137), which itself shows that Homer too was aware of a body of tradition about adventures of Odysseus later than the slaughter of the suitors: the seer's prophecy is in effect *post eventum*, and may be based on an early version of the *Thesprotis*. That is all the more likely if, as Pausanias (1.17.5) thought, the *Nekyomanteia* in the *Odyssey* was originally placed in the Thesprotian oracle of the dead at Ephyra by the Acheron.[1] Teiresias says: '. . . Then, when you have killed the suitors in your house, either by a trick or openly with the sharp bronze, depart, taking a well-smoothed oar with you, until you come to the men who know not the sea and eat not their food mixed with salt. They neither know ships with their crimson cheeks nor smooth oars that serve as wings for ships. Now I shall declare an exceeding clear sign to you, which shall not escape you. Whenever another traveller meets with you and declares that you have a winnowing fan on your bright shoulder, then fix your smooth oar

[1] For further arguments in favour of this identification see *P.P.* 61 (1958) 245–248.

in the ground and perform goodly sacrifices to Lord Poseidon – a ram, a bull and a breeding boar. Then return home and sacrifice holy hecatombs to the immortal gods who dwell in the broad heaven, to all of them in turn. But death shall come to you from the sea, a gentle one which may kill you when you are taken 'neath a delicate old age; and the people around you shall be blessed. . . .' Let us now relate these orders and predictions of the seer to the summary of Eugammon's *Telegoneia*.

The words of Teiresias ἐξ ἁλός 'from the sea' were also taken to mean in antiquity 'far from the sea', perhaps because in the *Thesprotis* Odysseus was in fact said to have died far inland in Epeiros, but in the later versions including those of the *Chrestomathy* and of the Apollodoran *Epitome* (7.36) Odysseus returns to Ithaka to die there at the hands of Telegonos. Apollodoros gives further details: Telegonos came to Ithaka and drove away some of the cattle. Odysseus defended them, but Telegonos wounded him with a spear barbed with the spine of a sting ray. Odysseus thus died of a death that came from the sea: we have here an ingenious adaptation, perhaps by Eugammon, of the words of Teiresias. This detail interested Sophokles who wrote about it in his *Odysseus Akanthoplex*.

It has been suggested that in the *Telegoneia*, the order by Teiresias to Odysseus to go inland to sacrifice to Poseidon was carried out in Epeiros.[1] An early tradition did indeed send Odysseus to Bouneima in Epeiros with his oar or to Trampya in the Pindos range[2] and Odysseus did have domains on the mainland (*Iliad* 2.635); but in the summary of the *Telegoneia* the sacrifice to Poseidon is omitted. Proklos does however mention the second set of sacrifices enjoined by Teiresias upon Odysseus; those are to all the other gods and are made after the hero has returned from his inland journey to placate Poseidon, but *before* his Epeirote adventures in Kallidike's kingdom. It follows that in the *Telegoneia* the inland sacrifices to Poseidon were made after the visit to Polyxenos, who was a king of Elis; they were therefore made inland from Elis, in *Arkadia* whose inhabitants were notoriously ignorant of nautical

[1] R. Merkelbach, *Untersuchungen zur Odyssee* (Munich 1951) 142–155.
[2] See Wilamowitz 189 n. 30. Hartmann, *Untersuchungen über die Sagen vom Tod des Odysseus* (Munich 1917).

matters. A confirmation of this inference is given by coins of the city of Mantineia in central Arkadia, upon which Odysseus is represented carrying an oar on his shoulder.[1] Since about Eugammon's time there were ties between Kyrene and Mantineia (Demonax went from Mantineia to give constitutional advice in the Libyan city[2]) we may surmise that the poet had the story of Odysseus and his oar at Mantineia in mind.

It is noteworthy that the Proklan summary of the *Telegoneia* begins with the burial of the suitors by their kinsfolk. This implies that the poem did not start where our *Odyssey* ends, because in the so-called *Continuation* of the *Odyssey* (24.417) the suitors are already buried. It is possible therefore that the *Odyssey* known to Eugammon ended before the *Continuation*, and it is worthy of remark, therefore, that two distinguished Hellenistic critics, Aristarchos and Aristophanes, believed the true limit (πέρας) of the *Odyssey* to come at 23.296. We are not told that the scholars had textual support for their belief, but they may well have been aware of the point at which the *Telegoneia* began.

The *Chrestomathy* shows that Eugammon digressed to tell the story of Augeias's treasury and how Trophonios built it. The point of the tale, as Charax of Pergamon shows (103 F 5), is the same as in the Herodotean account of the robbing of Rhampsinitos's treasury (Herodot. 2.121): Trophonios the architect, like the Egyptian thief, left a loose stone to enable the building to be entered and plundered. Eugammon presumably had this folktale from somebody in Kyrene with knowledge of Egypt. The robbery of the treasury was, almost certainly, said in the poem to have been shown on the crater presented by Polyxenos to Odysseus. Eugammon may even have had a real vase in mind; for a Lakonian vase fragment in Samos shows Trophonios erecting a tholos or treasury,[3] and a vase from Sparta with the same scene on it may have been exported to Kyrene, where Lakonian pottery was popular in the mid-sixth century B.C. The treasury of Trophonios like that in the Egyptian tale had a hole through which it could be plundered; this explains why Trophonios was chosen as architect in the Greek version of the tale: for the sanctuary of the divinised hero

[1] See *G.R.B.S.* 3 (1960) 26.   [2] Herodotos 4.161.2.
[3] E. A. Lane, *A.B.S.A.* 34 (1936) 165–166. Cf. A. Severyns, *A.C.* 31 (1962) 24.

Trophonios at Lebadeia was also entered through a narrow passage in the ground (Paus. 9.39.9–10).

Eugammon evidently wished to please the local dynasts of Kyrene, because, according to Eustathios (on *Od.* 16.118), 'the Kyrenaian who wrote the *Telegoneia*' said that Odysseus and Penelope had a son Arkesilaos. Since the poet flourished at a time when Arkesilaos II was king of Kyrene, it appears that a second son of Penelope was introduced to the *Telegoneia* to please the local king. Eustathios also states here that Odysseus had a son Telegonos or Teledamos by Kalypso, but Telegonos is elsewhere called a son of Kirke. Teledamos ($T\eta\lambda\epsilon\delta\check{a}\mu os$ as in $'I\pi\pi o\delta\check{a}\mu os$) is perhaps Kalypso's son; but, if so, we do not know what part he had in the *Telegoneia*.

The Brygoi or Bryges against whom Odysseus led the Thesprotians, according to Proklos, were, we may suppose, taken into the *Telegoneia* from the *Thesprotis*. They were a people of northern Greece or Macedonia and were thought to have been the European ancestors of the Phrygians of Asia Minor, who had immigrated thither in large numbers after the Trojan war.[1] Their war against the Thesprotians is perhaps a memory of an early stage in their migration. Odysseus and his troops may have been successful in checking their further progress southwards and have caused them to move eastwards through Thrace.[2]

The *Telegoneia* concluded with an extravaganza of marriages, of Penelope to Telegonos, and of Kirke to Telemachos. Herodotos reports an equally unexpected alliance of Penelope with the god Hermes, by whom she became the mother of Pan (2.145.4). Since Eugammon was interested in Arkadia, and since Penelope was thought by the Mantineians to have been buried near their city (Paus. 8.12.5–6), it is possible that this genealogy was mentioned, or even invented, by Eugammon; but we do not know that. Eugammon himself remains an obscure figure: a court poet perhaps, a drastic innovator and adapter of older poetry certainly; but a poet of whose work not a single verse survives. It is true that Athenaios (412 D) quotes an epic line to show that

[1] Strabo 680–681. See also *G.R.B.S.* 2 (1959) 98.

[2] Cf. N. G. L. Hammond, C.A.H.[2] II, xxxvi, 35. Hammond considers that epics ancestral to the *Nostoi* and *Thesprotis* originated in N.W. Greece as early as the twelfth century B.C. [*Epirus* (Oxford 1967) 386].

The Returns of the Heroes from Troy

Odysseus had a hearty appetite for meat and wine in old age – γέρων τε ὢν "ἤσθιεν ἁρπαλέως κρέα τ᾽ ἄσπετα καὶ μέθυ ἡδύ." The words could, as T. W. Allen suggested,[1] come from the *Thesprotis* or *Telegoneia*, but that is not certain.

[1] *C.R.* 27 (1913) 191.

XIII

The *Margites*

The *Margites* deserves at least a brief discussion in a book on epics because some ascribed it to Homer and because, if Eustratios[1] correctly stated that Archilochos mentioned the poem, it is one of the earliest known Ionian compositions. That the Parian poet was acquainted with the *Margites* is suggested by his trimeter:[2] πόλλ' οἶδ' ἀλώπηξ ἀλλ' ἐχῖνος ἓν μέγα, 'the fox knows many things, but the hedgehog one big thing'; that is, the fox knows many ways of outwitting his enemies but the hedgehog's one trick (curling himself up) defeats them all. The thought here resembles that of a verse in the *Margites* which was known to the writer of the Platonic *Alcibiades* II (147 B); the hexameter states that the comic hero of the poem 'knew many things but knew all badly' – πόλλ' ἠπίστατο ἔργα, κακῶς δ' ἠπίστατο πάντα, in this being markedly inferior even to the fox.

The poem, as Aristotle (*Poetics* 4.7) remarked, bore a similar relation to comedy as the *Iliad* and the *Odyssey* to tragedy. Its hero, a renowned ninny, was unable to count above five; he would not lie with his bride for fear that she would give a bad report on him to her mother; and when he had grown up, he still did not know whether it was his father or his mother who gave him birth (Suda s.v. Μαργίτης. Schol. Aisch. *In Ctes.* 160).

His sexual relations with his wife and the ruse she adopted to make him sleep with her seem to have been related in detail in the poem (Eustathios 1669, 41 and G. Knaack, *R.M.* 59 (1904) 315). A bedroom scene in a papyrus fragment (*P.Oxy.* 2309) could be an episode from this part of the poem, for a chamber pot, bedclothes and, possibly, a torch are all mentioned together in a succession of trimeters and

---

[1] Ap. Aristot. *N.E.* 6.7. See also O. Crusius, *Philologus* 8 (1895) 711.

[2] Cf. Bergk on Archilochos F 118. Zenobios, *Prov.* 5.68 ascribes the line to Homer.

hexameters. Ancient writers on metre agree that the *Margites* comprised groups of hexameters and trimeters arranged asymmetrically (see Hephaistion p. 59 Consbr. quoted by Lobel, *P.Oxy.* Vol. xxii, p. 1). There survive three verses from the poem, in which a trimeter follows two hexameters of heroic character (Allen, *Hom. Op.* V p. 156).

ἦλθέ τις εἰς Κολοφῶνα γέρων καὶ θεῖος ἀοιδός,
Μουσάων θεράπων καὶ ἑκηβόλου Ἀπόλλωνος,
φίλην ἔχων ἐν χερσὶν εὔφθογγον λύραν.

'There came to Kolophon an aged and divine singer, a servant of the Muses and of far-shooting Apollo, and in his hands he held a sweet-voiced lyre.' This bard, then, was no rhapsode with a staff, but a chanter to the lyre, like Phemios or Demodokos in the *Odyssey*, both of whom had a *phorminx*. But unlike them, the bard in the *Margites* fragment seems to be a wanderer; he resembles Thamyris and, as many believed, Homer himself. Who he was, and what he did in Kolophon, we do not know. With no better evidence, perhaps, than these verses the Kolophonians, however, claimed that Homer had composed the *Margites* in their city. It may be that the verses come from the beginning of the poem; if so, the aged bard may well have been said to have related the story of *Margites* to its author.[1]

The incompetence of the ninny-hero became proverbial. Two hexameters, noted by Aristotle (*N.E.* 6.7) and believed by him to be Homer's in the *Margites*, emphasise again the lack of ability: 'the gods had taught him neither to dig, nor to plough, nor any other skill; he failed in every craft.'

τὸν δ' οὔτ' ἄρ σκαπτῆρα θεοὶ θέσαν οὔτ' ἀροτῆρα
οὔτ' ἄλλως τι σοφόν. ⟨πάσης δ' ἡμάρτανε τέχνης.⟩

None would he heed and no work would he do, reported Theodoros Metochites (ap. Allen *Hom. Op.* V 159), whose words perhaps echo a trimeter.[2]

The asymmetrical arrangement of hexameter and trimeters in the *Margites* was not unique in early Greek poetry. A trimeter followed by two hexameters appears in one of the most ancient Greek inscriptions,

[1] H. Langerbeck, *H.S.C.P.* 63 (1958) 58.
[2] O. Immisch, *Philologus* 64 (1905) 633–634 suggests μηδὲν πονεῦντα μηδ' ἐπαΐοντά τευ.

written retrograde on the 'cup of Nestor' from Pithekoussai;[1] and a very early inscription of the Ainianes consists of hexameters and pentameters arranged asymmetrically, if the text of the verses in the pseudo-Aristotelian *Mirabilia* is in order (133. See also *G.R.B.S.* 8 (1967) 88). Thus while we cannot claim the *Margites* for Homer, it may well have been composed by an epic poet in Homer's time, in a moment of relaxation from the sublimity of heroic tradition or as a change from hymns of praise; for to mock a buffoon was as much to a bard's liking, as to honour Odysseus, to pour scorn on Thersites, or to laud Apollo.

[1] Jeffery 235–236.

XIV

Panyassis

A poet who was accounted the superior of Hesiod in his choice of subject matter and of Antimachos of Kolophon in the arranging of it can have been no mean practitioner of the epic art; the fragments of Panyassis do not refute, even if they do not confirm, this judgement by Quintilian (*Inst. Or.* 10.1.54), which accords with the view of so discerning a critic as Dionysios of Halikarnassos (*Vett. scr. cens.* 2.4). But the literary remains of the last great epic poet of archaic Greece give so ample a testimony to his industry and ingenuity that the loss of his *Ionika* and of his *Herakleias* or *Herakleia*, a poem said to have extended to nine thousand verses in fourteen books (Suda s.v. Πανύασις), is to be deplored.

Panyassis son of Polyarchos, a Halikarnassian, was a kinsman of Herodotos. The true relationship between them was disputed, some maintaining that Polyarchos was a brother of Lyxes, the historian's father, others that Rhoio the mother of Herodotos was a sister of Panyassis. Whether Panyassis was a cousin of Herodotos or his uncle, the fact of their kinship need not be doubted. Both had suffered in civil tumult in their native city, and it may well be that Panyassis, like Herodotos, had been forced into exile in Samos; Douris (76 F 64) indeed even claimed Panyassis as a Samian. Local political troubles proved the eventual ruin of the poet, who was put to death by Lygdamis, tyrant of Halikarnassos. Herodotos himself returned from Samos and overthrew the tyranny in his native city according to the Suda. This can hardly have happened later than 448 B.C., since we have to allow some time before Herodotos was himself again expelled and took up residence in Athens in the mid 440s (McLeod, *Phoenix* 20 (1966) 100–101). Panyassis, then, is likely to have died in the fifties of the fifth century B.C.

It is remarkable that Herodotos his kinsman never mentions Panyassis in his *Histories*. Nor are direct borrowings by Herodotos from the *Ionika* or the *Herakleias* easily identified. Twice however he differs from Panyassis: (1) In 1.7.4 he states that the Herakleidai of Lydia are descended from a slave woman of Iardanes and Herakles. The offspring of their marriage was Alkaios, whose great-grandson Agron was the first of the Herakleidai to be king at Sardeis (1.7.2). Panyassis had declared that Herakles had a son Acheles (who became king of Lydia) by Omphale, the Lydian queen (Schol. Vict. ad. Hom. *Il.* 24.616). Yet another version was given by Hellanikos (4 F 112) who stated that Herakles had a son Akeles by Malis, a slave woman of Omphale. (2) The historian asserts that the story of the Egyptians who led Herakles to be sacrificed to Zeus at an altar is ridiculous (2.45.1); but Seleukos the grammarian quoted from Panyassis a line taken from the poet's description of a human sacrifice in Egypt:

$$\pi \acute{\epsilon} \mu \mu \alpha \tau \alpha \ \pi o \lambda \lambda' \ \acute{\epsilon} \pi \iota \theta \epsilon \grave{\iota} \varsigma \ \pi o \lambda \lambda \grave{\alpha} \varsigma \ \delta \acute{\epsilon} \ \tau \epsilon \ \nu o \sigma \sigma \acute{\alpha} \delta \alpha \varsigma \ \ddot{o} \rho \nu \iota \varsigma$$

(F 26 Kinkel).[1]

The priest 'added many cakes and many baby birds' to the sacrificial feast; so we may surmise the context. The intended victim was almost certainly Herakles here. Thus Herodotos, it seems, tacitly disagreed with his kinsman.

Amongst early poets charged with plagiarism by Clement is Panyassis (*Strom.* 6.25) who, he claims, took the *Sack of Oichalia* from Kreophylos. This change entails no more than that Panyassis treated the subject in traditional epic language in his *Herakleias*. Three long fragments, all in strongly traditional diction, are reasonably assigned to the story of the sack. All come from the context of the feast at the house of Eurytos when Herakles, drunk with wine (cf. Sophokles, *Trach.* 268-269 and Stoessl, *R.E.* 18.3. (1949) 884), was roughly expelled by his host. The first consists of eighteen hexameters in praise of wine (F 12 Kinkel). Here Eurytos perhaps invites his guest to drink because he must not 'sit stuffed with food, like a child,[2] overflowing, and forgetful of good cheer' (lines 17-18):

$$\ldots \mu \eta \delta \grave{\epsilon} \ \beta o \rho \hat{\eta} \varsigma \ \kappa \epsilon \kappa o \rho \eta \mu \acute{\epsilon} \nu o \nu \ \mathring{\eta} \mathring{\upsilon} \tau \epsilon \ \pi \alpha \hat{\iota} \delta \alpha$$
$$\mathring{\eta} \sigma \theta \alpha \iota \ \pi \lambda \eta \mu \mu \acute{\upsilon} \rho o \nu \tau \alpha \ \lambda \epsilon \lambda \eta \sigma \mu \acute{\epsilon} \nu o \nu \ \epsilon \mathring{\upsilon} \phi \rho o \sigma \upsilon \nu \acute{\alpha} \omega \nu.$$

[1] Athen. 172D. See also Meineke, *Analecta Alexandrina* (Berlin 1843) 368.
[2] Or, alternatively, 'like a vulture' $\mathring{\eta} \mathring{\upsilon} \tau \epsilon \ \gamma \hat{\upsilon} \pi \alpha$.

Earlier (line 13) wine is called ἀλεξίκακος, 'averter of ills', in a polite borrowing of a title given to Herakles himself.

The second fragment offers advice to the guest not to exceed the two draughts prescribed by convention. Already Eurytos is perturbed by Herakles's capacity, and must be regretting his earlier exhortation to drink with a will εὖ καὶ ἐπισταμένως (F 12, 3). The first draught is for the Graces, the Hours, and Dionysos; the second for Aphrodite and Dionysos again; but the third for Hybris and Ate (F 13 Kinkel = Athenaios 36 D). Eurytos bids Herakles desist before the third draught, lest Outrage, inciting his spirit within, put an evil end to their fair entertainment: 'drink not to excess':

δείδια γὰρ τριτάτης μοίρης μελιηδέος οἴνου
πινομένης, μή σ' "Υβρις ἐνὶ φρεσὶ θυμὸν ἀέρσῃ,
ἐσθλοῖς δὲ ξενίοισι κακὴν ἐπιθῇσι τελευτήν.
ἀλλὰ πιθοῦ καὶ παῦε πολὺν πότον.

(F 13, 12–15 Kinkel)

Eurytos also urges Herakles to put his comrades to bed and to go himself to his wedded wife:

στεῖχε παρὰ μνηστὴν ἄλοχον, κοίμιζε δ' ἑταίρους

(F 13, 11).

Deianeira is perhaps meant. The remark was specially pointed if Herakles was already overwhelmed by a passion for Iole, whom Eurytos had declined to give to him.

The merits and dangers of wine are again described by Panyassis in a quotation in Athenaios (37 AB); the verses may well come from the same context. 'Wine is for mortals the best of gifts from the gods, beauteous wine, to which are suited all songs, all dancings, and all delightful lovemaking. All pains does it drive from the hearts of men when it is taken in due measure, but beyond measure is wine less of a boon.'

οἶνος ⟨γὰρ⟩ θνητοῖσι θεῶν πάρα δῶρον ἄριστον,
ἀγλαός· ᾧ πᾶσαι μὲν ἐφαρμόζουσιν ἀοιδαί,
πάντες δ' ὀρχησμοί, πᾶσαι δ' ἐραταὶ φιλότητες.
πάσας δ' ἐκ κραδίας ἀνίας ἀνδρῶν ἀλαπάζει
πινόμενος κατὰ μέτρον· ὑπὲρ μέτρον δὲ χερείων

(F 14 Kinkel)

Not long after this violent feast Iphitos, son of Eurytos, having lost twelve mares, came in search of them to Herakles, who killed him in his own house and kept the mares (*Od.* 21.23–30). Trying to rid himself of the blood guilt, Herakles came to Delphi; but the priestess answered him not. So he plundered the temple and carried off the tripod, intending to set up an oracle of his own (Apollod. *Lib.* 2.6.2). The story of a struggle between Apollo and Herakles for the oracular tripod is early; it is first represented in Greek art in the late eighth century B.C. on the leg of a bronze tripod from Olympia.[1] In late archaic times it was popular, because it had become symbolically associated with the First Sacred War. Panyassis certainly mentioned this well-worn theme, because, as a punishment for the robbery of the tripod, Herakles was required to serve Omphale, daughter of Iardanes, in Lydia; and, as the fragments show, in the *Herakleias* the humiliating Lydian adventure was treated in detail by the poet. Two verses may describe the arrival of Herakles at Delphi before his rebuff by the Pythia: 'After crossing on his rapid feet snowy Parnassos he came to the immortal water of Kastalia, daughter of Acheloos.'

$$\Pi\alpha\rho\nu\eta\sigma\grave{o}\nu \ \nu\iota\phi\acute{o}\epsilon\nu\tau\alpha \ \theta o o\hat{\iota}\varsigma \ \delta\iota\grave{\alpha} \ \pi o\sigma\sigma\grave{\iota} \ \pi\epsilon\rho\acute{\eta}\sigma\alpha\varsigma$$
$$\iota\kappa\epsilon\tau o \ K\alpha\sigma\tau\alpha\lambda\acute{\iota}\eta\varsigma \ ^{\prime}A\chi\epsilon\lambda\omega\acute{\iota}\delta o\varsigma \ \ddot{\alpha}\mu\beta\rho o\tau o\nu \ \ddot{\upsilon}\delta\omega\rho.$$

(Paus. 10.8.9 = F 15 Kinkel)

Pausanias treats the Kastalian fount at Delphi as a daughter of Acheloos; but Panyassis also used Acheloos as an alternative name for Okeanos (see *infra*); so it is possible that he thought the spring to be part of the ocean's streams.

Herakles objected to his enforced slavery, but he was offered comfort, perhaps by Hermes who sold him to Omphale (Apollod. *Lib.* 2.6.3): 'Demeter endured, the famous Lame-one endured, Poseidon endured, Apollo of the silver bow endured, to serve for a year in the company of a mortal man. Stout-spirited Ares too endured 'neath the compulsion of his father.' Thus Herakles, the speaker implies, ought not to resent his temporary enslavement. The life of Demeter amongst mortals was described by Panyassis, perhaps in this context: the poet said that the goddess came to Triptolemos, who was a son of Eleusis (Apollod. *Lib.*

[1] Kunze, *Olympische Forschungen* 2.115. See also H. W. Parke and J. Boardman, *J.H.S.* 77 (1957) 278.

1.5.2); but another possible context for this fragment is the initiation of Herakles into the Eleusinian mysteries (R. Rapetti, *P.P.* 107 (1967) 131–135).

When Herakles was in Lydia he fell ill but was cured, or cleansed, by the river Hyllos; hence he called two of his sons Hyllos, according to Panyassis (Schol. Ap. Rhod. 4.1149–1150, p. 308 Wendel). A tributary of the Lydian Hyllos was the river Achelesios. This too provided the name of a son of Herakles, Acheles, who was his child by Omphale (Schol. Vict. Hom. *Il.* 24.616). The rivers Hyllos and Achelesios are said to have given up warm waters to heal him (Schol. Hom. *loc. cit.* = Panyassis F 17). The occasion may well have been his purification from the murder of Iphitos. Panyassis also mentioned here river nymphs called Acheletides, who must have helped in the cleansing. The association of warm springs with Herakles appears already in Peisandros (F 7 Kinkel), but the idea is widespread and Panyassis need not have borrowed from him.

Asiatic allusions in the *Herakleias* are to be expected in a poet born in Karia, whose very name is not Greek but Karian. (Compare Tod 25, where the name Panyassis appears in a Halikarnassian inscription of the mid-fifth century B.C.). Not far from Halikarnassos the tough Lykians kept their freedom in their mountain redoubts. It was natural for Panyassis to match his Herakles against them (Plut. *Theseus* 11), and to be interested enough in them to provide a genealogical explanation of their origins. Herodotos, who almost certainly follows his kinsman in this matter, states that the old name of the Lykians was Termilai; they were still so called by their neighbours in the historian's time (1.173.3). A form of the name is also found in Lykian inscriptions of the fifth and fourth centuries B.C. Panyassis (Steph. Byz. s.v. Τρεμίλη) wrote about their eponymous ancestor Termiles or Tremiles who lived in Lykia: 'There did great Tremiles dwell and wed a daughter, his bride Ogygie, whom they call Praxidike, by the silvery Sibros alongside the eddying river. Her deadly sons were fair-haired Tloos, Pinaros and Kragos, who in his power plundered all the fields.'

> ἔνθα δ' ἔναιε μέγας Τρεμίλης καὶ ἔγημε θύγατρα,
> νύμφην Ὠγυγίην, ἣν Πραξιδίκην καλέουσι,
> Σίβρῳ ἐπ' ἀργυρέῳ ποταμῷ παρὰ δινήεντι·

Greek Epic Poetry

τῆς ὀλοοὶ παῖδες Τλῶος ξανθὸς Πίναρός τε
5   καὶ Κράγος, ὃς κρατέων πάσας ληίζετ' ἀρούρας.

4. Ξανθὸς Kinkel ξανθὸς Schneider.

The slightly uneven wording of the two lines at the start is remarkable; Panyassis had wanted to say 'daughter of Ogygos' but 'Ωγύγου (– ◡ –) would not scan in a hexameter, so he changed the construction in mid-sentence. The accumulation of datives in the third line is somewhat awkward too. The multiple genitives in a papyrus fragment (P.Oxy. 221, p. 64, 8–11), identified as being Panyassian by Wilamowitz (see Powell, Collectanea Alexandrina 248) are comparable. The papyrus states that the lines were quoted by the grammarian Seleukos from the fifth book of the Herakleia:

πῶς δ' ἐπορεύθης ῥεῦμ' 'Αχελωίου ἀργυροδίνα
'Ωκεανοῦ ποταμοῖο δι' εὐρέος ὑγρὰ κέλευθα;

The infelicities are notable; but there is no reason to claim that Panyassis, being of Karian stock, was not at home in the Greek language.[1] Herakles is here in the papyrus being asked, perhaps by Geryon at earth's limit beside Okeanos, 'how did you cross the flood of silvery eddying Acheloos,[2] the watery paths, o'er broad Ocean's stream?' The answer to the question would be 'in the bowl of the Sun, which he gave to me when he heated me too much on my way west. I drew my bow at him, whereat he being amazed at my boldness granted it to me, and I made my way to the island of Erytheia' (see Apollod. Lib. 2.5.10. Athenaios 469 D. Macrobius, Sat. 5.21.19).

The sons of Praxidike in the Tremilian fragment are eponymous heroes of the Lykian places Tlos, Pinara and Kragos. The robber Kragos, an Anatolian Antaios or Skeiron, was perhaps the opponent of Herakles when the son of Zeus came to Lykia.[3]

Having mentioned Geryon we may now turn to the treatment of the Labours by Panyassis. The canonical twelve appeared (though hardly for the first time) during his lifespan, in the metopes at Olympia; the poet too may have listed a round dozen. The Nemean Lion was mentioned in the first book according to Stephanos of Byzantion (s.v.

[1] Cf. Stoessl R.E. 18.3 (1949) 877.
[2] The equation Acheloos=sea perhaps recalls an ancient root αχ- meaning 'water'. Cf. Acheron.
[3] For more detail about this fragment see G.R.B.S. 5 (1964) 29–33.

Panyassis

Βέμβινα), unless πρωτῇ means here that it was the first of the Labours. Two lines are quoted by Stephanos

δέρμα τε θήρειον Βεμβινήταο λέοντος

and

καὶ Βεμβινήταο πελώρου δέρμα λέοντος.

Both mentions of the Lion skin link the creature with Bembina, a small village near Nemea, rather than with Nemea itself. For this detail Panyassis was perhaps indebted to some Ionian geographer, for example the great Hekataios himself. The placename and its duplication suggest a touch of pedantry in the epic poet. Of such tendencies his kinsman was delightfully innocent.

When Herakles fought the Hydra at Lerna, a crab leapt up from the marsh and bit his foot. Our hero then squashed it underfoot, but Hera took pity on it and placed the creature as a group of stars, Cancer, in the heavens (Eratosth. *Katast.* 11). This detail would have appealed to the poet's sense of the quaint or grotesque; but it was not original with him, since it already appears on a bronze fibula of the seventh century B.C. from Thebes (Schefold, Plate 6); it may even have appeared in the poem of Peisandros. Another catasterism mentioned by Panyassis (F 10 Kinkel) was that of the unsleeping serpent which had guarded the golden apples of the Hesperides against Herakles.

Two hexameters are said by Athenaios (498 D) to come from the third book:

τοῦ κεράσας κρητῆρα μέγαν χρυσοῖο φαεινόν
σκύπφους αἰνύμενος θαμέας πότον ἡδὺν ἔπινεν.

'After mixing his great bright golden bowl he took hold of the close-packed cups and drank the sweet draught.' The context is not explained by Athenaios, but a suitable occasion would be the entertainment of Herakles by the Centaur Pholos. Also said to be from the third book is a verse in which Thyone is given as the name, not of Semele mother of Dionysos, but of that god's nurse; 'he (Dionysos) leapt from the bosom of his nurse Thyone':

καί ῥ' ὃ μὲν ἐκ κόλποιο τροφοῦ θόρε ποσσὶ Θυώνης.

(Schol. Pind. *Pyth* 3.177; 2.88 Drachmann)

The reference is evidently to the god's precocious infancy, but the context in the *Herakleia* is lost. Panyassis could hardly have omitted

183

Greek Epic Poetry

some detail from the childhood of Herakles himself in Thebes. The hero's marriage to Megara there and the murder of their children also found a place in the epic, as we learn from Pausanias (9.11.2).[1]

Our texts of Athenaios (469 D), assign the voyage in the cup westwards to Erytheia to the first book, but the number here seems to be corrupt. Deubner plausibly suggested that the journey was described in the *fourth* book (see Kinkel p. 256). The arrival in the far west was described in the fifth book, if we have correctly interpreted the papyrus quotation from Seleukos in which Acheloos means 'Ocean' (Powell, *Collectanea Alexandrina* 248). The only other fragment assigned to a book is taken from the eleventh by Stephanos of Byzantion (s.v. 'Ασπίς). Stephanos, discussing the various islands called Aspis, 'shield', says that 'there was also one beyond Pisa, as Panyassis says in the eleventh book of his *Herakleia*'. The words 'beyond Pisa', πέραν Πίσης, perhaps are taken from Panyassis. The Eleian Pisa can hardly be meant here since an island 'beyond Pisa' in inland Elis makes no sense. The text is probably in disorder. There is no reason to think that the fragment comes from an account of the founding of the Olympic games by Herakles. Stephanos seems to be following a certain Kleon of Syracuse here – he is quoted just before in the same article and is known to have written on islands (Schol. Ap. Rhod. *Arg.* 2.297b. p. 150, 9 Wendel). Apollodoros (*Lib.* 2.6.3) says that Herakles on his way to Omphale in Lydia saw the body of Ikaros washed ashore and buried it on the island of Doliche 'Long Island', which he then called Ikaria. In return Daidalos made a portrait statue of Herakles 'at Pisa', which Herakles mistook at night for a living person; so he threw a stone and hit it. Pisa, therefore, in the Stephanos fragment may be a small island near Ikaria in the southeastern Aegean.[2] We have here perhaps a local detail gathered by Panyassis in his Samian exile.

[1] Panyassis may well have mentioned Amphion the Theban too: [Probus] in Verg. *Buc.* 2.23 (*Appendix Serviana* ed. H. Hagen [Leipzig 1902] 329, 23–25) reports: *Panyasis et Alexander* (perhaps the Aetolian) *lyram a Mercurio* (sc. *Amphioni*) *muneri datam dicunt, quod primus †Euianarum liberaverit. Panyassis: Panocus* codd. *Pannyasis* Egnatii ed. princ. *Phanocles* Schneidewin. *Phanodicus* Deubner. For the obelized word Meineke (*Analecta Alexandrina* [Berlin 1843] 251) proposed *ei in ara*. *liberaverit: libaverit* Meineke. But if this really is a fragment of Panyassis, the context is quite lost.

[2] Stoessl, *R.E.* 18.3. 889.

Panyassis

Two fragments dealing with the descent of Herakles to Hades may be treated together. One declares that Theseus and Peirithoos grew to the rock on which they sat (Pausanias 10.29.9). The occasion had also been described in the *Theseides*. In the second fragment a punishment of Sisyphos in the underworld is reported: '... as he spake the water of Styx did cover him.'

ὡς ἄρα μιν εἰπόντα κατασ[τέγασε Στυγὸς] ὕδωρ.

(Antimachi Colophonii Fragmenta p. 85 Wyss)

μιν is naturally short; Panyassis may respect the original digamma of Ϝειπόντα here. Sisyphos is in constant danger of drowning; the reverse punishment is here given to him to that of Tantalos in the *Odyssey*. The stone-pushing of Sisyphos in the *Odyssey* (11.593 ff) is inconsistent with this punishment in the *Herakleia*; so Panyassis is unlikely to have described it.

Panyassis also differed from the *Odyssey* in his account of the cattle of the Sun (amongst which he may have brought his Herakles on the way home from Erytheia). In the *Odyssey* the watchers of the cattle and sheep are the Sun's daughters Phaethousa and Lampetie (12.132 and 375). But according to Panyassis, their guardian was male (Schol. Hom. *Od.* 12.301 = F 8 Kinkel). His name is corrupt in the texts; and it is not clear where Panyassis placed the cattle. Herodotos however (9.93.1) knew of specially protected flocks belonging to the Sun at the Corinthian colony of Apollonia on the Ionian Gulf, not so far from Ithaka. These flocks had watchers chosen from amongst the local noblemen, and may well have been known to Panyassis too.

Not content with making Herakles draw his bow against the Sun, Panyassis asserted that the hero wounded both Hades and Hera (Arnobius, *Adv. Gent.* 4.25 = Panyassis F 21 Kinkel). In this he followed Homer (*Iliad* 5.381 ff) who makes Dione recall how Otos and Ephialtes had bound Ares – the words τλῆ μὲν ῎Αρης were echoed by Panyassis himself (cf. F 16 with *Il.* 5.385) – and how Herakles had wounded both Hades and Hera amongst the shades of the dead in Pylos. Homer relates how Herakles shot Hera in the right breast and caused Hades, wounded in the shoulder, to hasten to Olympos for first aid from Paieon the healer (5.392–402). Clement (*Protrept.* 2.36 = Panyassis F 20 Kinkel) quotes the traditional cliché ἐν Πύλῳ ἠμαθόεντι 'in sandy Pylos' from

Greek Epic Poetry

the episode of Hera's wounding. The presence of Hades in this context suggests that Herakles made one of his descents to the underworld in Pylos. The fight was part of his massacre of the sons of Neleus (Apollod. *Lib.* 2.7.3); in it Ares too was wounded: Herakles thrust his spear into the god's thigh and threw him in the dust (see *Shield* 359–367).

From Pylos Herakles went to punish the Hippokoontids and to restore Tyndareus (Apollod. *Lib.* 2.7.3). It is likely that Panyassis told this story also because one fragment (Apollod. *Lib.* 3.10.3) mentions Tyndareus and says that Asklepios raised him from the dead. But his revival may, alternatively, have been mentioned in connexion with the recovery of Alkestis (cf. Schol. Eur. *Alc.* 1). This is the last of the fragments which can with certainty be claimed for the *Herakleia*.

Not a single quotation is assigned by any extant ancient writer to the *Ionika* which according to the Suda (s.v. Πανύασις) was concerned with Kodros, Neleus and the Ionian colonial settlements; the poem was alleged to be 7000 verses long ἐν πενταμέτρῳ, which perhaps means in elegiacs. The subject of the Neleid and Pylian leaders of the Ionian migration had already been treated in prose by the Athenian Pherekydes about 500 B.C. (*F.Gr.Hist.* 3 F 155) and earlier still by the Milesian Kadmos. Panyassis may have used these works, but we have no proof. Nor is there any demonstrable connexion between the treatment of Ionian prehistory in Book I of Herodotos and the poem of Panyassis. One fragment may however be plausibly assigned to the *Ionika* rather than to the *Herakleia*; this tells the story of Smyrna and her son Adonis, and is perhaps part of an explanation of Smyrna the city's pre-Ionian origins and of the non-Hellenic sources of the Adonis cult.

Smyrna, according to Panyassis (Apollod. *Lib.* 3.14.4), was a daughter of Theias, king of Assyria. Thus much is certain; that what follows is a piece of Hellenistic romanticism, not a genuine fragment of Panyassis, is possible: Smyrna dishonoured Aphrodite who in fury caused her to conceive a passion for her father. With the help of her nurse she was enabled to share her father's bed for twelve nights. But when he discovered that he had been sleeping with his daughter he pursued her with a drawn sword. She, being overtaken, prayed that she might be made invisible; so the gods changed her into a tree called 'smyrna' the myrrh tree. Ten months later the tree burst open to reveal Adonis, an

186

infant of wondrous beauty. Aphrodite put him in a chest which she entrusted to Persephone, but when Persephone saw him she would not give him back. Finally Zeus had to arbitrate. He ruled that Adonis should stay by himself for one part of the year, with Persephone for another part and with Aphrodite for the rest. Part or all of this story is likely to have interested the Halikarnassians, whose month Adonion implies that there was an Adonis cult in the city. The strongly erotic content is perhaps better suited to an elegiac poem than to epic, but the story of Ares and Aphrodite in the *Odyssey*, for example, shows that such topics were quite at home in hexameter poetry.

In an isolated fragment Panyassis uses the word μῦθος as Anakreon does (F 8 Page), in its Ionian sense of στάσις 'dispute'. (See Powell, *Collectanea Alexandrina* 248-249, following Reitzenstein on Etymol. Gen. s.v. μῦθος): καὶ Ἀνακρέων ἐν τῷ β΄ τῶν μελῶν μυθιητὰς τοὺς στασιαστὰς ἐπὶ τῶν ἁλιέων λέγει, καὶ Πανύασσις διχθάδιός ποτε μῦθος· ἄναξ μετεμέμβλετο λαῶν. (So Reitzenstein. ἄλλα δὲ μετεμέμβετο λαῶν Cod. A.) The context of the dispute is lost: the Ionism is no proof that the hexameter comes from the *Ionika*; and the king (if ἄναξ is the correct emendation) remains unidentified. Another peculiarity of the poet's vocabulary was his use of the rare word βηλά meaning 'sandals' (F 23 Kinkel). Here too the context is lost and there is no place for conjecture.

Ancient critics' estimates of Panyassis are at least not refuted by the testimony of his fragments. He was an able practitioner of epic techniques with a thorough grounding in epic language; yet he had also a fondness for strange or unusual locutions. The traditional tales he accepted, but in his embroidering of them he freely indulged his taste for the quaint or the rare. This taste is seen, for example, in the encounter of Herakles with the Sun. He could moralise at length, as the fragments on wine reveal; and he knew that even divinities have their powers limited at times. Even Demeter had to serve in a mortal king's household; even Hades was wounded by the poet's hero; and the valiant Herakles himself had to serve a foreign queen. We may surmise that the half-Karian Panyassis relished the Lydian episode above all, and delighted to tell how his hero submitted to menial tasks imposed by a barbarian and a woman.

Because he was both industrious and versatile, the loss of the epics of Panyassis is specially to be lamented; but even so, his remains provide many valuable details concerning Hellenic myth and legend, and we must be grateful that so much of his work survives from the wreckage of early Greek literature. It appears too, if the Suda's description of him as a τερατοσκόπος may be trusted, that he continued the ancient Epimenidean tradition of the poet-prophets.

One other Halikarnassian poet, an exponent of a debased epic tradition, deserves notice. The Suda (s.v. Πίγρης) confusingly declare that Pigres, 'a Karian of Halikarnassos, was a brother of Artemisia who was distinguished in war' (this would be the lady who fought at Salamis in 480 B.C.) 'and wife of Mausolos' (presumably the dynast of the fourth century B.C.). Pigres is thus undatable, but if he really was a brother of the older Artemisia, then he flourished before Panyassis. He is said to have converted the *Iliad* into elegiacs in the following manner (Suda. *loc. cit.*).

μῆνιν ἄειδε θεὰ Πηληιάδεω Ἀχιλῆος,
Μοῦσα, σὺ γὰρ πάσης πείρατ᾽ ἔχεις σοφίης.

His reputation as a wit led some to ascribe to him the (extant) *Battle of Frogs and Mice*, a parody of epic, whose author wrote with tablet on knee, as he himself tells us, but made considerable use of epic clichés;[1] the *Margites* was by some also thought to be his.

[1] See G. S. Kirk, *Yale Classical Studies* 20 (1966) 161.

Epilogue

With Panyassis the primary period of Greek epic may fitly be said to end. About the secondary epics in the classical age of Greece even less evidence survives, but the fragments of Antimachos of Kolophon suffice to show that already by the end of the fifth century B.C., their manner was, in comparison with what had gone before, less spontaneous, more allusive, and even deliberately pedantic. There is no place for them in this book.

We have followed the lost hexameter poetry (apart from the Hesiodic corpus) in subject matter from the sublime to the obscene and in time from the eighth century B.C. to the mid-fifth. The few fragments give us a partial view of a vast body of poetry long ago lost for ever. The poetry was composed in traditional, but constantly developing, language of high antiquity, and much of it may have been transmitted orally, even in places where writing was well known. On the other hand, the art of writing was increasingly practised in Greece from about 725 B.C. onwards, and there is no reason why Greeks should not have written epics down so early as that – the shorter epics perhaps first, the longer later according to the availability of papyrus, wood, skins or other writing materials. For we must not fall into the trap of supposing that because the language of a poem is traditional (or to use a fashionable, but loose, expression 'formulaic') its author composed orally, rather than with pen in hand. Nor must we assume that because a poem was recited, no texts of it had yet been written. Milman Parry's great achievement[1] is to have demonstrated the complex economy of the ancient hexametric epic verse, which was inherited by the bards of archaic Greece from generations of illiterate forerunners. What Parry did not prove is that poets in an increasingly literate society after about 700, who used these traditional verses or parts of verses, were all oral rather than literate composers. Many of the earliest Greek inscriptions are in verse: autograph epic texts contemporary with those inscriptions,

---

[1] Most plainly seen in his articles on Epic Technique in *H.S.C.P.* 41 (1930) 73 ff and 43 (1932) 1 ff.

having been written on more perishable materials, have all been lost, but we need not doubt that from the time of Eumelos, Hesiod and Homer onwards they existed.

In this book we have been entirely concerned with verse. But there are many peoples whose earliest extant epics are in prose or in a combination of prose and verse; the Ulster cycle in Ireland is an example of such a mingling of prose with lyrics. In Greece as much legendary lore may have passed from one generation to another in prose – even 'formulaic' prose – as in verse. Such prose epics would have been the archetypes of the accounts of legend in prose by the earliest logographoi such as Hekataios about 500 B.C., and perhaps also of the prose work that passed under the name of 'Eumelos'. A traditional story teller is not limited to verse; he suits the manner and the length of his recitation to the circumstances in which he is required to perform. If verse was preferred, the poet chose it because his memory was aided thereby, or because verse was more suited to the occasion; but it would be a mistake to suppose that all early Greek story tellers were reciters or singers of verse, or that no rhapsode ever told a myth or legend in prose.

When so much is still uncertain about the precise manner of composition of the great extant epics, the *Iliad* and the *Odyssey* and the *Theogony* of Hesiod, we cannot hope for a clear picture of the way in which lost epics, such as those of Asios, or of Epimenides, were recorded for posterity. I have therefore avoided speculation about problems of composition and confined the greater part of this book to examining the fragments in the contexts of the traditional tales. With how much, or how little, success that has been done, the reader must judge; but I trust that he will agree on one point; early Greece is peopled with the shades of great poets and the loss of their entire works is deeply to be lamented.

APPENDIX

Some Irish Analogies

Comparative studies of oral and written literatures are illuminating because they show that what happened in one society may well have happened in another. What they can never show is that any practice observed in one society *must* have occurred in another. Only a lively faith in, for example, analogies between twentieth-century Serbo-Croat poetry in its decline and eighth century B.C. early Ionian poetry in its ascendant would compel us to admit that Homer *must* have dictated, because oral poets in Yugoslavia who can write down poems are known invariably to produce inferior work to that of their dictating, reciting or improvising colleagues.[1]

It is because analogies between mediaeval Irish and early Hellenic poetical practice seem to me close that I draw attention to them here. The Irish evidence proves nothing about early Greek epics, but it does suggest possible explanations of certain known facts about *aoidoi* and *rhapsodoi* and the society in which they moved.

Both societies were essentially and exclusively aristocratic. Eumelos, the Bacchiad nobleman who provided Corinth with a synthetic history, would have recognised the technique and appreciated the motives of the Hibernian poets who in the *Lebor Gabála* or 'Book of Occupations' compiled for their patrons in the eleventh century A.D. and earlier a metrical pseudo-prehistory of Ireland. He corresponds closely to the Irish professional poet-historian the *senchaid*; and like many a *senchaid* he was of high birth.

As with the Homeridai in Chios or the Ametoridai in Eleutherna, competence in poetry ran in families, of whom perhaps the most famous were the O'Dalys of Westmeath. To be the son of a poet and the grandson of another was in Ireland a title to the highest professional standing within a highly privileged class; but the privileges of receiving

---

[1] Cf. A. B. Lord, 'Homer's Originality: Oral Dictated Texts' in Kirk, 68–78.

gifts from his king, of eulogy, and of satire (including incitement to war), were retained only by the strict observance of professional obligations. A poet had to keep a high standard of composition; he must avoid slovenly diction and neologisms; and for his inspiration he required 'purity of hand and of wedlock, purity of lips and of learning'.

The highest class of poet, the *fili*, was, like the Roman *vates*, originally a diviner and a seer, indeed a kind of druid (*drui*). Thus Néde, son of Adna, a pre-Patrician figure, was known as the ollave (*ollamh*) or leading professional in divination and in poetry, and much of the Church's early opposition to the class of poets was due, not to their verses, but to their occult gifts. The versatility of the *filid* as prophets, judges, and preservers of tradition as well as poets, continued until the death of the native society in the seventeenth century. As late as 1651 the English apothecary Thomas Smyth of Dublin distinguished four types of Rhymer. The first was the Brehound or Judge; the second, the Shankee (*senchaid*), recited pedigrees; the third were the ordinary bards, and the fourth were the (more exalted) poets, the *filid*: 'These men have great store of cattle and use all the trades of the others with an addition of prophecies.' Epimenides would have recognised a fellow professional (in poetry and in prophecy) in any leading Irish ollave or *fili*. Equally striking is the analogy with the versifying prophet of the line of Melampous in the retinue of Peisistratos of Athens. Nor, when the Irish evidence is considered, does the story of Hesiod's instruction in divination by the Akarnanians look at all implausible. We may with more confidence ascribe the *Days* to Hesiod, the author of the *Works*, and perhaps add the *Ornithomanteia* to his compositions, since it was clearly linked to the *Works*.[1]

In Ireland poetical language was kept pure and uniform by the strict discipline of the bardic schools, from which local idioms were rigorously excluded. After seven terms in a school a pupil was usually eligible for the title *ollamh* and could serve a lord; to achieve the desired qualification an aspirant would travel far. In the sixteenth century Eochaidh O'Hussey studied for long in Munster though he was a Fermanagh man. He tells us, half seriously, that he is tempted to stay in the realms of learning in the south, but, of course, the claims of his native land are

---

[1] Cf. G. Murray, *Greek Studies* (Oxford 1946) 28.

Appendix

too great and he must return to the service of his chieftain, a Maguire. No great effort of imagination is required to visualise Stasinos coming to a Homeric school in Chios from Cyprus, or Arktinos, allegedly a pupil of Homer, returning from Chios to serve a Neleid prince in Miletos, as Homer himself perhaps served a descendant of king Hektor in Chios.[1] The standardised character of the epic-Ionic dialect, whose uniformity is far more impressive than its variety, is perhaps to be explained by a vigorous tradition of bardic schools like those in Ireland. Such a tradition would account for the almost entirely successful exclusion of Boiotian dialect from Hesiod, of Laconisms from Tyrtaios, and of Doric from the hexametric Κορινθιακά ascribed to Eumelos; but it is still an open question whether this uniformity of language is to be explained by Ionian influences rather than by a shared Mycenaean heritage.[2]

As in archaic Greece, Irish poets regularly performed at fairs and there competed with other poets. The conditions at the Ionian Panegyris in Delos, which was the occasion of the Homeric Hymn to the Delian Apollo, are not dissimilar; there is also a memory of a 'contention of bards' at the fair in Delos in the verses alleging a contest between Hesiod and Homer (Hesiod F 265 Rzach). In Ireland the 'contentions' sometimes centred on geographical claims – whether the Shannon should be accounted part of Munster or of Connaught, for example – and a poet, especially if he was a *senchaid*, was expected to have ready for recitation much detailed topographical knowledge in metre with which he could, if need be, assert his chief's claim to a disputed territory. There is a close Hellenic analogy in the hexameters of the Catalogue of Ships, which was often invoked in territorial disputes in early Greece. An Irish poet who did not know his place names well might incur his chief's or his tutor's grave disfavour. There is a story in the *Yellow Book of Lecan* of Ilrechtach, harper of the great bard Mac Liag; because the unfortunate man was unable to recite for his master a poem on the place names in the Slieve Aughty range, west of Lough Derg, Mac Liag threatened to hang him up. Fortunately another poet, Mac Lonáin, arrived in time, ordered the harper to be released, and spoke the poem himself.

[1] Cf. Wade-Gery 6–8. [2] Cf. J. A. Notopoulos, *H.S.C.P.* 68 (1964) 43.

In the period covered by this book Greek epic was handed down in both oral and written traditions. We have seen that in Athens written texts may have been used to control recitations, and it is possible that rhapsodes memorised certain poems from manuscripts. But there seems little doubt that oral and scribal traditions existed side by side, often with little interaction, until the art of oral composition died out. A similar situation existed in Ireland, where monastic scribes preserved poems and prose epics in part or in outline, but were unable to record the oral tradition in all its variety. In view of the fashionable theory that Homer dictated, Irish evidence for oral dictated texts is of particular interest. Dictation, far from enabling an Irish oral poet or story teller to dwell in loving detail at leisure on all parts of a story, caused both reciter and scribe to weary rapidly. The ninth-century story of Cano, son of Gartnián, begins with elaborate detail, but soon the detail is lost and the descriptions are hinted at. Later still, the incidents are given in summary, and all artistry is lost. The reason for this is surely that the reciter wearied quickly, because he had not the sympathy of the audience to urge him on, nor could his pace be adapted to that of the increasingly weary scribe.[1] A similar problem would have arisen if the poet had been writing: he would still have lacked an audience to encourage him to high artistic achievement. In short, a literate or dictating poet is unlikely, to judge from Irish conditions, in an oral tradition to produce poetry of the highest quality. Yet it is hard to believe that the *Iliad* shows Homer not at his best; are we then bound to declare that Homer did not write? And if we are, in what sense can we call the *Iliad* and the *Odyssey* his?

Irish analogies present a possible escape from this problem. In Ireland a clear distinction was made between poets, who composed, and reciters, who declaimed. A *fili* might have a number of bards in his retinue to recite or chant his compositions. The words 'reciter' (*recaire*) and *bard* are often treated as synonymous, but in a recitation it was the *bard*, not the *fili*, who was responsible for the music, as we learn from the *Dissertation* prefixed to the Clanricarde Memoirs (Dublin 1722), which looks back to a time when the native tradition still flourished. 'The action and pronunciation of the poem in ⟨the⟩ presence . . . of the

---

[1] See G. Murphy, *Saga and Myth in Ancient Ireland* (Dublin 1961) 9.

Appendix

principal person it related to, was performed with a great deal of ceremony, in a concert of vocal and instrumental music. The poet himself said nothing, but directed and took care, that everybody else did his part right. The Bards having first had the composition from him, got it well by heart, and now pronounced it orderly, keeping pace with a harp, touched upon that occasion; no other musical instrument being allowed for the said purpose than this alone.' It is not fanciful to think that a number of Homeridai, each having had a part of the *Iliad* from Homer, 'got it well by heart' and 'pronounced it orderly' to a scribe over a number of days. With the successive recitation of the bards we may compare the rhapsodic recitations of Homer ἐξ ὑποβολῆς, said to have been prescribed in Athens by a 'Solonian' law. Once we grasp that composer and reciter need not be the same person, the essentially oral, spontaneous, and non-scribal aspect of the *Iliad* and the *Odyssey* is perhaps seen to be less puzzling. To ensure that his *Iliad* was preserved in writing Homer perhaps had first to see that his school 'got it well by heart' and 'pronounced it orderly'; he did not have to undergo the inhibiting experience of dictating or writing it himself. In Ireland the existence of reciters meant that a poet did not have to travel to make certain that his work was widely known; there are mentions of poems being sent by the 'horseman of poetry' (the declaimer) to the chief addressed, while the *fili* himself stayed at home. It is not difficult to imagine a similar practice in early Greece: indeed the bard of the Delian Hymn to Apollo, whose author was, in the view of Thucydides, Homer himself, can be conceived as having come from Chios to Delos with the hymn, having 'got it well by heart' from the Master. May we not have in the roles of *fili* and reciter (or bard) an analogy with the original functions of the ἀοιδός who composed and the rhapsode who declaimed?[1]

The method used in composing a poem by a *fili* is explained in the Dissertation already mentioned, the anonymous author of which was shown to be Thomas O'Sullevane.[2] The poet entered a dark room or cell, where he lay down on a couch. He could then take his time in composing his verses in perfect quiet. In a late sixteenth century poem

---

[1] For the distinction between *aoidos* and rhapsode see Kirk, in Kirk 88.
[2] R. Flower, *The Irish Tradition* (Oxford 1947) 95.

Greek Epic Poetry

Fear Flatha O'Gnimh upbraids another poet for composing on horse-back in the open air and says '. . . I like a thing which keeps me from error, a barrier to keep out the sunlight, and dim couches to guard me. If I did not close my eyelids between me and the bright rays as a pro-tecting veil against the daylight it would ruin my artistry' (E. Knott, *Irish Classical Poetry* (Dublin 1960) 57). If poets profited by darkness, blind poets had a special advantage, but we do not hear of an outstand-ing Irish blind poet, a Hibernian 'blind Maeonides'.

In the *Book of Leinster* a prophecy of ill to come declares that there will be no poets, only bards. In Ireland the oral epic tradition was permanently maimed by the English butcheries of the seventeenth century. In Greece the tradition of oral epic composition by *aoidoi* died a more natural death as writing became widespread and imperial Athens set the literary standards of Hellas.[1] But, as in Ireland, the chief reason for the decline of epic composition was this: the Pindaric world of the international aristocracies who fostered such poetry had been swept away, and with them the noble patronage upon which the poets depended for their status and their livelihood. When Panyassis died fighting for his family's honour in Halikarnassos, an entire tradition of poetry died with him.

[1] It must not however be assumed that literacy everywhere killed the power of poets to improvise orally: a classic counter-example is Antipater of Sidon who could compose extempore in hexameters and other metres (Cicero, *De Oratore* 3.194).

Supplementary Notes

p. 26   For new fragments of Stesichoros' *Garyonais* in *P. Oxy.* 2617 see Page and Barrett in D. L. Page, *Lyrica Graeca Selecta* (Oxford 1968) 263–268.

p. 32   (*a*) Idaian Daktyls: See also K. Thraede, 'Das Lob des Erfinders' *R.M.* 105 (1962) 161. (*b*) *P. Oxy.* 1241, Col. iv, 3–4: [ἐν δικασ]τήριον suppl. Wilamowitz.

p. 33 n. 1   Io Kallithyessa: See further Pfeiffer on Kallimachos Frag. Incert Auct. (Hesiod?) 769.

p. 34   Eriounios: This epithet of Hermes could perhaps be an Arcado-Cypriot word meaning 'good-runner': see Hesych. s. vv. οὖνον and οὖνει. F. Bechtel, *Lexilogus zu Homer* (reprint Hildesheim 1964) 138. There is a new fragment of the *Phoronis* in *P. Oxy.* 2260, Col. i, 3–7, in which a hexameter is cited to show that δολιχάορος can mean 'having a long *spear*'. Athene is the subject (cf. Philetas F23 Powell):

ούδ'έτι κούρ[η]] ἀρκέσει ἐγρεμάχ[η δο]λιχάορος ἀγρομε[. cf. Hom. Hymn. 2.4 Δήμητρος Χρυσαόρου where D. has, presumably, a golden *sickle*. κούρ[η]: fort. κούρ[οις].

p. 36   Hephaistos and Athena in the *Danais*: Zeus gave birth to Athena after swallowing Metis; Hera gave birth to Hephaistos without Zeus's aid. (See esp. West on Hesiod, *Theogony* 886–900.) The attempt of Hephaistos to mate with Athena would be a logical development of the story. Owing to the god's wickedness the Rhodians did not employ fire in their sacrifices (Apoll. Rhod. F 11 Powell, which does not necessarily come from a *Rhodou Ktisis* of the poet.)

p. 36 n. 1   Another Argolic spring named from a Danaid was Physadeia: Schol. Kall. *Hymn.* 5.47 f.

p. 40   (*a*) Haimon: In some versions (e.g. E. *Phoen.* 758) Haimon survives to be betrothed to Antigone, but this does not seem to be the early form of the tale in the *Thebais* or *Oidipodeia*, in which he was a victim of the Sphinx (Schol. cod. Mon. 560 on E. *Phoen.* 1760 Schwartz, cited by Allen *loc. cit.*).

(*b*) The great length of the entire Theban cycle: According to Tkatsch, *Die arabische Uebersetzung der Poetik des Aristoteles*[2] 150 [noted by A. W. Pickard-Cambridge, 'The *Niobe* of Aeschylus' in *Greek Poetry and Life* (Essays Presented to Gilbert Murray) (Oxford 1936) 119] the original of the Arabic version of Aristotle, *Poet.* 18 (1456a 17) 'probably read' not Νιόβην but Θηβαΐδα. The variant *Thebais* suits the context in the *Poetics* well.

197

p. 78 For bees as βουγενέας see also Philetas F22 Powell.

p. 82 Endymion and Epimenides: The Nemean Lion also dwelt in a cave (Apollod. *Bibl.* 2.5.1 and Pfeiffer on Kall. F55). Selene, too, had a cave in Arkadia: Porph. *De. Antr. Nymph.* 20. Nemea herself seems to have been regarded as a daughter of the Moon: see Drachmann's text of Hypothesis *c* to Pindar *Nemeans* (Vol. 3, p. 3, 22).

p. 88 Nikostratos: In the Hesiodic fragment about him (F175 M.W.) Quincey proposes ὁπλότερον. West supposes that in the original the two lines were not so closely linked. The Spartans gave to Menelaos and Helen a third child, Aithiolas [Schol. Il. 3. 175 (1. 148 Dindorf)].

p. 90 If this Oineus is not an immigrant, but an autochthonous Samian, in the scheme of Asios, then he perhaps belongs to the vine-mountain Ampelos which rises behind Samos town; but Strabo (637) denies that Ampelos is well suited to wine-making. Oineus son of Aigyptos was held to have been killed by a Danaid (Apollod. *Bibl.* 2.1.5); so he could not, in any case, have settled permanently in Samos.

p. 91 Parthenope and Naples: G. Pugliese Carratelli, *P.P.* 7 (1952) 245.

p. 101 According to Pediasmos, Herakles shot at the Sun owing to the excessive heat at midday, when he had set up the Pillars at the limits of the earth; the Sun in amazement then gave the *depas* to him (10. p. 257 *Mythogr. Gr.* 1 ed. R. Wagner); in it he crossed Ocean to Erytheia.

p. 102 In poetry the canonical Twelve-Labour Cycle of Herakles is almost certainly as early as Pindar: see *P. Oxy.* 2450, B43 and C. Pavese, *H.S.C.P.* 72 (1968) 83.

p. 103 Hot springs, including those at Lindian Thermydrai, are discussed by J. H. Croon in *Mnemosyne* 4.6(1953) esp. 288-289. For the connexion with Herakles see his book, *The Herdsman of the Dead* (Utrecht 1952).

p. 105 For the position of Euboian Oichalia (perhaps near Aulonari) see W. P. Wallace, *Hesperia* 16(1947) 140.

p. 107 It would appear from Philodemos π.ε. p. 5 and 14 Gomperz (Hesiod F 295 M.W.) that the *Aigimios* included a reference to the daughters of Phorkos with their one tooth and one eye between them; this fragment, together with the mention of Io in the poem(s), shows that the *Aigimios* ranged far into legends not immediately relevant to the visit of Herakles to Aigimios. The war of Herakles against Theiodamas and the Dryopes, who were expelled by him from the vicinity of Mount Parnassos to Asine in Peloponnese and elsewhere, may well have been included in the *Aigimios* (for the story see Pfeiffer on Kall. F 24-25).

p. 108 In the fragment of Sophokles, *Inachos* in *P. Oxy.* 2369, F 1 it seems that Zeus in the form of a blackamoor had already seduced Io before she was turned into a cow. It is possible that in the early versions of the story she was already with child (the 'dusky' Epaphos, cf. Aesch. *P.V.* 851), or at least had been seduced, before her wanderings began and before her metamorphosis in the Argolid, as in Apollod. *Bibl.* 2.1.3.

p. 113   For the Molione in Attic Geometric vase painting see now J. N. Coldstream, *Greek Geometric Pottery* (London 1968) 351.

p. 119   The high antiquity of the pre-Homeric Kalydonian Meleager epic is emphasised by J. Th. Kakridis in his *Homeric Researches* (Lund 1949) 23.

p. 120   Theseus and the battle of Aphidna: E. Prigge, *De Thesei rebus quaestionum capita duo* (Marpurgi Cattorum 1891) 51.

p. 124   The relationship of Homer's poetry to that of Orpheus and Mousaios was examined, not long after Herodotos, by Glaukos of Rhegion: see, for discussion of Glaukos' fragments, *G.R.B.S.* 9 (1968) 47–54.

p. 126 and p. 162   Antimachos of Teos is alleged by Plutarch, *Rom.*12, to have lived as early as Olymp. 6. 3. Apart from his possible authorship of a *Nostoi*, he may have composed an *Epigonoi*: Schol. Aldin. ad Aristoph. *Pac.* 1270 declares of the line

νῦν αὖθ' ὁπλοτέρων ἀνδρῶν ἀρχώμεθα, Μοῦσαι· —
ἀρχὴ δὲ τῶν 'Επιγόνων 'Αντιμάχου.

Antimachos of Kolophon can hardly be intended here. Cf. Powell, *Collectanea Alexandrina* p. 247. The gnomic line

ἐκ γὰρ δώρων πολλὰ κακ' ἀνθρώποισι πέλονται

was ascribed to the Teian Antimachos (Kinkel p. 247).

p. 126 ff.   E. Bethe's edition of the fragments of the Trojan cycle has been reprinted as *Der Troische Epenkreis* (B. G. Teubner, Stuttgart 1966).

p. 155–156   Lesches and Polygnotos: See now M. Robertson, 'Conjectures on Polygnotos' Troy', *A.B.S.A.* 62 (1967) 5–12.

p. 156   *Little Iliad* F 19 (Allen). Lines 6 to 11 of this fragment are assigned by Scholia, MD on Euripides, *Andromache* 14 to Simias of Rhodes (F 6 Powell), not to Lesches, but there is almost certainly a lacuna before the six lines are quoted in the scholia. The order of events in the complete fragment is not logical. A possible rearrangement is to put the verses in the following order: 6, 7, 8, 3, 4, 5, 1, 2, 9, 10, 11. H. Fraenkel (*De Simia Rhodio* (Göttingen 1915) 37) also claims the fragment for a *Little Iliad*.

p. 160   M. L. West (*C.Q.* 17 (1967) 439) would reject the words 'as Lesches says'.

p. 168   The lineage of Odysseus in Homer, Hesiod, the *Telegoneia*, the *Alkmaionis* and in Asios has recently been explored by M. Miller, *Studies in Greek Genealogy* (Leiden 1968) 292–305.

p. 174   M. Forderer, *Zum Homerischen Margites* (Amsterdam 1960) 5 ff. (not read by me) argues against the attribution of *P. Oxy.* 2309 to the *Margites*. For sober discussion of the poem see R. Pfeiffer, *History of Classical Scholarship* (Oxford 1968) 74.

p. 175   The words 'he failed in every craft' are added from Clement, *Strom.* 1.4.1: see Allen, *loc. cit.*

p. 177   There is a detailed study of Panyassis by V. J. Matthews (Diss. Belfast 1968).

p. 179   For the place of the Graces in symposia see Erkinger Schwarzenberg, *Die Grazien* (Bonn 1966) 56.

p. 182 n. 2   For the equivalence Acheloos = Water see also Sophokles F 5 Pearson.

p. 183   Bembina: The wording in the Stephanos article does not quite guarantee that the second hexameter is by Panyassis. It could perhaps, for example, be an imitation of Panyassis by Rhianos, who is mentioned earlier in the same article. Note that the skin here mentioned may not be the one worn by Herakles. Some held him to have worn the skin, not of the Nemean Lion, but of the Lion of Kithairon (see Pfeiffer on Kall. F 677 and Apollod. *Bibl.* 2. 4. 10). Of Bembina as a district Pliny (*N.H.* 4. 20) declares: '. . . Clitorium, Cleonae, inter quae duo oppida regio Nemea est Bembinadia vocitata.'

p. 188.   For the addition of pentameters to Homeric hexameters see also Suda s.v. *Ἰδαῖος* *Ῥόδιος*.

p. 191   For the view that Kynaithos the Chian was a descendant of Homer see especially Wade-Gery, *Poet* 25.

p. 191.   Irish poetics: See now James Carney, *The Irish Bardic Poet* (Dolmen Press/Irish Inst. Adv. Stud. 1967). I am grateful to Mr K. O'Nolan for allowing me to see the proof of his original and illuminating article on the techniques of Irish and Homeric storytelling (*C.Q.* forthcoming). A useful corrective to the excess of formulism in contemporary Homeric scholarship is provided by Douglas Young in 'Never Blotted a Line?' (*Arion*, Autumn 1967).

p. 195.   Complete memorisation of the *Iliad* and the *Odyssey* may have been not unusual in early Greece. In Xen. *Symp.* 3. 5–6 Nikeratos claims that his father required him to learn the whole of Homer by heart, with the result that he can recite the poems, *ἀπὸ στόματος εἰπεῖν*. In the same passage it is said that rhapsodes, too, know the epics by heart.

Index

Greek Epic Poetry

Index

Index

Index

Index

Index

Index